T0196051

MY SISTER, MY ENEMY

A Memoir on the Joy and Pain of Sisterhood

Dr. Pamela Renee Applewhite, PhD

Archway Publishing books may be ordered through booksellers or by contacting:

Archway Publishing
1663 Liberty Drive
Bloomington, IN 47403
www.archwaypublishing.com
844-669-3957

Because of the dynamic nature of the Internet, any web addresses or links contained in this book may have changed since publication and may no longer be valid. The views expressed in this work are solely those of the author and do not necessarily reflect the views of the publisher, and the publisher hereby disclaims any responsibility for them.

Any people depicted in stock imagery provided by Getty Images are models, and such images are being used for illustrative purposes only.
Certain stock imagery © Getty Images.

Interior Image Credit: Devon Ford

Scripture taken from the King James Version of the Bible.

ISBN: 978-1-6657-0320-8 (sc)
ISBN: 978-1-6657-0321-5 (e)

Library of Congress Control Number: 2021903369

Print information available on the last page.

Archway Publishing rev. date: 5/21/2021

"Me, My Mother and Sisters (Unspoken Love)"

Introduction, Acknowledgement & Dedication Page

I am Dr. Pamela Applewhite, I wrote this book with several years of exploration, inner reflection, research, observation and experience. I will share a little about myself. I am a Mental Health Professional, Minister, Author, Wife, Mother of 5 boys and Non Profit Director of a Child Placing Agency. I have taught psychology courses at several online schools, as well as brick and mortar colleges. I love learning, growing, and experiencing, but most of all, I love giving. I believe that writing this book and finally and- I mean finally publishing this book, I want to thank God! He guided my thoughts, my emotions and my spirit into this book for you. I would be remised if I did not give God his glory for this book! This book is his expression of love towards sisters and their plight. God wants to restore and redeem the plight of sisters. I won't elaborate NOW, as I want you to read the book and lastly I truly thank God for my husband, Kenyatta Applewhite for putting up with me reading this book to him all through the night, and years and being my guide and critique. Thanks baby! Lets do it! Sisters- read this book and be totally transformed, blessed, restored and renewed!

This book took me several years to write. I started many, many years ago, after watching a Law and Order Episode about two blood sisters that were enemies. The Lord hit my spirit with the title of My Sister, My Enemy, and later over the years added the sub-title of "The Joy and Pain of Sisterhood". I have cried, fell asleep, did research, had revelations and ephiphanies, while pushing through the atmosphere- about this book. I saw it in my dream, I saw it in my sleep. I am self-publishing this book going into my 54th birthday in 2021. I am too excited to finally present this book. I edited this book, read this book and typed this book, all by myself-likened to Tyler Perry-written, produced and written (lol) (so if you see any mistakes, count it to my rookiness, but it will get better). I pray you much deliverance and freedom after reading this book. Look for my up and coming books on "Black Soot, a Twisted tale about a Girl from a small town", "Emotional Intelligence in the Church" "The Kim, you never knew an un- authorized fictional book on the life of Kim Porter".

This is my dedication page. I am dedicating this book to My Aunts. I want to elaborate on the dedication portion, as I know things are often taken out of context. This portion of my book is only to cite a model of how I learned about sisters, but not to say (hear me readers, family and friends) that this book is about them in particular. this page is only about the dedication and, who I am dedicating it to, although I am using examples that I perceived to be useful and teachable. I caution myself, as I know that some will think it is SOLELY about them, and its NOT, its about life, and the journey of sisters. It is an awareness!. It is about what we have been as sisters, and where we need to go as sisters. It is a journey! So know that as I dedicate this book! Let's take this ride! I pray you are totally fulfilled and in love with this book, until you want more and more and more!

"Satan can twist love and turn it to hate". "And a man's enemies shall be one of their own household (Matthew 10:36, New International Version, NIV) "Love Believes in, hopes, bears and takes all things (I Corinthians 13:7 New King James Version, NKJV)"

Dedication to my Aunts—"Sansbury Sisters"—"The Model Sisters"

To My Aunts Patricia "Ann", Rosa Mae, Jack, Gloria, Janice and Elaine Sansbury (maiden names, except Elaine) are a portrait of the best sisters I know, they love, they disagree, dispute, but they stay together. They truthfully, allow each sister to play their role without stepping on one another's toes, most of the time, by what I can tell. I have noticed with my aunts that even in the midst of difficult times in all their lives, they (in my eyes) have been the best sisters I know. I will talk about them SOME in the book, and what their sisterhood example, has brought to my life through their actions, their declarations, and the examples they have bred in the lives of their family members, acquaintances, and the communities that they live.

I will demonstrate a little bit of their lives to the good. These are my Aunts, the " Originall Sansbury Sisters"! I know life has not been easy for them as sisters, but what I do know, is that is they are close and bonded, even when they think they are not! Hint! Hint! I dedicate this book to them primarily and then to all sisters, because through them, I was able to write this book and explain and elaborate on sisterhood.

I will walk us all through sisterhood; using various sister examples, traits, personalities, thoughts, whims, notions, you name it, as- I have seen in lots of sisters-not just my aunts! This book is a total reflection of sisterhood. It will hurt, it will help, it will even make you mad, and most definitely make you cry! I will use various sisters in my book to show us all, how we have been, how we have not been, and what we need to do to get it right. I will inevitably walk us through this journey of sisterhood. All in all, this book it is about getting back to love, to closeness and to sharing.

Special shout outs in dedication to the Wright Sisters formerly from my hometown of Timmonsvlle, South Carolina. Cynthia (Cymp), Glenene (Lynn), Angie, Debbie, and Shoan (Shawn, is how we pronounce it), that lived down the street from us and to, my cousins "The Graham sisters (my first cousins)", Traci, Candace and Krystle, They are ALL Model SISTERS!!! And to my sisters the two on the cover and the back of the book, Stefanie and Jenny, Love is always love with you two guys!

Read this book for encouragement, support, deliverance, eye-opening revelations, renewal and/or straight awareness! Read it for what it is, as we say now in the 21st century " As-It is what it is"!

Love, Peace and Blessings! This one is for you! Sisters of the World!

Dr. Pamela Renee Applewhite, PhD

Prelude/Introduction

The Story of Sisters

What is a sister? What should a sister be? How do you relate to your sister (In childhood, adult hood, and throughout life) What are the characteristics and traits of sisters? What are the personalities of sisters? Are there particular types of sister groups? What is the "Wall of the Mind" of a Sister? I am going to attempt to respond to these questions through examples of real-life instances that I witnessed, experienced, saw, interrogated, researched and inquired about through my many days and nights pondering the thoughts of what sisterhood is, what it is not, what it can become, so on and so on. There will be pictures within the pages of this book to show, express and illustrate how sister hood is, can be and how sisters express themselves. I want you to get excited about this writing! It will truly bless your soul, mind and spirit! "I ask you", to use the pictures to visualize in your minds the "mood and mode" of a sister and sisters. I hope and pray the words and the pictures of this book enlighten, brighten, allow you to transcend through time to be healed and stabilized within your sisterhood journey (Watch for Special Notes and Key Points throughout the book).

Now to The cover and back of this book is an actual picture of me and my sisters taken many, many years, ago, we were all in our late teens, early 20s, as I was praying, searching and seeking God for a picture that connected to this book, I saw this picture at our mother's house and there it came to me this is it! So I dedicate the cover of this book to us, me and My Sisters, Jenny, Steffie, and Pam—"(The Sansbury Sisters)".

Additionally, I dedicate this entire book to SISTERS (as well as to my Aunts) out there in the world that have experienced joys, pains, happiness, trials, tribulations, sadness, loneliness, death of a sister and revivals of sisterhood, this is all located in this book! Enjoy your journey of this book!

My Aunts, the "Original Sansbury Sisters
(Strong, Deep, and Bonded Sister Love)"

Sisters. So many thoughts came to my mind when God gave me this book, but one in particular was during a "Law and Order" episode where two sisters were rivals and hated each other, while fighting for their inheritance and vying to be their daddy's favorite. This ultimately prompted my title, as I was laying in my bed watching it. It sparked the thought, _she is my sister, yet she is my enemy._

Hold fast as you read this book though, as through this report, and experience for some, yet real-life testimony for others. It will at times be painful, devastating, and mind-blowing. This story is one that many of us have experienced. I want to take a look at the various forms of sisterhood, sister personalities, actions, activities, conversations, and thoughts. Consequently when someone doesn't have a blood sister, one may fall in the category of ending up with persons that we are close to, that we deem as a sister. This memoir will touch basis on sisters that are linked and connected to the heart, although not by blood this- will be mentioned and highlighted in the book. Furthermore, a sister may be someone that we were reared with or have come to know in some association or link. She is someone we decided to make our sister or create that sister bond. Because of this I want to look at as many avenues of sisterhood as possible, to expose what sisterhood is and what it is not. I want to bring forth healing in the form of sisterhood, or in some cases it maybe just- simple- awareness. First I want to describe a spiritual aspect of the mind when it comes to sisterhood revealed to me by God. It was strange to me at first, but I knew my mind didn't stumble upon mental rubble, so hear goes. Read on!

God gave me a phrase, referring to it as "The Wall of the Mind of a Sister". He described and showed me a place where sisterhood lives and breaths! The wall of the mind of a sister is a distinct and unique entity of it's own. God showed me what goes on in this place and how it has been handled throughout the time and how it is being handled now. God want us to understand this place and how to function in the mind of a sister, as a functioning operation. Read on readers, let's get started.

Defining "The Wall of the Mind of a Sister", is the place that the creation of sisterhood starts and resides. It is the place where the sister looks out from, and into the world of sisterhood, as well as life. It is the place that she measures, explores, cries from, and identifies from, in who she is as a sister. The wall of the mind of a sister presents a place of comradery, togetherness, oneness, pureness, and wholeness, if played and operated in sync with the soul and spirit of one another (the sisters, that is). The wall of the mind of a sister replicates an upright structure, an upright position and a being that is combined- as a legendary whole, for all sisters involved and pushed through, the same 'womb". The wall of the mind of a sister is a place where we are totaled in nature and as one. There is nothing like this place within the wall of the mind of a sister. It can take you places of glory and places of victory that no other place can. It is us! This place can also take you to dark places. Places where one cannot talk, speak or utter, due to things that happen with, to and among sisters. It can be shameful, hurtful, dark and cold. Let's explore further!

Consequently sisterhood is a beautiful place. If we are tied together within our souls, something keeps us together, bonded, and securely knitted. Yet some out there may need a release from sisterhood in some way, shape, or form. It's sad to say, because some of us who are sisters may have been hurt, distorted, used, abused, and bound. We end up in the devilish or soulish realm of attachment to our sister or sisters. Some -have been waiting for some form of confirmation or release from the binding factor that holds together the ungodly or inappropriate sister, relationship, especially if it- is treacherous, evil, or malicious.

Some sister relationships are not good and are not bound by God's love and connectedness. There is, and can be a lot of manipulation, strife, stress, backbiting, subtle aggressiveness, and trickery when it comes to sisterhood. (Yes I have to go there.) We will touch on the good and the bad of sisterhood and the relationships involved. When in a relationship with one's sister, God does not want us to be stuck not believing in our own ability, or feeling as if we are looked down upon or are not adequate in our sister's eyes—no matter what and to anyone, no matter who it is. Sisterhood should be a group, a team, a machine. Although this is supposed to be so, there are indiscretions in sisterhood.

There are sisters out there who have really great relationships with their sister or sisters. This is inevitably a part of this writing too, so don't fret. This is not a curse your sister book. Consequently, It can be-that a sister may be in a recluse state, or just too afraid to say or mention what she really feels about being a sister. She may want to create her own sense of self, and in doing so, seem to isolate all other sisters in the group, this is not uncommon. This area will be explored. This book is to help you unravel thoughts, feelings, emotions, long-time, pent-up, harbored stuff that you may not actually be able to get out, or rightly say or do -regarding one's sister, and within the sister consciousness and path.

This memoir is to aid all of us sisters in building one's confidence, strength, power, and identity, and to speak out and tell one's truths as a sister. It is time out for crazy doings with sisterhood. As I move forward in a new decade, although I initially started this book over seven or eight years ago, I have come to realize a lot more stuff when it comes to sisterhood. I have been revealed to by the most Holy Father, what it is that sisters do, have done, and will do, in times past, and in times to come. I have stopped, started, and stopped and started this book again, and again. God wanted me totally endowed and informed to aid my sisters, and other sisters out there with power, strength, and love. God would not have it any other way sisters!

It is time for us to attack what Is binding and blocking us from staying jelled as sisters. The all and the in-between- that needs to be rooted up, or out to get us there, is what this book is about. It will make you laugh, it will make you cry, and it will probably make you want to put it down for a few days! That is my prayer, that it is too deep to read all at once, and that it is too- breath alluring and intense to stop at one sentence. I hope and pray that it will be a marker for your life until you have to pick it up and reference it again, again, and again! Thank you God for this memoir, I give you praise! Let's move forward.

Sisters, as your eyes begin to open up, when reading this memoir, if there are areas that have left sore spots or strongholds in your mind regarding sisterhood, then know that one can mend- by focusing, addressing, and unleashing, in which will be explained "time and time again within this book. Take the proper steps to cautiously destroy the strongholds in one's life in order to become useful, free and productive. This book/memoir has taken me years to write, as God would slow me down at times, and I would draw a blank at other times. This book/ memoir is not to tear the mold of sisterhood down, but to build and restore it up, in a lot of cases. If, though, you are one that has or still is in a relationship with your sister, and she has treated you cruelly and unusually, then you might want to read this and hold on to your seat. Experience this story around issues with sisters that bond, but secretly hate, experience the story of sisters that feel, and think, but never speak- outloud, on the but-so-obvious issues that need to be spoken on. Let's move forward!

We, as sisters often have and carry thoughts in our minds that just "stay there (and won't move that can be incredulous, delusional or incomprehensible)"! You will see this noted a lot throughout the book and how it has affected our relationships. Unspoken or pint up thoughts that have been kept in holding and they have ultimately become a "strong figment or hold" inside our minds. Lets read what having a strong hold means.

Special Note: Stronghold: A belief that is strongly held or stored and is often the reason for misunderstandings when it comes to being a sister. One sister, or the other may believe that one has done something to her or against her. Various strongholds exist among sisters, identity, unhealthy comparisons, spite, envy, finances, family relational stuff, parental stuff, issues with spouses or significant others and lots more (fill in the blank with yours).

__Problems and Issues as Sisters__. With some of us, let's first start out with the severe, yet serious stuff. We, as sisters, often bind unseen cloaks around the necks of our sister or sisters, through life-long hindrances such as guilt, jealousies, rivalries, miseriesims (a word God gave me, the root word is derived from misery), things not meant to be said, things meant to be said, and the like. There are some sisters out there that are bound by their sister's power. Each one of you inevitably need this book to help you or her, come back to herself. And to divulge into the individual sister that God wants you to be, as well as not continuously live in the shadow of your sister. This book is to help you, my dear sister, be delivered and set free, to help you get out of your sister's prison and create your own true sense of self and identity. This writing is to aid you in your own development and to aid you in unlocking your own sense of confidence and get up, and not be held in a sisterly prison anymore! This book is to squash the timidity and bring about courage! This book is *say it* girl, *do it* girl, right in front of your sister-girl (type of thing). I mean nothing bad, I do not promote self-injurious or self-sabotaging behaviors, and this is all about *empowerment*. Furthermore, this book is, and can be about pure joy to make room for more joy, as a loving and beholding sister. Everyone will have a different perspective, outlook, choose yours, as you read this memoir.

__Moving on__ Some sisters out there reading this may want to take their own step away from their sister or sisters in order to become a better and unique sister, but they have been fearful to make that move. Some have been waiting all their lives to hear these words because they knew that their sister or sisters had them bound and gagged. But they had no sound proof, no solid evidence that this psychological pin-up was occurring. You ultimately lacked substance and feared who God created you to be. You allowed the mayhem and disarray to live in the sister circle for most of your life. You strived for your own identity, so much so until-. You did not want to be called "so-n-so's sister". You wanted to be identified by your name, your God GIVEN talent and gifts and not hers," now there is an expansion of this, but that will come later, because there will be a part of some sisters that have developed, evolved and sprouted, because of their sister's name, fame and title, but we shall talk on that later, this is for the sister that all she knows is being "her sister" and it has been haunting you for all or most of your life, lets dig!

The words of being labeled by your sister's name is - often to some sisters- like daggers! It is okay, to feel this way, but it is not okay to stay this way. As there are several ways to approach and unapproach the trap of the sister bond, that binds, controls and holds one hostage. When one is sickly close to your sister, and it seems you cannot let go unto yourself, then there is a problem. What do you mean when you say sickly? This means that one is bonded, yet in a manner that is ungodly, unfeasible and to the point of having a pathological scar. This is the type that your entire make up is centered around her being, what you do, what you don't do, how you dress, always thinking what she will think if she hears, sees, or knows you are doing or saying something, contrary to her "so-called standards"-this is what I mean. Furthermore, Not being able to create one's own path, without fear of what she will think or say. This my dear is not what God intended or meant for it to be when it comes to any form of sisterhood. There is a level of abnormal attachment to one's sister or sister group, if this is occurring. God intended for us to be together and move together in sync, but not to the point that we are not our own selves. We have to understand who God created us to be and not who our sister is, now there is a point of mating where we come together to evolve and grow, create, and most definitely prosper, but the key is to always remember that you are not to do so at the expense of your own soul! Never, ever! A sister should bring life, not take it! If you and your sister are in a relationship where you are feeling taken, then you need to deal with this issue straight on! No one needs to be hanging by a thread and not be able to speak or breath in a relationship with one's sister, where she is not being seen, heard or identified. I am going to get to all the bad stuff first, okay girls, so hold on, as you read forward! !he bad stuff out -and the good stuff in (BREATH)- The BEST is saved for last! Keep on!

Sister Rucus.There are some sisters that seem like they are caught up in a scandal of a type of "lifetime movie, bellowing out for help" with how they relate to their sisters. For instance,if - one is so caught in the mental barrage of sister entrapment, it can somehow feel like a strand that you cannot pull yourself away from, no matter how hard you try. It can be likened unto a show on the cartoon network that my son's watched when they were younger, I cannot remember the name, but they were sisters and the one said, you took "my doll" and you destroyed it, and you "blacked the eye out, when we were little." These sisters were totally at war, the one was stronger than the other and the weaker one played her role to the "t," she was weak and she allowed her sister to manipulate her, trick her and steal from her, emotionally and physically for a long period of time and they became cartoon rivals, the fought like cats and dogs! Ongoing confusion and rucus! It gets better! Let's keep going!

The action of the sister, at the onset of childhood was what drove one sister to do much evil, while the other thought she did much good, but did not. It had turned into a really "fire hot mess"! Yes some sisters really do this, don't we? I heard a girl say this one day when I was shopping in the Dollar Tree Store, she said, to someone- that she was shopping with (out loud, as I was shopping on the very same isle with her), that, "There is no way I can live with my sister, I love her, but I cannot live with her"! She said she is the partying type and I am not! That said a lot to me. She openly expressed that they had two types of personalities, and there is nothing wrong with that and that it just could not work for them living together, at least she knew their differences, do you know your difference as sisters? Do you know where the line stops and where it begins? Do you know when to say "no" when you are sisters, without it being a federal offense to deal with (so-to-speak)"?. We have to know and acknowledge, as this lady did that we are different, yet can be the same, knowing how to function as such, is one main key to sisterhood. This lady in the store, openly acknowledged, that they were not a good match when it came to them living together, and this is just one example. How many of us, stay in a partial relationship with our sister or sisters in areas- where we know there is no match! How many of us continue to eat ourselves alive- about something that just don't click for "us" with you, your sister, or sisters! We should know where we mate at and where we don't there are differences in all walks of live, why do we make it so difficult in sisterhood? Why do we do this? Now I am not saying that we have to keep or kick- one's sister out of our lives, in this instance, let me be clear, by no means am I saying this! I will acknowledge though, that in some instances there will be separation issues that occur throughout the life of our sisterhood. That we can't do anything about. But then there are times when sisters need to be close. Let's learn which is which.

Genetics. Each of us have different genes/ genetics, although we have them all- the same if you know what I mean. I will say that we all have certain inner workings, that is why I uses genetics, as we are all the same, but different. Even if there are identical twin sisters, there is always a varied aspect of traits, with each sister. Sisters take the time to know yourself, take the time to explore who you are through reading up on your God given name, your characteristic traits, such as, am I an introvert, extrovert, am I shy, sensitive, hyper, focused, lazy, not In-tune, non- chalant, head strong, haughty, I mean, the list is endless; know who you are, do some psychological research on your personality, the things you like, the things your sister does not like. I mean work by yourself to know yourself, I promise you in the long run It will not only improve you, but improve who you all are as individuals, and as sisters. Sisters take the LEAP! Start thinking about this now!

Sisters we are all in all different, but the same I remember being a teenager my-self and, having my "own specific type of ways," my hormones began springing up and me and my sisters began to have attitudes, feelings and emotions that were different, then when we were just outside playing. Not only did they come upon us as individuals, but as sisters as a whole-- I remember us having "things" against each other that we kept secret, at least, I can say so for myself. Confession Time (What is your confession about your sister, think of it RIGHT HERE AND RIGHT NOW): I used to hate when I was on the telephone talking to my friend, and she would always interrupt me, I would find something to argue back with her, rather than just say, "Hey, I don't like it when you interrupt my conversations, when I am on the phone with my friends, I never interrupt you, when you are talking to your boyfriend)." I never had the nerve to do it! I just let it happen. How many times do we "just let things happen," with our sisters when we know we shouldn't? Why don't we speak up in the way we should, when we should, in order to let our sister know how we feel, without getting and staying mad forever. I am totally guilty of this and no longer am I ashamed, but free! Sisters it is time for us to let each other know, and know the truth and all the truth! Why do we think that it is not ok to talk to each other from the depths of our soul, why? Why are we afraid to really say what we feel? Why can't we talk to each other about what it is that you did that was wrong in my eyes, or what you said that was wrong to my hearing? What is wrong with that (getting to the bottom of the issue)? I say this to the "up building of the bond," we need to start being open and honest, and eliminate the forfeiture of our connection, by what our sisterhood bond does to us when we are not totally upfront and truthful. It's is okay to get upset and mad at times, but so long as we get it all out. This is one of the most important facts that need to be adhered to- when it comes to sister mating. When sisters bond or mate, there has to be a stiff connection. A connection that is so tight that you can almost read your sisters mind, body language and actions. If there are things that stifle this, the mating process will always not be secure and tight! Furthermore in mating there are lots of issues to contend with and a lot of times insecurity is a "biggie"! For instance- one sister can feel inferior to one or the other one, for one reason or the other, by means of any word, act or deed that occurred at childhood, the tender years, during adolescence up until adulthood. When this insecurity hit, it was never addressed and was left "hanging" within the sister's soul for a life time almost or until it is noticed and addressed. Out of convenience the situation was left overlooked and not attacked to conquer the fear that was within! Some of us think, when we are offended or hit with on offense that leads to insecure feelings for or with our sister or sisters that just because- this is "my blood, this is my sister, "how can I," "How can she," it goes both ways, it goes "all ways," but I have come with God almighty to release some sisters out there, in an entrapped state of being, free, yes to set you free with this memoir- today! I pray to you, that you can- receive these words! Read on!

Special Note. In the wake and rise of sisterhood, the pressing problems of being a sister has- come up on shows such as Iyanla Fix My Life,as well as in various scenes in movies with all kinds of races and nationalities of sisters being described. With this depiction of sister relationships it has shown sisterhood as being debilitating and degrading!

The sister pact or crew can be rehabilitating or it can be debilitating. Which sister group are you in? Do you get along with your sister and cannot do without her, or is your every awakening moment centered around your sister what she thinks, what she might think about you, your decisions, your children, your mate, your purchases, I know yawl know what I am talking about, or do you, argue, bicker, fuss and fight to the point of seemingly no return, does it seems like "She is your

Enemy often times, more than not"? Is the bond of sister-hood ever violated or broken or does it stay solid all the time. I can say yes to both. We all can, say that at some point and time, whether openly or ***secretly*** - that our sister has not been our friend "all the time", she (the sister) in some instances, has caused so much anger, rage and disillusionment, until my sister has totally been an enemy to my heart and my soul. This is due to fear and suppression of feelings thoughts and other non important stuff that is carred around as baggage! Some people that- I have interviewed or talked to, have said that they were just simply- intimidated by their sister for no viable reason whatsoever, it can just be that she is (you fill in the blanks)! Others in terms of sisterhood- have been betrayed, buckled and kept down, but not anymore, this psychological prison chain has to be broken. Let the tie that is binding- you loose you and set you free!

Some of you have been so repressed by your sister, or sisters- to the point that you don't want to see, speak, smell or hear them! A broken heart she/they swept and kept on you! She/they took your heart and trampled all over it, yes, this has happened to some and if not all of us in some way, shape or form, when it comes to sisters. I know someone out there has felt looked down upon, but God has come to rescue you from the PIT of being drowned by your forever thoughts, acts of "looking over your shoulder," when your sister is on the horizon. I mean this may be your own sister or it can be someone that you naturally or spiritually adopted as your sister, because you had none of your own. Don't let her manipulate your any more. Don't let the actions that took you by the neck, and kept your heart and mind wrapped right in their little fingers and hands keep you any longer. God wants deliverance and godliness. He wants good and fruitful relationships, not dead, intrusive, and binding connections. You sister, I am here for you today, God has come so that you can have life, and have it more abundantly (John 10:10, King James Version).

More over Sisters, when these things occur we need to seek shelter. We need to seek comfort. We need to find ourselves and our own souls to refocus, relive, and relift! We do things that are treacherous to each other too often, it is NOW- time out for that! We have done this, so much, so to the point that sisters have literally, ended up worse than enemies. Sisters, we can often tear through the bond of love and pull it down, and force the bond into a lull of malice, deception and sometimes even in the worst of cases; death (yes this is true). I have seen stories on CNN and Fox where sisters have destroyed their sister's life deliberately! We may say, "Oh no" it will never be that way for me, and for most of us it won't, but for some, there are cases where it IS. I have seen horrifying scenarios and stories on social media, and television out there, where sisters have set each other up, taken one's partner, one's inheritance, one's child, one's money, and it goes on. I have taken hold of the sister space to see what it holds, what it entails and what it does. By God's divine pouring and unctioning, I deliver this memoir to my fellow sisters, of all races, colors and creeds in the words of the famous Marvin Gaye "Here My Dear, Hear it is"- this memoir is to serve the bond of sister hood and to STRETCH it to its FULL capacity.

There is a bitter pill that has put itself out here with, and for sisters, let's taste that pill, so we can swallow it and get better. The bitter pill that you have tasted all of your life for your sister can now be changed. This pill can be reverted to a sweet savor and touch for the attachment and connection for sisterhood. Let's take hold of it and delve into its darkest place, so we can come out shining and on top. Let's deal with the lonely place of sisterhood, lets deal with the darkest places of sisterhood, then we will deal with the fulfilled, and brightest place of sisterhood. It is okay for us to explore all aspects of sisterhood, God has sent me to bring forth an opening to help your eyes become enlightened, to help you to become empowered, endowed and set free, so that you can, if at all possible- enjoy the place of sisterhood. God wants to give us a sword, (to slash- any all problems, indiscretions and troubles that carry itself within sisterhood)- at the root! A door to rid the animosity that you, as a sister have been carrying for a very long time in order to- release the burden of feelings, and the concept that is inside of your head that states,, "what a mistake this was to birth me into this group of girls"! Yes, I have heard it said by some that will remain nameless!

__My Sister/My Enemy__. Stories of how your sister has become and is, your enemy are tragic in the flesh and tragic in the spirit/soulish realm. Hopefully somewhere in this book you will find a way to break the bitter pill up and not allow it to become toxic, in the way that some are doing these days. In the wake of reality shows and sisters often being depicted as arch enemies. I wanted to shed some light on how sisters can become one another's keeper instead of one's enemy. This is the book, that I have been writing for years, "My Sister, My Enemy," on the Wake of my 16th wedding anniversary, to my wonderful husband Kenyatta Applewhite (September 8, 2019). I want to, and will continue to finish my book. I want to talk about how sisters become sisters and how sisters become enemies, yet how to grow in either direction to the good (meaning seeing the good that can come out of the bad- that occurs with sisters)!

The Meaning. The meaning of sisters is defined by several different dictionaries as "a woman or girl related to one through being somebody's daughter", and another description says a "close friend or associate." So with that being said, I will explore this option, as well, a surrogate sister. So in saying this, are you telling me that a sister can be a friend or close associate? That is what I hear some say. I have witnessed, experienced and observed sisters getting along, being the best and closest of friends, with a sound and secure identity in place, while on the other hand, I have seen it not be so and a surrogate sisters steps in an "fills in the blanks, where a real sister should be (say it aint so, just kidding and lol)"!

Moving right along.I have seen the unspeakable happen with sisters to cause enemy ground to be established! I have witnessed sisters, seducing their sister's closest friend, husband or significant other, I have witnessed, heard and saw stories of sisters fighting over inheritances and their deceased parents properties, to the death. I have heard it all, as I have listened closely, took notes, wrote on napkins, wrote in the annuls of my mind, and as I walk along grocery stores, the malls, at church, sitting at the light, the revelation poured out to me and I kept it inside so that I can tell you guys what being a sister is all about, the good bad and the "real" ugly! I have read, explored and researched, stories, situations and documentaries of sisters and how they behave unto one another. Consequently, sisters it is time for us to take a real look at what sisters are and what they should be. This memoir will attempt to go in as many directions that God allows and directs, in order to aid sisters in finding a "release". Let's start with the bond.

The Bond. What is a bond? A bond is defined as something closely tied together, an agreement with, a force, or something joined together by chemicals. Is this us, as sisters (ask yourselves), are we a force joined together that will never cease, are we chemically bound or unbound? What is your sister bond to you? What should it be? ARE you trying hard to keep it in tact or are you secretly "side eyeing" your sister because you think- what she thinks about you? Is it this or is it that "? My, My, My, this is all a bunch of "Malarkey (as used by Joe Biden in one of the debates during President Obama's last election)." What should sisters have, when it comes to a bond? Are we supposed to be fighting with or picking at each- other, or are we to be that support in any situation that presents itself to aid our sister in whatever situation that she or the group faces. What is a bond, then- I ask? Sisterhood is, and should be a force, as listed above- to be reckoned, with as a- functioning force. Do we see our sisterhood space like that? Having a sister bond is not "just fighting with her against her husband or boyfriend," Nope, that is not what sisterhood is about! Although, for some of you "Young SISTERS, out there, you are muttering, "OH YES IT IS"! LOL!!!

There are variances of opinions of what sisters are, and how they should bond. Yet one needs to explore your sister bond for where it stood in the past and where it is today. Do constant maintenance on your sister group. That is why I am featuring the WRIGHT sisters, because they are sisters that I grew up with in my neighborhood, Cymp, Shoan, Debbie, Lynn and Angie. They started their trip, in what I can tell to keep their bond close, while experiencing, love, laughter, good times and life with each other once a year, while they still can.

They post their actions on Face Book and do live features! This just- lights my fire! Exactly- because they are living examples of what sisters should be. During this trip they do things that identify closeness, excitement, endearment, love, and caring. While showing how much they cherished their sister bond. I noticed during their trips, that the last few days they do a color matching scene or day, when they all wear the same colors. This is so symbolic of sisterhood. Coming together, being together, listening together, laughing together, letting your hair down together, crying together, sharing together. I have watched and experienced the Wright Sisters for a good portion of my life, even though half of them moved away, all I ever saw was togetherness, even at a distance, living in different cities, they would always find their place of "TOGETHER".

"The Wright Sisters (Fun and dedicated Sister love)"

This is a key word that all sisters should use and look for and that is "together" being in, and within one another, knowing that no matter what we are sisters! Can I get a AMEN? Knowing that we were sisters- when we came out of our mothers womb. My little granddaughers Krissy and Melianna, ages 2 and 5 months are the perfect example. When I was babysitting them one night, I watched their bond. I watched Krissy, look into Meliania's eyes and Melania (*The Eldest-see below*) into hers, they were so in sync with each other, as my youngest grandbaby- the 5 month old, was chirping, cooing and waving her little hands to the sound of her sisters vibe, she was so in-tune with her and she smiled and laughted at every turn when her sister came near. I put her close to her sisters face, as to allow her to grab her and kiss her and I saw the smiles and the geers that meant so much to the two of them, it was a glorious episode of sisterhood, that flashed "right before my eyes". I was marvelled at how much they love each other, at the very little ripe ages of know nothing in this world. This should show us, big "gals" that we are far behind. It reminded me of the scripture that says "And a child shall lead them (latter part of verse 6 in the 11th chaper of the book of Isaiah)". It takes children to show us the right way and my grandchildren allowed Gods grace and mercy to shine through them to show me how true sisterhood should be (View their picture in this book on the last page). Sisters continue to understand what it means to grow and be a sister- knowing that we were sisters, before we were married, sisters before we had our children, sisters in time and sisters on the earth! God created and designed the mold, for us to be just that and that is - sisters. Lets take notes from the Wright Sisters and my little grandbabies to see that, togetherness is the key. I am always excited to see what they have up next for their sister trip and am waiting for the next, although I know with COVID-19 in tow, they may have to wait a while. Keep it "lit"- my dear sisters from another -mother--. A really good example of sister bonding and maintenance. "Ode to the Wright Sisters, Keep it going girls!"

"Melianna/I am the big Sister)"

**Ongoing and forever.** We need to explore our bond as sisters? Take note of which experiences "where we are as a group, or as- individuals ". Learn of what you are dealing with now, or have dealt with for most of or, all of one's lives when it comes to sisterhood. Explore any or all hindrances that are occupying your sister bond. Are you still stuck, as a sister where you feel trapped, where you feel like all of your other sisters have made it and you have not, which leaves the bond incomplete? Do you have thoughts, feeling and emotions that leave you feeling insecure, of any kind within the sister bond? Do you feel like you are less than at times, because you maybe a half sister, do you feel deep downwardly inadequate, like you cannot put your finger on it?

Do you feel she has the personality that money cannot buy? Do you feel that she has the friends that you desire to have? Do you see her as the soul that stole yours and left you without? How do you see your connectedness to your sister (good or bad)? What is it that she has that makes you feel special, what is it about your sister that she has that makes you feel nullified and without? What is it that you want to imitate or as we used to say back in the days "copy"? Do you secretly wish you were her, or could be like her, for the good and bad, I have seen it happen both ways? A sister that loves her sister, looks up to her, and wants to be like her and gleans from her cup to the good! Then I see another in the same token that wants to be like her, act like her, talk like her, but secretly, snides at her, and decides to take the alternate route and rob her sister's soul, by illegally taking her ways, thoughts, feelings, and emotions into a secret cup of her own and create a world, to combat her sister with her OWN stuff (ain't that a blip), that is not by no means, nice, but it just needs to be said. Let's explore these issues, write them down and talk to ourselves, a therapist or even God about your true feelings that you have about your sister. It is the time to get it all out!

Additionally- Do you feel that physical- beauty didn't catch you, motivation, drive, authenticity or the like, as much as it did your sisters, do you feel like you are the " unattractive ugly duckling, or have the Cinderella sister syndrome "? Do- you walk around with "weird sister complexes"? I have heard countless stories, face-to-face, word of mouth that sisters have endured and experienced similar to the ones mentioned - that has caused them to have an unfortunate complex (when it comes to sisters), God has allowed me all this time, to jot down experiences, emotions and actions of sisters in the table of my heart, in order to write it in this book. Some sisters have felt like they will never amount up to the next sister and what she has done, achieved and even what she looks like. This is a tradgesty, I will talk throughout the book on what sisters should really be like. Let's first look at it, face it and deal with it, sister's now is the time!

I want to say first, that in my opinion with the, observation and research on and about sisters, I think that the sister bond, should be the closest one on the planet! Your sister can be your complete "same" and your complete "opposite (at the same time)." Being the complete opposite and the complete same is often times grounding for good matching to take place with sisters. Some of us think that because we are different than our sisters, that it is an awful place to be, but it is not, every sister should bring something to the table. Everyone one of us! I have heard my friend and confidant Ms. Gertha James, say that "Sisters can be at times closer to each other than they are to their own mothers"! I wondered to myself why and how, while realizing that this is true, some sisters tell each other's things that they would not dare say to their mother and some do the total opposite. I am not saying either is wrong, but there is grounding and validity in both means.

Furthermore on bonding, bonding is a time of special intimacy. It is a time that we lull together in "nothingness." A time when we talk about nothing that often times lead to nothing, or leads to something, when we sleep together, when we cry together when we are totally enmeshed and full of each other. When sisters take the time to do this, often times the relationship flourishes throughout time, but without it, it diminishes. Have you ever experienced this type of bonding and mating with your sister in your life, or did It fall short of the closeness that it was meant to be? I want you to think, as you read the words, of this memoir or book, which sister are you, what type of sister are you? Where do you meet your sister, at spiritually, mentally, and emotionally or do you do it at all? Do you take your sister for granted, do you not show her the same respect and regard as she has for you, which is it? There is so much that sisters go through, until it is totally crazy. Issues that arise such as: jealousy of one's relationship with their mother, their father, their other siblings, achievements, personalities, there are so many things that sisters go through. Let's walk this thing "all the way out" so we can figure out which sister you are, where is the core of your being that is connecting or detaching you, to or from your sister or sister group. Where does your ingestion flow to and from, when it comes to the tie that binds you with the person that is so much like you, but yet is so much different than you! It is time to propose healing in this area, it is time to lift up the banner of success, victory and triumph when it comes to sisterhood! Let's do this!

Special Note:Some people out there; sadly have lost their sister or sisters to death, and have had not had the chance to say, "I am sorry," nor time to reconcile or "bond" your efforts or issues with your sister. It is okay, but it is not okay. God has sent this unique writing to you, as a form of recompense. God has sent me to tell you that this book is to help you get there, this book is to make you the sister, that you wish- you could be, or could have been. In addition, to enhance the one that you already are. Forwardly, I saw a movie that a lady wrote to her deceased daughter. Her daughter was adopted out, when she was little, and she never got to meet her prior to her death, as they had been distanced by the adoption (where she willfully gave her up-the mother tried to get to her, but before- she could and right near the time they were almost there, the daughter, that she gave away for adoption passed away), She later- met her daughter (that passed away) through her daughter (that survived via child birth) She saw who her daughter could have been to her and the relationship that they could have had, had time allowed it. She decided to write her everything she wish she could have said to her, this can be for the living or the dead. If you need to get your feelings out sisters to someone that has gone on, do so! It will be relieving and refreshing. God sent this message to you, so that you can say everything that you need to say! Force the regrets into a place of forgetfulness, by taking action and resisting the enemy's agony that is constantly going back and forwards in your mind, saying "What if I would have or "I wish I would had"! Pour your heart and pain out in a letter, you will feel so much better! Take your time, even if you need private counseling or help, -do so, but write that letter and read it out loud!

The force/The Bond. Push the force together, do what is necessary to recreate the place, the journey, the aspiring projection of what it means to be a sister. Being in a relationship with one's sister is something that is to be an 'intertwined (a never ending circle that goes around and around)'. A force that is not able to be 'untied (in my own words)'. Sisters are to have an automatic or "unloose able bond." Do you remember, when you got into little spats with your sister about whose turn it was to "play jack stones' or "who was going to wear the good jacket today" or "Who was going to sit in the front seat or who was going to tell momma"? Those were arguments that you would forget about the next day, or in some cases the very next few minutes? Our bond was priority back then, but over time the bond changed. When did your bond change with your sister? When did the connection, short circuit? When did it break loose? Explore this to trace the origin of your pain, explore why this is so. Rachel in the book of Genesis Chapter 29, King James Version knew her pain, although she didn't voice it, she knew it was because her sister could bear their husband's children (yes they shared a husband) and she was barren. Rachel at the time could not. What is it that your sister "bares" that you cannot, what is it, that is holding you back? What area of productivity is it that your sister yields that causes you to "flinch" every time you see her or hear of her name? What destinies are at total contrast of each other, yet the same? Rachel and Leah were different, but held a similar position, they were both married to the same man and they were sisters, although this is not what we practice in our culture today, it was then, and they had that one thing in common.

Sister Fighting. Sisters can fight over anything, money men, children, parents, positions, being "right", :being wrong"- defending one "sister over the other", taking sides, inheritances, what she said, what you said about my child, "my job", "my walk", "my talk", "the way I address my kids", "the way I take care of my kids", "the way I react and respond to my husband", the way I love and do for my grandchild", the list goes on and on and on! Let's take for example Rachel and Leah-again- (two biblical sisters, Genesis 29:1-28 King James Version), the bible notes that Rachel was loved by Jacob (her husband), while Leah was despised in her husband's eyes. Leah was the eldest daughter, but got overlooked due to her appearance. Leah was actually the first wife of Jacob, although he desired Rachel first and foremost, because of how she looked. Amongst other things, the Bible tells us that- he loved her madly and worked to have her for a total of 14 years (seven at first and seven later, when he found out he had to marry the oldest first according to customs)., Neither sister knew who they were, they both had no sense of identity, no sense of self, as sisters or individuals. Both relied upon, the other's ability. One had the babies, (Leah) and one WANTED babies (Rachel), but could not, as she was, BARREN (Rachel), they both thought that this gave them identities, in the long run it didn't work out well for them, internally! The text goes on to describe Leah as being "weary eyed," "tender eyed" meaning soft or weak eyed, I have heard some teach that she was "crossed-eyed," making her less desirable in her husband's eyes and the other (Rachel) was desired. Often times one sister gets preference over the other in many different ways, and causes the other to be left feeling useless, unuseful, and worthless, physically, naturally and internally. Leah had a sense of doubt and low confidence in how she looked because of that one physical issue. In this situation, the younger sister got preferred over the older, in which caused the older sister to become depressed and sad often times. How many times do we put ourselves down because this is how we face life, this is how we see ourselves when we are in our group of sisters. "Oh everybody sees her as this, and does not see me as that, this is what happened to Leah, and she lessened who she was because of her deep rooted insecurity. How many of you sisters have a deep-rooted insecurity that you have left unaddressed. Leah, though, had a position of power and acknowledged she bore seven of Jacobs children. Leah knew this and sometimes flaunted it. Leah held on to the only piece of security that she had at times, to show that she had something. We as sisters need to rise to the occasion to see that we need to have a identify of our own apart from our kids. We, yes love them and cherish them, but we need to build up what we are and who we are in God. Don't get my wrong, because I love my kids too, but we have to pull ourselves away from having our "sole" identity tied into our children.

Going right along, with the two sisters Rachel and Leah, her sister only bare two (Rachel), she (Leah) wasted her time focusing on the wrong thing about herself and her sister, consequently. She was subconsciously blinded by what she thought her sister had and she didn't and then her sister Rachel was blinded by the same, in the reverse, as Rachel longed for children that she could not have at the time, both - sisters were at a loss- and didn't see their worth or value in God's eyes, or within themselves. Is that you? Are you wasting time worrying about what your sister has, and what you don't have? Let's regroup and stop this. You are throwing away your blessing, and your most precious time. You are slowly gnawing away at your God given position, time and royalty! Take the time, to explore who you are, what you are, and what God has given you to produce to your identity and not your sister's. Let that go and "go for yours," it's time.

"Rachel and Leah (The battle of Sister Love)"

Leah and Rachel they both had something in common. They both had to bare God's seed to expand their families to bring Gods purpose into the earth, neither knew this. On another note, Hebrew custom required the eldest daughter to be married first. Side note—Are there a few sisters out there that feel your sister, took something that was yours? It does not necessarily mean a man, it could have been something else that you were due to inherit or receive? Did she take a blessing, a word, a thought, a stance, a spiritual position, a natural position, or deed that was yours to gain, yours to inherit? Do you feel slighted, by her actions? If so, we need to deal with those feelings now. You need to first confess it, and then figure out a way to get this issue out in the open, so it can no longer hinder or haunt you. Now I do not force anybody in this memoir to do anything, these are just suggestions and you have to do it of your own free will. I have seen what I am telling you, work for some sister groups. So I am informing you, so that you will know what can work, and help you. Do all things in - prayer and supplication, make every request known unto God regarding your issue with your sister, before moving forward. (Philippians 4:6 NKJV) It is time to explore this so that you can be set free, once you explore this and acknowledge your pain and inner conflict you can grow and produce too! God has given us all fruit to bare, but we have to identify with it on our own, we cannot continue to blame our sister or sisters because we do not have the same skill set or production skills that she has, it was not meant to be that way! God intended for us to use our own fruit, our own talents, our own mind, or our own creativity, to build or enhance ourselves first and then experience the fruit what we 'yield' as sisters.

**Sister mating**, Let's talk about this process. This is a process where sisters coming together such as we did in the old days, when sisterhood was valued and highly esteemed. Sister mating is when one comes together to reap and sow, to build and tear down, to move and stay (rock and go steady), it is simply a time to come to-gether as a group and as individuals. Yet knowing and understand our roles, our resources, our integrities, our spiritualties, our homes our loves. I mean knowing, what we have to give, even if it is a little pain, that invokes strength, "all goes for" the mating session. When we was sit back, in the old times, sisters -and would be laughing and outside playing, jump roping it, hopscotching it, double dutching it and other types of games to stay close and bond, with each other. Those were the good ole days, sitting outside on the porch on Sundays, talking, laughing, running our mouths, sisterhood was at its best back then, but then we all "grew up (I am sure you can all can relate, to where I am going with this)". When we grew up, we some how left some parts out. We skipped over what it means to grow in sisterhood, we just left it and did not learn of it. Learning of sisterhood as adults is totally different than that of it, when it is in the childhood phase. We have to learn how to belt together and be together as adults. You know how a belt has a buckle and you find the hole that fits, so that it can fit your current size, that is how growing sisterhood is, we have to figure out which "hole" fits for us, now as we grow in size and stature! Read on!

**Growing Up Sisters, Aunts and our children (another side of bonding)**. When we grow up and our size changes, we have children, we get married, we go to college, we do so much. Growing up as sisters was, good, but there is yet another angle of sisterhood, that I want to tap into. A area that is vital to sisterhood is how we treat one another's kids when we have them. A lot has changed since the times when I grew up, yet - when we were growing up, all of my aunts had the right to spank out little behinds, and nothing would be said, we had the assurance (meaning family) that one's aunt had their niece or nephew's best interests at heart, so, if one of our aunts needed to spank us, it was done. Now the latter has taken place, now, in these days and times, if a sister, spanks another sister's child, or even say a cross word in the manner of correction, this will most definitely be a fight. Why is this so? This is also a great wedge in sisterhood, how we handle and love each others kids. Whatever happened to the trust we had in chastisement of one another's children (grown or small). Why do we get so mad and angry when our children act out (grown or adult, because- we have some grown-up baby-nieces and nephews that need chastisement and we as sisters get mad because our sister has something to say, there has been really high offense in this area, girl don't say "nothing and I mean nothing" to my child, what if your sister can reach your child better than you can, maybe she can pull your child out of the pit that he or she is on, but oh, now, we fight to the death to keep our sister from saying anything to our children, when this should not be so) Why does conflict immediately arise among sisters, why do we get an attitude, when someone says something to our kids, I am only talking about sisters right now, nothing else, think, think and think, on this? I say not much more on this topic, as I am sure those that know this, know that this is true, that we got to keep the bond connected even with our kids. We must let them know, through our connection that what goes for one goes for all, with extremes being sought out with the sister at hand. I get so weary of hearing stories on the internet rang out of countless stories on Facebook and Twitter of Sisters fighting, arguing and battling each other about their kids' situations. We should have an unearthly understanding to work together to help each other with our children, but not abuse. Believe it or not- that is the way the bond was back many "times" ago. My Aunt Rosa Mae kept us, while my parents worked, she chastised us, fed us and kept us in check. Sisters were trustworthy with one another's children, normally if a child told something to their Mom that their Aunt did they would get another spanking, but times have changed, I only speak to the bond, and how sisters were able to trust their sisters with anything even their lives, but that is not the case today. So sad!

__Further sister conflict__. I heard a story that was reported a few years back on two different accounts of "identical twin sisters' setting the opposite sister "Up to Die" and succeeding. This is a horror! I could not believe what I was hearing. Yet I had to ask myself what was it that could have caused so much hate, so much animosity, what could have caused so much destruction, in one sister's heart towards the other? Somewhere in there, the bond was broken. It was destroyed and blinded. Is your sister bond broken? Is it crippled? Ask yourself? Is it strong as the new forms of super glue (sounds a little corny, but is it true or is it not so true). Check your sister bond out. Explore it, wring it out, all the way out, to see if it is pliable, if it is secure. What can cause sisters to loose the tie that binds? Think of a rope, when you were a little child and you tied a rope to a tree to hang from it and you had to make sure that the tree was tight enough so that you would not fall or hurt yourself, is your bond not so tight? Is it that the bond is not properly knitted together to endure the pressure? Do you have barrier and boundaries clearly set, so that you can and do understand your sister and she understands you, or have you allowed the distant shadow that follows the bond to spill out into spooky images?

Do you allow your sister's thoughts to delve into a place that you know it shouldn't be, or do you immediately talk to her and let her know what is real and what is not or vice versa, all of us, as sisters have a responsibility to be true to who we are and not hide, not hold what we feel inside for years and years and have this "green or hateful eye" stirring at the very presence or sight of one's sister, a secret sin, a secret hate, a secret insecurity, after all your sister is you, she is your mirror, in some way, somehow, you look like her, or act like her or even smell like her, maybe all three, maybe one or two, but somewhere in your soul, and your spirit you are, or have become your sister, whether, you like it or not.

Work to secure the tie that binds, remember the tree, how you made sure It was secure, before swinging wildly or carelessly on it. Work on securing that bond, tie that "knot" tight. WE all know when we swung on tree swings, that we wanted to make sure our ride was fun and right! Make sure your "rope" is tight! Make sure that it won't come aloose and when it does seem that the knot is loosening up, do all you can to tighten it! Talk, work it out, visit, strive, push, get your bond back to that tightness it once had!

Do what it takes to, take the time to get to know who you are and who your sister really is, not who you think she is, take the time, to realize her worth and vice versa, take the time to know what times she likes to get with or be with you, know if she really has the money to loan, know if her feelings where hurt when you didn't call, write or text her back when she needed you. Know if words you spoke were belittling or demeaning! Learn to explore one another's feelings to keep the bond connected. Think on your responsibility as a sister if you need to call or text her back, or go to her grave site and get it right with her, or simply get on your knees, wherever the place is that you feel that you lost, or hurt your sisterly connection, please work to mend it, to tie it, to bring it back together.

The Gibbons Sister Twins. I have noticed too, even though, I have seen lots of sisters all over the world, some I know and some I do not. I now want to take a observational look at a set of African American twin sisters, that I came across doing my reading research -regarding sisters, that were so close that they would not speak to anyone.The Gibons Sisters were a set of twin born in Wales. The Gibbons sisters' language they spoke "between themselves (them two only) was unique to them that --only they knew it, nor would they share it. June and Jennifer Gibbons, they grew up, being known as the "Silent Twins." The twins were born in Wales and had some issues that were quiet disturbing for their family, they talked to each other in tones that were annoying, they had mimicking, squealing, and wierd sounding behaviors, that caused doctors and psychiatrists to only believe that they were psychotic in some way. Strangely, they lived a totally isolated life, they had a bond that was so deep, until it was psychotic. They refused to be alone, so much so, until when they were 14, their parents sent them to separate boarding schools, the separation was unbearable for the two and they became psychologically burdened, until they had to be re-united and once reunited they went directly back into isolation. The twins had grew and became violent, rebellious, insolent, and in some cases criminal, they had fights, and competitions, all in "evil." The girls, even though- they grew into psychological experiments, amongst other things, they remained united, and they remained tied to each other. They were ultimately bonded to the good and bonded to the bad.

Are you like the Gibbons sisters, are you too close, and connected until there is some pathology involved or are you not bonded at all and there too stands pathology? Is there some trace of infidelity in the link of blood? Some envy, some spite, some word, that was passed through your ear canal, through a mutual acquaintance, relative or even someone you trusted dearly someone you shared the womb, with your mom? IS there something that links you, but yet so much separates, you as it did the Gibbons Sister/Twins? Some of us, are bonded negatively to our sisters. Sisters, we don't want to be comrades of the devil, and his cohorts, as these two were (my opinion). We want to be sister servants of the most High! Yes, we have our secret- ques, codes and notions, that connect us, but let's make the lines clear, as to not fall into states of obliviousness. Let's talk to each other in ways that are socially acceptable for us. Let's not fall in the trap that keeps us bound forever in a negative manner. Let's fight to get out. Let's not end up sisterly "mute" Let's not allow pathology to destroy our unit, such as this case. Psychological harm can turn in so many different directions. It can cause a sister bond to be irretrivacabily broken. It can cause life to take a sister by the throat and choke the life out of her, if not dealt with.

"Sister/Pathology"

On the other side of things, Furthermore-I have seen people that do not have a sister, want and long for a sister, while the ones that do have one- wish the opposite. I have seen some that wish that they never knew a sister. I have heard people say things, like, "That is your sister, you should love her and get along with her and - I have gotten responses, like, she is not my sister, you really don't know her." She is not really a sister, she is more like my enemy, true story. Comments of the sort breaks the sister bond down and sabotage the inner and mental connection. The Gibbons sisters were so close that they agonized one another's presences, because the could not break apart from each other. They were so connected until it was scientifically baffling to professionals and the closeness caused their untimely demise. Sisters don't allow your miscommunication or "the strangest of fruit type" connection tear your connection down with your sister. There is a song called "Strange Fruit," the song is sung by Billie Holiday, that was the rendition of a poem that was referencing African American Lynching's. We don't want the good of something such as the sweet melodies of this song to turn up into a visual of turmoil and/or chaos. The name of this song, says nothing for the true meaning of the song. Don't allow the "Melodies of Sister Hood" to end up like the unwrentched antonym of this lyrical song; end up in your fellowship, forbid "strange fruit's entrance" into what God ordained as abundancy.

Furthermore, there were unavoidable negative and positive issues surrounding the story of the Gibbons Twins. Being close and bonded to one's sister does not mean that one is to use, abuse, or take advantage of one's sister's kindness, weaknesses or strengths. Some sisters can even take advantage of one' sister's strength, by neglecting it, yes neglecting her sister's strength. During an interview, I watched Solange, and Beyoncé in an old interview. Solange, made a statement along the lines of saying that "She would not interview or do a show with Beyoncé," I wondered, to myself, why not. It seems that she didn't want the advantage that her sister's fame could bring her, she wanted her own. That is how it should be, yet lets not be abrasive about it and subtily sinical! We all should have our own identity, but let me caution you, not to the point of rebellion (this is a double-edged sword). Some of us, do not realize that our distaste or dislike for what our sister has produced, causes subtle levels of bitterness and rebellion. That is not how it is supposed to be. I am not saying that is what was the case for Solange, or was it (my opinion)? We all as sisters should take the time to learn how we can benefit from each other, after knowing without a doubt who we are. See some times we can break the bond of sisterhood without knowing it, remember the rope, mentioned early, we can damage the tie of the bond, by not knowing and understanding our false innuendos that we develop through the falsities of our own mind, when it comes to our sisters, taking advantage or not taking advantage of the privilege of having a sister, loosens the rope that secures the bond. Making clear bounds or stopping points can enhance one's relationship with one's sister. Are you constantly unmanteling the tie? Work on securing it by knowing yourself, knowing your sister, knowing your limitation, knowing her limitations. Get to work! It will be worth it in the long run! Understanding the advancement of sisterhood will make your life a whole lot easier! Take it from me!

When we were little my Momma would grease our scalp, after putting it in pony tails or braids. She would tell us that greasing our scalp made our hair grow-in order to stay healthy and keep it from being dry. Are "we greasing up" our relationships with our sisters? Are we using the proper grooming materials to keep our relationships healthy or are we just ignoring the process, ignoring the upkeep of the interconnection? Are we constantly making one or the other feel like we are really sisters? Are we initiating calls, initiating times together, pulling together outings for our kids, making sure our kids are in relationship with each other, in order to model, this relationship skill.

"Sisters, Lets jump roap"

A little bit on famous sisters. One thing that I did notice about another set of famous sisters the Atkins sisters, Mary, Mary (Gospel Singers), Erica and Tina Campbell, they fuss and fight on national television, but they make it clear to all, on television that they are close, and that no matter how mad the get, they never, ever cross the line of what it means to be a sister. They have expressed in their pain that they go to the ends of the world to push sisterhood, even when they fall out. I have seen one of the sisters chase the other one down to lasso them right back to the place that they were created through their mother's womb-that, is the channel of sisterhood. The Atkins sisters (all of them, as it is a total of 6 of them) demonstrate a really good version on my list of sisters, in which I will demonstrate others lists later that show, that although they have gone "through it" so to speak, they still keep and make the bond tighter. It seems to me by my observation the harder it gets with the Atkins Sisters the closer they get! I applaud them Sisters! I know that because of their relationship with their Lord and Savior, that his divine grace and mercy has kept them together and solid!

There are so many compartments to being a sister, which compartment are you a part of? Take a look at your sister bond to see if it is greased properly in order to take a look at the tie that secures- you closely with your sister to see if it is toxic or if it is sweet? See if the relationship is one of moral benefit or moral demise. Check out the area that you connect and the area that you and them- disconnect in order to produce more fruit. "Jesus said cut it so that it may bear more fruit (**John, 15; 2, KJV**)"Do you get pleasure- out of seeing your sister down and out? Are you feeling like you deserve it and your sister does not, if you do, then, you need to do, like my husband tells me, when I am thinking too hard to "Get out of your head." Get like the Atkins Sisters (Mary, Mary, Gospel Singers) and fight for the love, fight for the togetherness, follow the way of endearment of the sister path. Don't just let it die, sisters, you need to bring it all back to reality and explore and research what it is that is causing these things to occur. Is it something that was said to you, at a very young age, is it something that you overheard (I repeat this throughout the memoir for a reason), was it something that you perceived, something that you saw, something that you tasted, and you just cannot shake it, is it a thought that the devil put in your mind about how you see your sisters or how they see you? Explore this very issue! Determine what is it that makes you cringe?

Sisters Some More. Is having a sister the best thing in the world or the worst thing in the world? As you read on, I would like to share cases that show sisters that are explicitly "enemies," but yet still "Sisters." I want to discuss, report, explain and divulge in the deep dark stories, secrets and accounts of stories where sisters have become the arch rivals and nemesis, yet they still love each other. I want to report on historical events that point directly to the enemy of our blood, the enemy in our own household and that is or can be one's own sister, the one that you passed through the same birth canal. Some may look at this book in "disdain" or some may even trash it, I am prepared for both! While some may embrace and lock this book in the door of their heart! This book I am hoping will be liberating in either sense.

In life, it has been taboo to say, think or act on sister rivalry. Yet we see where some are open and some are discreet. There are sisters out there that feel they are entitled in some particular area, that the other sister is not and have acted on this particular way of thinking all of their lives. Some sisters have a "pinned up belief that their sister hates them." It has been cited that making comments or saying "I don't care for, or like my sister period" is shameful. This is because the position of sisterhood is supposed to be "sacred and regarded highly." Sisters are supposed to have each other's back at all times, be supportive, be like a spare tire when one goes out, but in the 21st century it seems that 'being a sister has changed, for a lot of us . A very good percentage of us have let go of what it means to be a sister, and in some cases we have totally let go of our relationship or dis-owned our sister. Several reasons may emerge as to why this has taken place. It may be due to some indiscretion or another, either from her or you (yep, we are all guilty, even though we don't want to admit it). Breaking a sister bond is one of the most treacherous events, but in the day of reality shows, social media and free speech, what it means to be a sister has been diminished, tarnished and almost nonexistent. Some are saying that is not totally true, and you are right, it is not, but I come now in the name of the sister that is being seen as -the enemy (not the enemy, but just being seen that way-keep reading). I will talk later on sisters that represent the real meaning of "sister." Keep reading!J

It is safe to say that we all have done somethings to our sisters "knowingly or unknowingly" that may have sabotaged or damaged our unique relationship,

Dr. Pamela Renee Applewhite, PhD

whether we want to admit or not. Understandably though being a sister is special and is always supposed to be. When referring to one's sister, the sound of saying just "my sister" elicits specialty. It speaks automatically to someone that is there at all times, or at least it should be. A sister will or is supposed to "get out of the bed" for you, at any time of the day or night and fend for, and with you. Ask yourself is this so?

Special Note: Let's finish this statement, "I think of my sister as-_____ _____to me" Think on this after filling in the blank (This is good for sister conversations and mating times).

A sister's relationship is supposed to be one that you cherish and should be a standout encounter. The fruits of being a sister should ripen as one gets old, but we often fail to realize that at a young age that having a sister only gets better with time. That having some one- to love you, in spite of, at all times, no matter how much money you have, no matter how much education you have,no matter how many properties you have, no matter how many contracts you have, no matter how broke you are, no matter how unattractive you feel or less than you "think" you maybe. I listed these- because- just because a person has material possessions, it does not mean that they are at their best, not everyone with tangible items are as happy as we think they are! Let's stop having the immature thought that a person is alright because they have money or things, nothing could be farther from the truth. Let's not think that a sister is totally- complete because they seem to have it all materially. It is not so. Money, power, prestige and things-do not make for- total happness and inner joy (sometimes, but it is not everlasting) ! It is all vanity! Something inside of a person still wants and longs for something that you cannot explain, even when you "so-call make it or reach it"! We all have in our lives, sisters- reached our goals, whether tangibilly (something you can touch and feel) or intangibly (something that is not touchable, mostly inner things). But there is always something else, still!

So, sister if you are looking at your sister through those set of eyes, maybe you need to refocus your view, it is not the absolute truth in a lot of cases. See, I know some of you think that I am referring to one particular type (skin color-wise), but

I am not this thing of sisterhood comes in all shapes, colors, personality types, classes, financial brackets, it catches us all "big or small." I have seen good looking, I mean beautiful women that are White, Black, Indian, Jamacian, Italaian and a lot more, admit that they feel insecure, hopeless, helpless, and worthless, and not as worthy or fulfilled, as their other sister or - sisters think she does. In the way that the opposite sister- thinks she does or sees- about herself. I have witnessed women with lots of money talk on severe depression and feelings of emptiness, loneliness, worthlessness, confusion, and inferiority. I have heard the smartest, and most achieved women that are high ranking in society, the community in celebritism, and the gospel (ministry) say that didn't feel worth "a thing".

Furthermore, sisters, I have taken polls all of my life on sisters, their reactions and behaviors, even my own aunts (paternal and maternal) that are sisters, and my sisters - on behaviors, actions, feelings and emotions towards each other, and with each other. I was paying attention since I was very, young to the dynamics of sisters. I have realized through my family members, that they have held on to their integrity and position as sisters, even when it was bad. I will have to say that, I have never heard them (my aunts-that are sisters) openly betray one another, in any facit, at all. They have always through- whatever they have faced as sisters remain, just that. I have even heard, my momma say often, "That is my sister"! Those few words hold deep! But not with ALL!!

Let's move on! I challenge each sister, as you read this book to open your heart and mind to what is being revealed in this, controversial writing, that is coming solely from my heart, spirit and soul- to yours. Now I caution you, some things being said will be highly disputable and debatable, but true, some may not even fit you, and some may "fit just right", but it is okay, this book is to "hit the right spots" to get to the core of what it means to be a sister and to bring realization to the lives of sisters. This book will help you to become the sister that you desire and need, to be, whether it is to set yourself free from bondage from your sister of it is to enhance the relationship that you already have. This writing will hit the core of your sister situation being, so outright and so true, until some of the writings will bring fear to your soul, and even make you shutter. It will be like listening to the preacher, when revelation is revealed, and you are totally astonished at "how on earth could this have been known, unless by his spirit." early cautioning! Keep reading.

Okay, lets' all face it, for those of us that have been there, there have been times when you asked yourself, "wait a minute, is this the same person, I knew as child, that we played together, slept together,"played Barbie or Cher with, I don't think I know her anymore. This is not the person that was there with me, slept with me, played outside and slid down hills with, laughed with, braided or fixed my hair, snickered with- about others, this is not my sister, not the one that I know. Somehow she has changed, and I am not sure why or who this person is. I speculate it maybe because I left,- went to college and made something of myself, because I married him, because I had them, because I did or didn't say this, or did or didn't stay that. I really don't know why my sister is behaving this way, this is not the comfort of my sister's support that I felt when we played "hopscotch" or "jackstones," this now is in fact "My Enemy" … … Why I don't know.

Special Note: As I go forward sisters, find your place in this book, because even though this book is revealing and may seem "down trodden", there is some good in sisterhood that will be revealed. Keep reading!

Now moving on, let's be honest, there are times when we cover things up and hold things back, but never really say what we really feel, and we go out and talk about it (meaning things that occur with and among our sisters) to other people or we say nothing at all. It's almost like, what we see portrayed in the movies. We develop a world of our own based on the world of our sister, and we are stuck there for most of our lives, looking through that tiny speck of insecurity and even basing- how we conversate with her and others, through those callously bred eyes (for those of you that know what callouses are). It is time for your deliverance, my dear sisters! Lets go forward!

Isolated occurrences can cause us to talk to everybody and somebody- about how we feel about what "our sister has done to us or against us" except telling them ourselves. This is a rule violation- this is where we should be close enough to our sister to speak how we feel. I saw two sisters on The Chow (back on a-2015 edition), and they were competing on who could make the best Thanksgiving dressing, one was traditional and the other one was spicy, one had shrimp and all kinds of goodies. The sisters were highly competitive, but both wanted their dish to win. Both were noted as extremely good, by a guy that sits on the panel, but only one got chosen and that was the non-traditional dressing. You see, we all have to be able to accept that in life some sisters will win, and some will lose, but we are all still sisters, in it all! With this instance, the other sister doted on her sister (the one that won), even after the win- the sister that won, kept the competition going, but kept it mild, it was all fun in love and war! Whether we win or not- our sister wins, we are still one and the same, although we are different- meaning that because she has won, I "too have won," because she is my blood, my kin, my inner/kinsman redeemer (granted by God) We are all still one in the same. It is hard for sisters, in what I have observed to see their sisters excel. Some walk in fear of what their sister has achieved and they allow jealousy and envy to rise. This should be an immediate issue that should call for an active meeting or platform for conversation when this takes place with sisters. Jesus said that "The children of the world are wiser than the children of the light (Luke, 16:8, KJV). Don't let the world handle their affairs better than those of the kingdom. Lets talk, work and act better than as sisters! We need this philosophy, this concept sisters. Lets do something different, so that we can win as sisters!

When you think about corporations, businesses, non-profits, and when there are problems of debate or arguments on specific issues when meetings are held, forums of discussion and debates take place. Some are heated, some are rather professional and painstaking, yet it takes place I bring this point out, my dear sisters, to say that we as sisters need to sit and talk, if we want to be and remain close. The variations of how sisters exel and mate is wide and spread out- yet it needs to be done. Sisters, it is time for us to come together to solve these problems. Sisters, for this very thing, you have to bring your heart to a place of confidence, to an open table for discussion, in order to express your true self, to express how one feels about things that were either- said and done to you, or at least the perspective that is in your mind. You see, we all have a mind's eye and we all see things differently, maybe what you are seeing and what she is seeing is two different things. Take a chance and explore what is going on. After all, my sister- is supposed to be my support, my friend, my confidant, but lately in the 21st century, as stated before does this happen. The bond of sisterhood has really changed, and we all need to acknowledge this fact, for those of you that your-sister bond is great, then Hallelujah (I will say this a lot)!! But there are some of us, that our bonds are not so hooked, not so tight, or not even the slightest bit connected. It is time to come out of the closet, and acknowledge that at times, **_My sister can be my enemy_**! Although this can be and is true, that is not how we want it to stay! Let's keep in mind though- that through adversity, comes life!

Sister Examples of competitiveness, the right way!Venus and Serena Williams, play real live enemies on the tennis court, and they do it well. I say they do it well, because they play enemies to one another in the game of tennis, yet there seems to be understanding beyond the racket, that we are 'blood sisters'. There is no holding back in the game; they unleash their full creative tennis ability on the court, and they play enemies to the highest! After all they're defeating for cups that are world renown, yet the tie never breaks as, one sister to another unfolds with their each individual competitiveness. By observing and seeing this, this tells me in the natural scheme of life, there should always be room for some form of positive competition between sisters, just so long as one understand when I win, you lose, yet we are still of the same "stock," so all in all you still win, even when you lose or when I win, "sister-to-sister." There is no way, we as sisters can lose when we understand when I win, you win, when I lose, or you lose, we all still win!" I really like the idea that Venus and Serena, have an open and obvious respect for each, other as well as an open mind, they both seem to understand that once they pick up the tennis rackets, all bets are off. You see, they use being a sister's enemy in the right context. They understand, at this very moment, that my sister becomes my enemy, but only for this instance, and for this cause, only and only, for this space in time and once they are finished they have been noted as walking to the fence and hugging,embracing or even crying with each other! I simply love this! Sister's if we can adopt and conceptualize this concept, we will win every single time as sisters! Serena has been the victor in most cases, but what I have noticed that somewhere in the training process, when they were little elementary aged girls, Serena developed tenacity and an energy that was instilled in her and through her own nature and skill that God gave her. She appeared to have honed her craft fully and infused it more and more. As she grew, she developed in the game of tennis. Venus, you see, has a tenacity in another whole direction, although she is still a winner and always will be. She is still Serena's sister! She is her sister's confidant and competitor, all at the same time, what a match! If we all got this, what wonderful sisters we would be. You see girls and ladies, this is a great example of what sisterhood is. They never act out in public, they always support who they are as sisters and I have never seen them allow the media to tear them apart, no matter who is the victor! Some sisters, do not have the inner respect for one another when they fight, as Venus and Serena do. We fight with our fangs out, our lies out, our "belittles (belitting, talking over, dismissing)", we don't respect our sister's voice, we try to stamp her out with our own two feet! I have seen a instance, where a sister is with another sister at a family gathering, her insecurity is so steep until she cannot stand to hear her sister talk, and when she does, she clips her with her tongue, spits her out with total dominatrix venum and tears into her loins like a ferious lion. She (one sister) tries to diminish her (the other sister's) soul and spirit in anyway she can. She talks at her in subtle conscious "creeps" of "I am going to get you, if it kills me, you will not out do me, nor will you think you are better than me! I am going to show you in front of everybody, that I am just as good as you"! She fights, and fights with all she got and has in order to push her sister into in asylum (a place of mental illness) or an abyss (place of darkenss) or place of nothingness, so she can stand, in what she thinks is substantative hierchy! She thinks I have established my self and I am now somebody, because I have defeated and depleted my sister and then she walks off! She walks into what she thinks is authority, esteem, overcoming, when it is nothing by pure evil! Pure sinister ploys and schemes that never address the real issue. This is pure back-door ignorance. This is purse satanic indulgence and activity. God is calling for us as sisters to stop this type of inundated behavior. It is a delusional lie that the devil implants into the mind of an insecure, unsettled heart and soul of one sister to the next! I am sure that this is something that we all wanted to come out and hear, so here it is! Now you have it! So lets deal with this issue, for those of you that it's for, lets not just stop at the reading of this book, let's put "***feet on it***", as my brother, Stephen W. Sansbury stated in one of his sermons! Let's take care of the devils doings in our lives as sisters! I know this maybe hard for some of you to believe! But, yes, I have seen it done! Sister

Dr. Pamela Renee Applewhite, PhD

if this is you, it is time for you to stop doing this and sister that it is being done to, it is time for you to stop allowing it. It is time to call a natural and spiritual truce! Do you hear me, my dear sisters, it is time!

Furthermore, We all need to take a lesson from these two famous, world renown tennis creatures (not in a bad way, but phenomenal way)- Venus and Serena, they understand the difference between love and war. They understand where it is appropriate and how it should be used, to make them successful sisters. Even though, they fight like real live enemies on the court, as if one does not know- the other while- on the court, a necessary act at the particular time. They do it and they do it swiftly and they do it well! How many of us as sisters, know when the time is right to walk in competitiveness with our sister, all in love, fun and to produce? I am not sure we have this knack, as Serena and Venus do. Even though they have to put on a mind of competing against one another in the game of tennis, they keep their bond together and intact they way that they should. This team of sisters in my observation share - regardless of who wins, in my personal opinion. They are a true hallmark of what it means to be a sister. I think that their bond is unyielding, no matter how much they fight on the tennis court, they seem to have the understanding of connectedness, and that they know that one is going to lose, and the other is going to win. Let's look at this metaphorically.

If your sister is in a higher position to prosper, excel or reach certain levels than you, don't take it to heart, look to see what you can learn, grow or prosper from her in that particular area. We never really know what the one sister puts into what she is doing, so let's not pre-judge her or accuse her of the sacrifices she makes to get where she is. Let's either try to get better, or get on board with her in some way shape or form to support her. When this happens, the one sister to the other must release to this energy, and must acknowledge that this is how it is going to be. In life we must know that, there is always one person that reaches a "milestone" in one area and one that does not (or vice versa), but it is not to be taken as an offense, in the exact way that the Williams sister's does it, they do it "right," if I must say. They know how to be "abased and abound (based on Philippians 4:12, King James Version)"! "To all things, I have learned how to be full and how to suffer need." One person knows that one will be lifted up, while the other one "takes " down, but we all know that both girls/ladies Serena and Venus are stars in their own right, sometimes one wins and then sometimes the other sister wins, yet she walks in it and does not push to get into her sister's light when she is in the light! Hear me well sisters, don't evade your sister's light, let it be, let her shine when it is time to, stop being a light "hoarder"! Remember when she shines you shine! It is never over, when the other sister is in a place that you are not! When the bible says 'suffering need" it seems that no matter who wins or loses the circumstance will eventually pull you up. We are our sister's keeper! From today and moving forward, sisters if you are out there and you are having serious problems with your sister, take a note from the Williams sisters, ask yourself key questions, "Does my sister work hard at what she does"? "Am I being overly critical of her?" "Am I in support of my sister"? "What am I doing to represent a reflection of my sister?" Am I secretly criticized or putting her down or her efforts?" Am I connecting to her, the way I am supposed to? Am I in understanding, as to know- that what she does is not a threat to me? Ask yourself these questions. I want you to grow!

**A little more on the Williams sisters,** Sisters-Going forward. Know that no matter how hard the fight is, that we are still sisters? Know that nothing should override sisterhood! We should only fight for the cause of sisterhood, not against it! No matter what comes our way! I have noticed with Venus and Serena, when the media tries to strike barriers between them, their faithfulness to their sister bond is always the first to stand out! One does not belittle the other, but they state facts and that is it. Do we use their strategies as sisters (think about it)? Is this what happens between us, as sisters or is it not? I don't think so. In today's world of bitterness, mayhem, pestilence, confusion and such, the sister hood bond is becoming less and less. Not many of us think the way Venus and Serena do. Nor do we live the exemplary life or adhesiveness of their sisterly bond. Not many of us understand that if one sister wins, it's okay, and that we are all triumphant and that she can still love (the winner), but be "triumphant" still in her own special area. I may not be as tenacious or fearless or even victory seeking as you, but I bet I can hit a ball, I bet I can type 60 to 75 words per minute, I can sing like Aretha, I can dance like the Soul Train Dancers, what is it that you, sister, do not have that you sister, in all her fame, does not, or vice versa? We are all special, gifted and talented in our own way!

Sisters know this, you are losing the battle, and overshadowing your gift, by thinking erroneously. You as a sister need to change how you think towards your sister or sisters and stop being overly obsessed with what she has and – and every little petty thing that you are thinking your sister does! Wake up! Get up! Do your own thing, learn of yourself and who you are! As it has been quoted, "Do you" and watch the sister group multiply in its own time ! That is what I love about Venus and Serena, you see Venus is the oldest sister, but Serena is the younger and she is vivacious, hungry and ferocious when it comes to tennis! Yet they both benefit, Get it, they both benefit, they are both Williams, but women today, cannot get that, they just can't! It is time for us as sisters to "wake up!""We have got to focus and think about being sisters, now and not later'. " It is okay if we have to fight "sisters", but know your limits. Submit to the authority (energy) that is in control at the given time in order to profit from the relationship. See, Serena and Venus understood that there will always be a winner and there will be a loser (saying it again and again), so let's prepare ourselves for who is which one, but yet at the backdrop, ultimately they all and we all- both win! I don't know how these sisters feel in their heart, but I am sure, if they are like me or you, "plain human," they have feelings such as we all do. One was happy, victorious and the other may have been sad, but still yet, she knew that her sister triumphed and won, consequently, they both were still winners, because their family name carries on, no matter what. The famous tennis player Billie Jean King, did not even want to "comment" during the prelude of the battle that was to ensue between the sisters, because she knew both were "just that good" with their meeting in Wimbledon 2015.

Sisters it is time for us to mature and understand the sister thread. We need to stop thinking that one sister is "winning" over the other in a negative sense. That is warped thinking and it comes from the enemy. Do you think that the Williams sister's gained their name, by one alone one "sister gaining the fame, over the other," no they did not. They both gained the name of two of the best tennis players in the world, with the beaded hair, but they played the game as 'sisters' until they matured, developed into their own individual identifies and slowly but surely- they had to understand that we will "match up" one day, because we are both the best, so it was inevitable for either sister to think one would not be the "chosen "one. Am I saying they did not argue, no I am not, because I do not know them personally, I have just observed their behaviors and what has been depicted in their matches, their responses, some of the media, and past comments made by their Dad. I have seen how they react during matches, during interviews, on shows they appear on, etc., etc. They have led really good examples of what sisters should be and are. I think that sisters of all races, colors, creeds, tribes, broods, or "whatever," should truly examine their overall roles to determine their individual roles, at the same time. I say that because in today's time of 2017, we face lots of spiritual opposition "towards one another" and it seems that the sister relationship is in jeopardy. We see so many siblings fighting, not only sisters, but brothers too.

"The Game of Tennis and Sisterhood
(play it like Venus and Serena)".

Speaking of Sisters, My Aunts, Elaine, Jack, Janice, Gloria, Rosa Mae and Ann are similar to Venus and Serena, they are a perfect example of a "real life experience" where sisters "exemplify" and "validate, support and deal fairly with each other, no matter what (I know they have their issues and problems, but, there is always a but). Since I can remember, they have been totally bonded. They visit with each other, they help each other raise their children and they do what they can for each other. I can remember my aunts at family gatherings and how they all "chip" in to bring food and they never fight about it. I can always remember how Aunt Rosa Mae (2nd oldest of the girls) always fills in the gap, for anything or anyone, she knows birthdays, significant events, stories, occurrences, she is a real live, ancestry website walking! LOL, this is a true story, if you ask her anything about the family, she knows it, she is very resourceful, giving and supportive of the sister group and the family, that is totally her gift! Not one of my aunts is jealous of her ability to be resourceful in the family, as a matter of fact they depend on her! I hear them all the time, say throughout life, "I don't know; to this or that, Ask Rosa Mae, she knows, and she almost always does, and if she doesn't she will try her best to know it, or get to it." You see, she knows her part and has taken on her role, without boast or brag, she just walks in it. My Aunt Patricia better known as "Ann," the Oldest Girl- has always been the one that has been resourceful in another way. She has always traveled, as a military wife, but when she came, she brought with her, joy, hopefulness, and excitement! The entire family "stood still" when Aunt Ann came home, from far away countries and cities, we longed to see her, hear her voice and her stories, her presence meant a lot to the family when she "came and went" as she bought something that the family did not have, and that was expectancy and adventure! Aunt Ann was that sister, that all the sisters needed and desired, even though for most of her life- she was far away residentially ". Aunt Ann added adventure to her sisters and in my opinion, she invoked a sense of risk taking, as she stepped outside of the norm and did things that most of her siblings did not, she stepped away, she moved around, she took life as it came to her and she loved every minute of it, by what I could tell! You see, all sisters have to realize that there will always be the one sister that has a "risk taking spirit" and she is not afraid to step out into the world of the unknown to live her wife the way she chooses with no regret. I was always excited to see Aunt Ann come and go, she got the "red carpet welcome" every time, that she came! Love you Aunt Ann! Sisters realize which sister has that "it factor," some of us are not that type, some of us are content with who we are, let's not get upset or jealous with – or- of our sister if she chooses to live her life in a way, or if she chooses "not" to live outside of the norm for what we all know, think or believe it should be,because no matter what the very essence of each sister's path - makes our sister group "boil," it keeps the pot cooking, gives us hope, something to look forward to, something to talk about, let's applaud that sister, whether she is the oldest or the youngest for what she brings to the table and not the other way around.

On and on though, it seemed that, each of her sisters (my aunts), respected and looked forward to her return and were saddened that she had to leave, but doubly happy, that she would return every single time. My aunts that were not as "up front" and "in the spot light," too- had a part they played, and it seemed (in my eyes) it was played well. My Aunt Gloria, was always the smart, educated one, she was a "sports fanatic and can tell you everything from the player' number, their position, name and stat's yes, My Aunt Gloria, did that!" yet she was quiet and to herself at times, but she was who she was and nobody coined or branded her for it (negatively). My Aunt Gloria had a firm and solid presence and was totally respected for just that, - who she was, Aunt Gloria or as we call her "Aunt Glory"!My Aunt Gloria was esteemed differently than the others, as she had her own unique way of fitting in. No one pushed my Aunt Glory to be what they wanted her to be, nor did they (the sisters) force her in or out (so-to-speak), they always allowed her to be herself, whether she is or was "in or out," she was accepted! Her being quiet was acceptable and her being vocal, when she did, was acceptable. Aunt Glory rarely got challenged, as she was astute, tenacious and firm in her beliefs and she was and is smart! It was definitely her role or part to play in the Sansbury Sister Group! Now, I have my Aunt Jack (The 4rth Oldest), the Life of the party, Extrovert, Confrontational, and the "In Your face Type". Aunt Jack voiced her opinions at anyplace and anytime without any "pushback," she was who she was and when Aunt Jack got started, everyone knew it would take a freight train to stop her, so her confidant and friend the Baby Girl Aunt Elaine, was always there to be that pin that would let the hot air out! When she said "Jack", that was it! Somehow Aunt Jack calmed down, you see, they all played their roles, moving right along (sisters out there, do you see yourself and roles in my Aunts). All of my Aunts, the sister's would not have it any other way. We all need that sister who is ready to go down for the cause, she says what no one else has the guts to say, she is out of the box radical, and she has her own special personality that fire, that burns, that the sister group often needs. What I admire

DR. PAMELA RENEE APPLEWHITE, PHD

about my aunts is that they all know how to flow with each other and at times when they need to flow away from each other, they too, have the skills to do that too, yet each and every one of them will jump up at the drop of a dime and run to the aid of all.

Special Story. I remember when my Uncle Leo passed away, my oldest Aunt Patricia Ann's husband, before I knew anything about it they had all gotten out of their beds and ran to the aid of their sister, without reservations, that is how they are, and that in my opinion is the heart of a sister. Being there for you to the very end! Let's read on, there is my Aunt, My Bestie, My Partner in the Spirit, all though I love them all, Aunt Janice goes without saying. She is quiet and reserved, but always will find you an answer, through prayer and supplication, she is the sufferer of the girls, the prayer warrior, the secret strength of the sister group. Aunt Janice is special in her own way, she does what she does from her heart, she is not as vocal as the rest, but don't get me wrong, when she unleashes, she has a lot to say and it will all be in love and respect for God's word. Aunt Janice is the yelling baby, right above my Aunt Elaine, the baby. You see as I describe my Aunts, I want to present to other sisters out there their own individual upbringing, uniqueness, sameness, yet differences. My Grandmother, Mable, raised them to be individuals yet "tight (figure of speech)," and they somehow seem to have grasped this concept from childhood... Now, I am not saying my Aunts, did not struggle in their roles, but at the "end of the day (as we say in the 21st century)" their mind, body, and spirit, knew and where knitted together like-a weaven rope and they all knew where each piece belonged. Remember how puzzles were family fun "back in the days" and we would work hard to find that particular piece of the puzzle and when it was found, you felt "profound, awesome and brand new," that is how my aunts are, as sisters, when a piece is needed they look for the piece, put the piece where it belongs and they glory over the completion of the finished product (issue). They are internally satisfied when the proper pieces are in place, in terms of being sisters. I watched them all my life and I can say they are an excellent example of what sisters are and should be. Now let's keep plugging on! Love you all, my Aunts! There life of sisterhood is rubbing off on my cousins and their offspring in several sets of sisters, Krystle, Tracie and Candace, Jennifer and Janae, Nicole, Sonya, Veronica, my deceased beloved Erica!

"The Graham Sisters (Our Sister love is our Life)"

Should and Should not be! With sisters, there are some things that ought not to be so, though. We should learn what we are and what were are not. I say this constantly throughout. We need to learn how to function properly, as a "blood team." After all, that is what we are. There should be no other bond greater than a sister, remember this, I may say this several times throughout (some sisters are closer than a mother and a daughter is, given to me by Gertha James, I refer to her as Mother), and I am sure I will say this a lot more throughout this book. When I mentioned to a few people the "Title of my book," they could not believe it. Some were appalled, yet-because I am thinking the "chord" struck home, or because—yet- whether we realize it or not, whether we acknowledge it or not, our sister can often times, more than one, become our enemy. How many times have we said or thought to ourselves or secretly, "I just hate her." She thinks she's better, she thinks that "Momma loves her more" … (something to think about huHHHH)? Thoughts that we kept buried for years, but now as age creeps in and thoughts turn into words and words turn into actions, until as age creeps in the thoughts- began to manifest itself into actions. Remember when you would do things, just so your sister could get in trouble or you wished the worse for her, so that you could not be seen as "last" or not "as worthy as she is." These are secrets of the soul, things we often think, but dare not to say out loud Have you had any secret negative thoughts about your sister? Think about this, this is just a "soul stirring question," but think about it, as I proceed.

Sister Assignment Confess to yourself and Repent for I have had thoughts of my sister in the way of_____. I love her and I want to make it right with my soul, but I need your help, please help me to let what I hold in my heart towards her or them,release itself from my being, I want to be free to love her.

As we go forward-think on, mediate and savor-this book. This book will serve as a force of life! It will help us be honest and true to ourselves and one another, To our sisters, to our parents, to each other.

Let's proceed. I will give various forms of examples, of the types and kinds of sisters that I have observed in and throughout my life. This is my personal under-taking and spiritual travel from one place to another, when it comes to sisters, and how we act, think, feel and relate to and with one another. I will speak on all types and kinds of sisters, my sisters, celebrity sisters, sisters I see on the news, on reality shows, sit-coms or the like. This is my research and journey in the valley of sisters.

Additional definition of Sisters are defined as a girl or a woman who has one or both or one of the same parents (**_Merriam Free Online Dictionary_**). Some definitions that I have come across during my lifetime, tell me that sisters are supposed to be close and intimate, but that is not always the case. Furthermore, in the 21st century, it seems that sisters, are growing further and further apart. We hate each other, we talk about each other, we laugh and mock our sisters (some openly and some in private), when she fails, falls, or makes mistakes, some of us fight our sisters (with words) and and in the current time we fight with fists. I have seen countless You Tube videos where sisters are fighting and using profane language to belittle and overthrow (where I come from we call it "cussing each other out)." It has and is getting worse, as each awakening moment occurs, the bond of sister hood, it is severely broken and in some cases irretrievable. Some have been so wounded by their own "flesh and blood sister, that they do not want to look into their own sister's face," while there are some others, that 'just want to be friends and love their sister." Additionally, there are some that are becoming more of one's enemy than one's close confident, loved and cherished friend. Let's look into this issue.

Sisters when they are born, play with each other and some protect each other. I recall taking up for my sisters on several occasions in the yard in the small town we grew up in. I recall bossing them around, telling them, that I was "going to tell momma this or tell momma that, or say, what I would do to them if they did not listen." I remember being ready to fight anyone that posed a threat to my sisters. I remember me and my sisters playing in the living room with our doll babies, having fun with each other, playing hiding and go seek in the house and making prank hang up phone call asking people "Is your water running" and hanging up. Those were the "good ole days." I remember such times of joy, with my sisters when we were young. But as we grew older, it seems things changed. Our emotions changed, connections changed, how we interacted with each other changed, we turned into total "Sisterzillas (form of Godzilla)." We argued, fussed, called each other names, so on and so forth (me and my baby sister the most). Is there one sister that you just don't click with? Come on? If it is, then you need to face it, deal with it. It will be mighty, mighty painful, but at least she will know and so will you. Stop hiding behind the fake, sister act. It is all an act. The energy is always present, you know it and she does to. Step into it! Get it out and move on! Furthermore, me and my sisters' relationship changed as we got older, girls, this is a part of life, it will change. Don't get me wrong, as you grow, get married, have children being a sister will, and must change, but, I will say not to the point of disregard, disrespect, dishonesty and deceit. I can recall me and my sister arguing in Charlotte, NC (several years ago) in a parking lot, after shopping on "Black Friday," so much so, until we were seriously name calling and shouting profane things at each other, not only did we frighten the children, but my momma too. I am not proud of that day. It is nothing to brag about. Scars are evident and trust was broken at that time. Learning to accept your sister for who she is, is one of the most valuable things a sister can do, yet speaking the truth in love when it warrants it, is as, important. We must not allow our resentment that builds over years and years cause us to disgust, hate, or envy, one another or even blind-side us. We must not let the one little incident take our minds in to an oblivious state of seeing and viewing our sister as a being- that we cannot live up to or "stand her presence." I really hope this is touching somebody. We must understand the difference between our own self-worth, self-acceptance and self-assuredness, as well as our sister's. We must learn to respect, honor and cherish who our sister is.

I recall when Oprah found her sister, Patricia, she (Patricia) made a conscious decision to not say anything about being Oprah's sister or sell her story, to the media. She decided that based on who her sister was, that would be the ultimate betrayal. She did not want to see her role or position in Oprah's life, diminish before it got started, is what I was able to tell. She (Patricia, Oprah's sister) didn't want to make or profit from it. She built her connectedness, seemingly before the relationship even started. She immediately bonded to what she found out was her sister, long before things came to fruition, by what I heard and saw through their self reports, I am talking about sisters! Furthermore, although she hadn't known or related to her, for a large portion of her life, this act- made her be even more connected to her. Her support for Oprah in her actions said it all. She used her God given wisdom and common sense to know a person of her sister's caliber would bring on unsolicited media attempts and rallies, so she just left it alone and waited until it all came together and in the end, she was totally blessed by their union. Can we as sisters take on this mindset, can we learn to adapt to who God created us to be and stop looking at our own flesh and blood sister as if she is a monster or someone that was forged into the earth for our demise (although some of them are, but I will talk on that later). Can we begin to learn to accept one another, support one another and most of all protect one another as sisters? Our hidden heart, is often open for our sister see.

<u>Repeat this</u> : *"I will begin to protect and guard my sister's name, integrity, stance, position, power, authority, identify and reputation, I am forever her Keeper and* *blood affiliate, If I have failed in this area in the past, Dear Heavenly Father, please forgive me, Amen"!*

As the story continues, I can also remember manipulating my sisters, using my elder authority to make them do what I wanted them to do (that was not good) I must confess. We should never use the authority, God gave us to take things from our sisters or rob them of their existence (strengths or shortcomings), just because we know we can, we should not use our sisterly authority to gallivant around their (our sister's) premises of life just to exalt ours, this is wrong. Just because we know we maybe- a little bit quicker than them or quicker to the draw. We must remember that she is our sister, whether it is her emotions (playing on them) or her time, money, or anything valuable that your sister has, and you want it. There is enough sister room for everybody. Know this! If there is anything open-ended or plain ole, left in the "dirt." Just ask your sister, don't go around the "bin", as she already knows, when you call, text or write, it is not just to say hello. Your sister has already discerned it, she saw it when you were little and she sees it now!

So sisters out there that are manipulating your sisters for one reason or another, "STOP" she sees your soul and the actions of your heart, the bible says "What is in a man's heart, will come out of his mouth (Matthew 15:18, King James Version)." So believe me, you are not just getting something, she knows and sees your ways, "little sister" or "big sister," for that fact. I remember lots of things, that most elder sisters remember and use to their advantage to stay in control of who they are and their younger sisters too! I think there is nothing wrong with being the big sister, and staying in control in order to teach, help, learn, lead or advise your younger sister or sisters into power, knowledge, understanding and guidance, yet I can say,when a sister uses her role selfishly or in a manipulative way- that God has given, after she comes into knowing the truth, then it is wrong.

How many sisters act selfishly and "internally the same" 'NOW" as when they were children? Manipulating the younger or older sisters for that fact, with "what we used to do" or "how we used to do it." You see that is most of the problems with sisters, in the present- we do not "grow" out of childish things and into mature things-along- with each other, we continue to act as if we are out in the yard playing together, acting as if, we are still fixing each other's hair on the porch. We have to realize that we are not the same, as we grow- we need to-adjust our attitudes and thoughts accordingly, but do we do that? I don't thnk so! There are some of us, that we still act the same way as we did when we were a toddler. Read on.

Manipulation. I want to discuss manipulation. Manipulation is the act of handling or controlling something or someone in a skillful manner in order to get the outcome that they want or desire, in addition -it can be unfair cheating and tactless schemes. When someone uses their power in an unnoticeable or obvious way to get what they want, this is manipulation. Manipulation can be through certain actions and words. Manipulation can be in the form of crying, intimidation, threats by a sister saying things like, "I am going to tell or reveal this or tell or reval that (deep dark secret or story)". These are psychological tricks and actions. Manipulation is a power that has been used throughout time in all relationships and all situations. When something is done to skillfully handle or control another person it is not pleasing in the sight of God. Sisters, ask yourself do you do this to your sister or sisters, whether you are the youngest, middle or the oldest, do you skillfully handle your sister in order to get what you want? Do you pet her with a "smile" or do you "gut" her like a fish? Do you string her along with some darkness that chills her soul; some secret that you know frightens or intimidates the core of her being (that only you and she know about, if so, let her go, let yourself go, its been too long now, yes you, my dear, God sees- your secret, he wants you all to settle it now)"?

There are so many tools that a sister can use to trick, degrade, suppress or hold you in a soulful or spiritual "prison cell"A sister normally knows all of one's dirt or deep dark secrets. We all, as sisters, have learned each one's "mode of operation". When we learn each other's mode of operation, we play on it, use it, and sometimes, no-mainly a "lot of times", we abuse it. Sisters we all have either seen or heard "one or the other of us" say or do something that can expose, belittle, degrade, or cause friction in our sister relationships or the like. Some siblings sisters, I have seen use a sin (against their sister) that is- and 'decades' ago old.

The one sister uses this "strong hold" against the other sister to keep that sister in a "low down/knee-ed" position, yes you know how a dog "heals to his master"? This is how sometimes a sister may do if she knows a deep dark secret of the other sister. And believe it or not sisters, I have seen situations like this -happen in real life. The stories we see on television are stories from someone's mind or imagination, but of course most of our thoughts are patterned behind something or some story that we often know to be true, think about it (art imitating life)!

Question? Do you skillfully use another person- being your sister in the case of this memoir, to get what you want? Or do you control another sister's weakness to get your wanted responses or actions? Do you use your sisterly power to gain control or possess your sister's heart or reasoning? Do you take the butcher knife to her soul and chop at it daily, yearly or even from generation to generation? I have watched celebrity sisters, manipulate the other, because they are not as "in the light (so-to-speak)" as the other one and they tend to play on that, even so. I have seen a major celebrity play the victim, because their sister seems to be more popular than she is and she, in my opinion used that as her harness for her other sisters emotions, to make her feel as if she had to always make up excuses for her, or cove for her, or do some added feature for her, when all in all, it was manipulation. Manipulative tactics should not be used to strike your sister down or turn her spirit in the way that you want it, it will never get you far! Let's work on this my dear sisters, read on!

The elder sister in a show that I watched was seemingly, "masking her behaviors as love" not realizing her sister was manipulating her, due to her own selfish reasons. Sound familiar? Sister, Do you call, your sister only when you need something, smiling and laughing in her face as if you are concerned about something in her life (and you know you are not), but your ultimate goal is to "get money out of her or some other valued- so called "favor," just because you can?. Or do you filter your feelings through her to "get at other people." Do you use her strength and power to your benefit, "without her knowledge"? Do you tell yourself, "I know who I can use, I will use _____ (fill in the _SISTER_ that you are blatantly using)"? Do you purposely get what you want from her in a malicious way and then "turn your back on her later on"? You know, that you sister will feel sorry or "guilt ridden, (if she doesn't)" do what you want in the long run and you then try to internally punish her for lack of compliance to your requests.

Some sisters will punish their "sister on the run", but holding on to something invisible that she has concocted in her mind for most of her life about her sister and by constantly holding the hammer over her head, everytime she sees her, she finds fault, every place she "runs to" she is trying to take her sister down, she will say things that cut her sister to the core, but nobody notices it but you, she will snide in mid sentence at her sister when they are talking to keep her soul at bay or down beneath so that she can gain some type of mineral satisifaction. Yes there is this kind of warped level of thinking and being out there. A example of this treacherous behavior was depicted in a Life time movie, where there were twins, and one twin hated the other so much, that she set her sister, up, even to the point of possible death. There have been so many stories on the news where sisters have killed or destroyed each other. I saw a story, where an identical twin sister killed her sister in cold blood, by driving her off the cliff, while they were riding in a car. She (the evil sister) somehow, crafted a scenario that caused them both to be in a risking taking situation. She went to the point of risking her life, to "get over what she hated about her sister", she was just that evil, just that doubting, just that insecure, she didn't want her here anymore and was willing to take her life along with her to see her evil goal accomplished. What a horrible situation, but it is true, and it happens. It may not be as tragic or severe as attempting to murder one's sister, literally, but what other inner thoughts, secrets or atrocities, do you hold in your heart amd mind against your sister? I had to wonder, though, what would make an identical twin sister, that look so much alike, that-only their mom, knew the difference. As both were gorgeous, both were popular, both seemed to be "on point". But something on the inside of one of the sisters was very insecure, very self-loathing. She used all of her life's energy to destroy her other sister, because of this one issue embedded deep inside of her. I am sure her sister was devastated, as she realized her very own sister was taking her life, I would not be surprised if she gave up the ghost because of the devastation of seeing what was happening- and not the "blow from falling off the cliff." What is it that you "look behind your sister's back and see," when she is not looking, what is it that makes you hate her so much or "cannot stand her"? What is this dark place, this dark circle that has manifested itself within your heart? Is it the way she laughs, is it the way, she gets along with other people and connect with them in a way that you can't? Is the way, she is strong-willed enough to resist, reacting to your "set-ups," that you lay trap for her, at your will and intentionally? What is is that has severed the tie that binds in sister-hood? Think long, hard and deep…

If this is you, raise your hand. This is to help you, not hurt you. Don't close up in shame, face the honest truth of the matter that is tucked deep down in your heart and deep down in your soul. Don't continue to internally mock and laugh at her (your sister). There is someone (as I speak prophetically) out there where two sisters are working for a company, and one has one position and the other has another position, and one is trying so hard to "beat her sister" with this contract, or to win favor in a way that would "knock" her sister down or degrade her value. I feel that there is someone out there that is living this out right now and as, you read this book, you need to be healed by these words and turn back, stop the set up! It will hurt you in the long run, more than it will hurt your sister (I get prophetic unctions throughout the book, so beware and be cautioned of the level of deepness that will hit your heart, for those that It applies to). This book is set to bring forth instant healing, as the pages "come off the book" to the life, in your soul. Don't be the one that destroys your sister and on the other side of this- don't be the one that allows your sister to destroy you, "move out of the line of fire," one way or the other, it is time to realize what is really going on with your sister. Take the time to do so. If this is you, and you are taking advantage of your sister's kindness and its being done constantly, then stop it. Work on change now!

Rescuing the desolate sister example. I saw this other episode of Law and Order, where one of the cops, had a sister that was doing drugs, doing this, and doing that. Well her fellow cop mates tried to warn her of her sister's deceit, but she contended that "Well that's my baby sister (and she kept on "rescuing her)". There was, though- this one particular situation, that stuck out to me, was when she (the younger sister) was with her boyfriend that was abusing her and influencing her negatively. The younger sister called her to older sister her apartment or maybe she was just randomly visiting, and her boyfriend was "doing something to her (as she saw it)" and the other sister (the cop, the oldest sister) asked him to "get off of her" and he would not, and it ended up that she killed her sister's boyfriend, trying to protect her (the youngest). The sister (the youngest) had used her sister (the oldest) so much, until she (the oldest) nearly lost all that meant something to her, because she as the oldest- wanted to protect her sister all the time. The oldest sister was not the type that wanted or needed protection (actually), the eldest sister role, was bound to the youngest siste role- how many of us, dwell like that with our younger sisters to the bad?. They were bound by the inner connection that she (the oldest) vowed from her earlier phases of life. She vowed to herself according to the depiction of the character that she would or could- never leave her sister to perish. Her big mistake (the oldest sister) was that she didn't allow her sister (the youngest) to make her own mistakes and learn from them. The tie that bound them was the act of "enabling" and the chord of manipulation, usury and lies. The sister (the oldest) thought she was doing a good deed, and was ultimately, left holding the bag when the other one didn't even care and had no intention of changing. It was only until she got into trouble. Sound familiar, sure it does, it happens all the time. It may not happen in all sister groups or to that degree, but in one way, shape or form, we all have experienced some level of "bailing one sister" out of a situation. The key to this is to not allow the sister to become dependent on what you do for her, whether it is verbal consolation, advice or aid, learn how to give your sister enough room to grow. Learn to embark upon your sister's strengths and help teach her independence away from you, if this is happening to you, in your life.Furthermore, when we feed into her sister's indiscretions we are setting her up for bondage, we need to realize that not allowing freedom with one's sister is breeding ground for "mix-up, match-up intertwining souls" Lets not harness one anther's weaknesses and make evil out of it.

Note. Sisters, those of us that rescue our sister's out of practical, decisions that only they should make, over and over again, we are robbing them unjustly, we are taking their ability to learn of their mistakes. When you see your sister repeat the same behaviors over and over, after you have advised, counseled, argued, etc., we all have to learn to let it go. Especially if there are no modifications in the behaviors,. Sisters if we enable our sisters (or one another). We give permission and we open the door for emotional blackmail to set in. We allow torment to take us along with, little pieces of our heart and soul. If that is the case, we can classify ourselves just as twisted and demented as the next sister. Read on! Understand, though- that as a sister, we are there to protect, help and serve, don't get me wrong! We are supposed to without a doubt back one another up, as appropriately needed, but not after repeated attempts and tries to help. We must all learn to allow our sister's to take on their own personal sufferings. This can be hard, as the eldest, but often times with time and continual practice, along with saying or demonstrating the word "no" to one's sister, can aid her with independence.

A little bit more on the story, see the eldest sister in the episode on Law and Order, really cared about the younger one, yet she was so blind-sided by her need to protect her (gone in over drive). That she was blindsided -to seeing the deceit that she created, by enabling her sister. You see, there are almost always other factors in the sister, that we "ourselves generate or cause to happen", through our actions or non-actions, which ever applies. Sisters if there is a level of consciousness of this behavior, one needs to take,and get a grip of what is really happening and get it together.

Sisters allow yourself to see and know who you are as sisters. Learn what is beneficial for her and what is not. In the roles of the two sisters in the Law and Order episode mentioned earlier. The younger sister, did not have the sense of care to return the love or concern to her oldest sister. This was because she had been overshadowed with her sister taking up "the slack" so to speak, at every empty turn of her life. Is this you, is this your sister? Have you experienced or seen this in yourself or other sisters that you know?

In the Bible the scripture speaks of sparing the rod and spoiling the child (**Proverbs 13:24, KJV**), this scripture is used for disciplining children, but I will use the "rod of discipline" in the case of sisterhood. There is a level of discipline that we as sisters, should allow to take place or "wrap its little arms around (us or sisters, or each other) whether in childhood or adulthood, so that lessons can be learned, if we do not, we "spoil." Yes, we allow the terrible things to come out of us, if we are not disciplined and discreet in our relations within the sister group.

Whenever the act of allowing someone to learn their practical lessons is disbarred, this allows room for increased "ungodly" seeds or acts to manifest. See what happens is we as a sisters ultimately create room for dismissiveness of a serious problem, when we do not walk in total and complete truth towards one another as sisters, when the truth finally hits, and you cannot bear. the brunt of your sister's imperfections or issues, no matter what it is, you fall in the trap of accusations. For example, if you are the type of Elder Sister, in the sister hood brood, where you are accustomed to making excuses, salvaging problems and misfortunes, taking responsibility for your sisters issues, instead of allowing her to do so. When you finally come to the end of your rope and you confront her or them. The entire shift is made and projected upon you. The issues then, are poured on to you and you are now the stand out, you are the one being blamed. When this happens, you need to properly pace your interactions and responses to your sister in a truthful and proper way, As if you do not it will get "real ugly". Things will be compiled onto you in a way that is bombarding and it will be hard to get your points across. Being truthful throughout life is the best way for sisters, inabling and upholding turns into torment, agony, and relentless chaos among sisters.

Going back to the scene from Law and Order, I found that the sister that was the youngest of the two, the Cop and her Sister (for those of you that are *Law and Order fans*) on that particular episode -developed a subtle, yet hidden hatred for her sister, she saw her as the culprit, versus her savior, she began to hate her, inwardly, if one could read between the lines. The younger sister had no insight into what she was doing, she was just simply "doing her' in her place of comfort, by blatantly using and abusing her sister's goodness and kindness. She was set in a place- that her sister had put her in, for most of her life. How many of us, set our sisters in places that are hard for them to come out of later in life, because we spoiled them to "us". IN other words we have done everthing to please them, not realizing it is actually hurting them, solving their relationship problems, "taking up for them, when they know they are wrong", "giving them stuff, when we know all and all they don't need it", all the while making them inwardly and outwardly dependant on us and when we disagree, they turn "tail" on you, as if they did not know you? This is a set up! We as older or more responsible sisters should not do this, we should not ENABLE, our sisters, we should give and help, but not the detriment of the sister in need holding you, accountable for her! I know this is making sense! Keep reading!

How many of us, create real live traps for ourselves- in our relationships with our sisters? Are we always honest with how we feel, or do we hold it inside until we are mad enough to talk about our sister to someone else, or scream on her, or them, when we hadn't done it before? We then, make it seem like the other party is the one with the problem, when it is really us? Are you that kind of sister? Think about it.We as sisters, have to learn to take responsibility for the role that we play in all of this. We have to take responsibility for how we stand as a sister, learning our role or "roles" in the scheme of the sister- hood bond. We have to know without a shadow of a doubt that we are. and can be that "good sister," but honestly, discretely, "chastisingly" and "openly". This means that we need to activate all of the aforementioned traits to make for being a good elder sister. The ones that do everything, all the time, will end up with the bad end of the stick, as you will get overwhelmed and overburdened with "their stuff"! And believe "you me (a figure of speech)", you will regret it until you dying days. Now I have lived this, and God will have "us" authors live out a system, so we can perfect it for others to help them get better in the long run! So here it is, "yall" get better at it!

Roles. Knowing your role and position as the sister, can be vital to your relationship with your sister or sisters. One needs to first, or throughout life take little "spot checks" of what your role is, in being a sister. One needs to take time early on, to see what role do I play, if I am the oldest, how far do I go with my sisters when challenges are faced? What do I say to her, to push her to grow and learn as well as develop in crisis on her own and not "one me (if you know what I mean)", versus me enabling her or them, by being a crutch to be used constantly? How do I use my role as a sister to benefit our bond and relationship, versus destroy it over time? How can we make "sister maintenance," throughout our lives to keep the relationship "fluid'. What do I do, when my sister has hurt my feelings or I have hurt hers or we have crushed one another's soul? How does it all connect or how do we reconnect, if a disconnect has taken place? Ask yourself?

Furthermore, how do I approach talking to my sister confidently or lovingly to get my points across, with out always being told, you "are so offended" or being seen as if "I am the one with the problem"? Let's see how- every employer, if you notice define job descriptions and roles. We all need to consistently know and understand our roles as sisters. I have to ask the question, do you as a sister understand what your role is? Do you know your job description? Do you understand when to use your gift within your role to help you, or your sister? Or do you use your role to hinder your sister or sisters? Do you know how to apply your special skill set as a sister to make your sisterhood experience a good one, or do you just idly sit by and allow your gifts and talents to collide and diminish for lack of understanding of who you are and what you mean to the sister group? If we all knew our roles, duties and positions, it would make for the processing of sisters problems a lot better. Understanding and knowing what sisters go through would be a lot easier, if we knew this. A prime example is one of my aunts (The Sansbury Sisters, I spoke about early on in this book) had a cook out at her house and one of my kids did not have any swimming trunks the Eldest Sister, Aunt Ann, said to "Ask, the Middle Aunt (Rosa), she has everything, and sure enough she had an extra pair of swimming trunks that my son could use. So in saying this, what resources do you have that everyone in the sister group can use or benefit from? The swimming trunks are just symbolic of a resourcefulness that one sister carried. What is your resource? What is your natural "knack" that you have and contribute to your sister group? Which sister has an area that she specializes in that can help make the situation of sisters better or improved. This is how we can grow as sisters, if we are assured and confident in the role that we play amongst each other. Understanding your role and passage of 'rite' is one of the key things in understanding, your role, your sister group and your group's sister engagement. I will discuss rites of passage and birth rites later on in this memoir/book.

More on Enabling. Let's **_not_** take on the enabling role or position- of sisterhood, let's banish that activity from our circle, and let's do this now! Enablers are defined as, a person or thing that makes something possible, or a person that encourages or promotes self-sabotaging or negative behaviors. In our roles as sisters let's not allow one of us to "beat off of the other or the group of sisters (a figure of speech)" by continually "taking from us," taking from our souls, hearts and minds. Let's take our sister role in pride and stand in the gap and do this thing right. Let's give out of necessity, not out of obligation, whether it is for a particular financial situation or of her soul or spirit. Let's get this thing, and work it to the good of our sister, not to the detriment. I know of sisters, right now that wish that they had said something to their sister, or not had said a particular thing to their sister, because whatever it was she said or not said, it caused her sister emotional, mental or physical harm. No, you cannot change what happened to your sister, but you can move on, by forgiving yourself for the mistake you made in either enabling her to the point of her demise or missing the opportunity to open her eyes to the blind spot that she was missing, it is all okay, you now get, to- let go of the agony, you can get on our knees right now or where you are sitting and say,

"Dear Heavenly Father,"

I am so sorry for what I have done or not done to my sister (Name), I ask for forgiveness and I ask you to strengthen my heart to move past the guilt and pain that I have endured because I was fearful of what my actions or words would have caused. I know that maybe I could have changed the course of her life, had I taken action. I am so sorry, but now I want relief, I want to be rid of the guilt and agony that besets me so that I can live prosperously, as you want me to. Thank you Dear Lord for your promises, I know you are Yahweh, My God, My Savior, I love you and Bless You-- 'Yeah and Amen"!

God wants us to give out of care and concern, but not to allow the "giving" to become "abusive within itself." Time is not adequately taken to measure what is healthy and what is not healthy when it comes to "being a sister." There are so many shows 'coming out' now in the terms of "sisters" and how we act and behave towards one another. We are always either arguing, fussing, fighting or "backbiting." We are always "fighting each other" for the wrong cause. We are not fighting to "make our relationship" better, but it is mostly the opposite. We do not understand truly what it means to be a sister. We are always trying to "rob each other of our roles and positions." We are always either having jealousies or envies against one another or talking behind one another's back. I realize that even in watching the Kardashians, there are times when one sister is with the other, conversing about the other with something one did or didn't do. Let's not be that way, let's take it beyond that, it is time to change and the time is 'right now'.

PAUSE—WHEN YOU SEE PAUSE IN THE MIDDLE OF THE BOOK THAT MEANS THAT I AM GETTING A PROPHETIC UNCTION THAT I HAVE TO ADD TO THE BOOK AT THE VERY MOMENT. This unction has taken place during the proofreading of this book!

"I speak prophetically into someone's spirit, right now, the Lord is showing me that someone witnessed their sister get molested and kept it a secret for all of their lives. The God of your salvation is now telling you to release this burden, go and tell it, confess it, get if off of your chest, he is showing me that it is eating you alive and you can no longer carry it, you can no longer burden your heart with this issue, now it is time, seek help and let it go, seek guidance and let it be seared out of your consciousness, it is time!"

<u>**Roles, Continued**</u> … Do you know that your sister may be hurting because she sees how you are using her spirit, mind and soul?, Basically due to how your relationship has grown for most of your lives, she does not want to hurt you, so she goes along with it for the most part (because of parental pressure or helplessness), all the while, her eyes are straightly- opened to the games that you have played but neither of you can let go, ever since you were young and figured out how to do it so meticously. I want those of you that are reading this book to really think about this and ponder your very thoughts and depth of your soul to see if either person is you? If so, then some changes need to be made. Manipulating your sister is one of the biggest things that keep sisters torn apart and illegally bond together. One thing that Oprah said when she found out she had another sister, was that she was so "taken (in so many words)," by the fact that when her sister found out that they were sisters, she never even once considered 'talking to the media' about her new found sister or identity that linked her to Oprah that could have possibly produced countless stories to the "bad. Oprah's sister, did not "in so many words-go behind her back' to try take advantage of her positon or use it

for personal gain (is what I interpreted it as) and that within it itself, made Oprah feel loved and cared about as a sister and connected. The sense of sisterhood played itself out right before her eyes. No amount of money, title or fame could have separated the moment that Oprah and Patricia found out they were blood connected and spiritually bonded, and from what I can tell they still are today. Now I am going to talk about the Gayle type of thing later(sisterhood), yes the sister that you have that is not blood, that is yet- another whole different "sister thang (get my drift girls, I know you know it)."

Consequently, this is what sisterhood is about, at least one of the things- is protecting your sister's name at all costs (Oprah/Patricia), keeping your sister covered in all circumstances, even if you do have the opportunity to "bash" her name or create wealth, if your sister holds a position in society that carries "weight (so to speak)". I think it is safe to say, that in this regard to this concept that- Oprah's sister played her role, loyally and responsibly. Unfortunately, now a days, I think that is not happening with other sister groups out there! I think that we are all 'gathering' in on the discussions that occur "against" our sisters, for those that will listen to us. The population at hand (21st Century) won't stand to the challenge, a lot of times, and protect our sisters anymore, as we used to do "in the ole days." We really could care less about our sisters, at times. I had a conversation with a lady about my relationship with my sister and she said, I cannot believe that, me and my sisters, don't go a day without talking. She says, this is the newest thing, I have heard she says! I cannot live without hearing their voices (God Bless, her Soul, now deceased, Betty Moore, for those words). I don't think this should be so. I think that sisters need healing and restoration. I think that as a sister we need to understand who we are and what it means to be a sister, even if it is to another sister by blood or by adoption. Or it can be whomever you call a sister and know that you are connected to. Later on, then if changes need to be made, it is time to make them. That is what this book is about "understanding where we are, where we have been, and where we are going as sisters." Know and understand your role, whether you are the oldest, the second oldest, the "knee baby" the baby of the bunch, or anywhere in between. Know what you stand for, what your resources are and how you can use them to benefit your sister group, no matter what!

"Sister Love"

"Sister Epiphany of Me and My Sisters Jumping Rope"

The song by the singing group "Sister Sledge (*I don't own the rights to this song*)-" in one of the lyrics say, "Have faith in all you do, you want go wrong this is our family jewel" and continues to say, "we are family, we are family." I think that those of us that are sisters, should take this in (for those of you that know this group, listen to this sing and for those of you that don't listen to this song, you will see what those words about sisterhood really means, makes a world of sense to me). I think that we can pick up a few major points, if we go back and take a good listen, at every word, as sisters and see how they are together and what this song means. I have interpreted it as a family of beautiful women, that came together to share with the world, how they are successful as sisters! It seemed to have worked. They were really successful in their day! ASK yourselves sisters reading this book, if you can say that you are bonded enough together to allow the jewel of being a close and bonded sister group, work for you? This is what the "Sledge" sisters did, they made it work. Kudos, to them! Listen to their song, when you go on Sister Trips and when you are in your "Sister Mating Season"! My Wright Sisters (mentioned earlier in the book) got this on "lock (Cymp, Shoan, Debbie, Lynn and Angie)"!

Sister Types. The singing group called "Sister Sledge" sings a chorus in their songs about "We are family, I got all my sisters with me, as noted above." Do we all have our sisters with us, are we rocking to the very beat of the drum, with this particular song? Do we even care if we are all one? Do we want to be all one anymore? This is a question I want all sisters to explore, as you read this book.

The sister type can vary from family to family and generation to generation. You have various types of sister types.

1. Bonded/Close Knit
2. Close but not bonded
3. Distant and Detached Sisters (but will fight to protect the family name)
4. Supportive, but unattached.
5. Jealous, Conceited, Evil
6. Reality Show Type
7. Spiritual/Religious Type
8. Betrayal

I have seen all types of sisters groups throughout my life and have realized that they all have one thing in common whether they are rooted and bonded at the core or not, they are all still just that- sisters. Let's take a look at the first type of sister listed above.

The bonded/close knit type, this type of sister group, is bonded and, close, they do everything together, they take trips together, they talk often, they grow their kids together and make sure that they relate and know that they are cousins, they take care of their parents or any parent figures . They follow-up with each other, participate in marriage celebrations, educational accomplishments, child accomplishments or birth, job achievements, they are a team, the do not break the bond nor do they include outsiders in the 'crux' of who the real sisters are. They will give to their sister and her family in time of crisis or come together if one cannot do it and figure out a plan on how to get it done. They are very sister conscious and private of what goes on in this sister group. This group is very proactive and protective- of each other. They are balanced, and they will confront each other on serious issues, this type is mostly on the same political parties and they sit and discuss their views, even when it gets heated. This type of sister group is very organized and aligned. They understand all roles and they try hard not to cross the lines. They do pickups when one has a baby sitter call out, they do stand INS at schools when their sister is in need, on a trip or what have you- this sister type is proud, confident and assured. This sister type can be tender or they can be ferocious all in harmony at the same time! Don't let this sister group fool you, they are role followers and they will let anyone know outside of the sister group, if they are wrong and will let those within the sister group know they are wrong by having special meetings or conference calls, this sister type will not backbite and if one does 'clique' up with the other, they will report back to the group, their prior discussions, this sister group is exceptional. Sisterhood is their "Mantra". They live and breathe it! These sisters if they are married or have a significant other, is very respectful to their partner and let's their sisters know their priorties. They also let their spouses or significant others know the value of their sisters in their lives. When sisters are first they are first, when sisters are second to their marriages, they are second. They are very innovative in balancing it all, including their parents. Sisters of this sort value their parents and make it a pivotal point in their marriages, that they never disclude their parents in any special events in their lives. This sister groups do not pick mates that do not understand this level of functioning in their lives, they are very engaging with family things. They alert their spouse to all that is going on and they never, ever let their spouse or significant others feel left out, put to the side, or indifferent when dealing with their sisters. This sister group is phenomenal, they are on the money, they are emotionally intelligent, motivated, driven and successful within their own rites, they have money and if one is without the other takes the slack, they view success as profitable and not always money. They have a unspoken leader and unspoken follower and get this-- the roles change over time, and over the years and when the "shift" comes, they all fall in line and if they have to discuss it they will, but if it is something that happens to their spirits, they take note and go with it! These sisters are the example of what sisters are, there is more about this sister group! If I would go on and on the world could not contain all this sister group has, but I would be remised if I left this out, they all worship and love the God of their Salvation, Jehovah, Jesus their Lord and Savior, they don't push religion on each other, but they have the basis in their lives and when one strays, they know how to let go and let God work it to their sister's good, they are not "bottom feeders" and they are fearless, this sister group is one in a few, I mean a million, but they are there they are in the Universe that God created, if this is you, write me and testify to this spiritual description, given to me by God himself! Love you my Sisters!

Close but not bonded type. The close but not bonded type, are sisters that believe-that a sister is a sister, but for some issue- that has occurred throughout the course of life, they did not have the time to bond. It maybe parental issues, abuse, neglect, financial disparities or burdens in or on the family, the sisters were close, at one time and believe in backing up a sister or sister up, but only to a degree. They will not talk about their sister to anyone else, but they may discuss their issues with a close family member and/or friend. This sister type, does not have the tolerance for bonding their kids, their emotions or spirits, they just live through life and introduce their kids, as normal families would, but do not make any extra efforts to see that their kids or anyone else for that fact are all bonded and walk together as close family should. The can be disenfranchised unlearned, uncaring, distance and aloof. They respect having a sister but don't take it as close as the bonded sister type listed above.

Distant and Detached Sisters (but will fight to protect the family name). This sister type is an estranged group of sisters. They are sisters, and have known to be and live as they are sisters, growing up in the same household, but when the age of adulthood was reached, they left the group, where it was, and that was at home. This sister group is not relationally inclined, nor do they care to be. They will talk about their sister to anyone that is outside of the sister group, that they do not know- when they have a specific problem going on with the sisters; a stranger, but not someone they know, (for fear it will get back). This type of sister group will fuss, fight and argue with each other, but will not allow anyone outside of the sister group to talk about the "group itself (strange isn't it, but it strue)", even when they do. In this particular case. The are protective of the family group of sisters, but within the sister group, there is no care or concern They will use the sister for what she is worth and laugh, mock or ridicule the sister with other family members, but not outside persons, unless they are a total stranger. They strictly don't believe in "bashing" the family name within the community, a sense of warped pride or togetherness still exists within this sister type.

Supportive, but unattached. This type of sister is very supportive and will go out of her way to help her sister, there is no inner bond or attachment, only that they have the same parents. They don't visit each other's homes, but will meet at the house of their parents to provide any support that is needed. This type is unconcerned or does not know anything about the sister's personal life, only if she is in need and specifically calls for help, then they still tend to keep their distance. Financial responsibilities when It comes to sisters, is far and in between . This sister group, has been raised in a neglectful (emotional) environment.

Jealous, Conceited, hatred, or other type. This type of sister type, I must say is the worse. I have seen this trait, more than ever these days in the sister group. You have sisters that are jealous of one another, sometimes it is open and sometimes it is concealed. The type of sister group that is concealed, is often time the worst. This type won't support, applaud, or do anything for their sister. They are often entitled for one reason or another, can be rich or poor and they tend to hate each other. This type of sister group is jealous of the way their sister or sisters, walks, talks, acts and does "anything she or they do or does." This sister type envies the ground her sister or sisters walks on, it is always something with this type, all the time. She is a griper, a insulator, a busy body and totaltarium trouble maker. She or they are willing and eager to do anything she or they can to crush their sister or sisters. This is the one that can express her hatred openly through generations of hate or she can do it subtly day to day, bit by bit, or in her sister's face. This type of sister group is treacherous and evil. They can see their sister falling and laugh at her through secret messages she sends with body language. Furthermore, she will filtrate messages through their relatives, their parents or sisters they are close to, within the larger sum of sisters. This type is normally the larger sizes of sisters and can fall in to the more "rich and wealthy" type of sisters. The conflict may have surfaced during child hood through favoritism shown more so towards one sister or the next. This type of sister is hateful and conceited. It can lead to serious games of blackmail, torture, and tragedy, leading up to death or very serious situations. This type of sister, is ruthless and mean. They fight over inheritances, they have their sisters followed, investigated, and they invoke certain other serious elite crimes on their sisters. They are always in competition and it never ends until death takes one or the other home. They are evil, without conscious and they are relentless.

The various types of sisters listed above are categories that we see all over the world. Throughout each and every culture, religion, race, creed, or language. Look at the categories and see which one you fall into. You may have a trait or two outside of the traits listed, but which one are you primarily? Does your sister group need healing? Does your sister group need to be totally revamped and changed? What is your sister group dynamic? Do you desire change? If so read on.

There is a lot of jealousy that needs to be acknowledged amongst sisters that we have been covering up. Some may be inside of you, and then some may be inside of her (it just all depends). Some may be because of visible things we can touch and feel, some may not be. It may be how she acts, her confidence, how she looks, how she dresses, how she talks, how she walks, how she talks to your Momma, how she talks to your Daddy, or simply how she is. I have watched and observed sisters constantly. I have seen some sisters be so jealous of one sister that they have sabotaged special moments of another sister, by facilitating tragic events that caused the family to "halt" at her issues and take the reigns, so to speak, so that the attention is switched, and no longer the special moment for the sister "at hand." I have seen sisters manipulate their parents into believing lies they have told in order to get what they want, and get the other sister in trouble. These are not "Life Time" stories, these are real issues that I experienced, or saw happen with sisters. You see the focal point of this writing is for us to acknowledge what we have been feeling about or towards our sister, so we can be set free and live the good life that we were promised. Some people do not realize that they are hurting themselves by hating their own flesh and blood and holding internal hates and secret issues that are deep and "dark" felt -towards one's sister. Let's get to the bottom of these issues. Keep reading!

Reality Show Type. There is a trend out there of women, that are sisters that are creating reality shows, on live television, on You Tube, and other forms of social media. I am noticing a trend of sisters that are taking their lives to the eye sight, of the public, by allowing their relationships to be openly explored and exploited by the main stream media. These are the reality show sisters. It started out a decade or so ago, when one of the Hilton Girls did a reality show, it was not with her real sister, but with two girls that were made to be friends that made them-selves seem like sisters, Nicole Richie and Paris Hilton (this is where the terms BFF was coined). They went on this journey of their lives, while being followed by the camera. The current shows are now- focused on sisters that we came to know as the Kardashians, then there came the, Westbrooks (short-lived on BET), the Braxton's, and Mary, Mary just to name a few. The reality show type are the sisters that put their lives and private affairs on social media for the "show of it." It seems to be the dawning of a new era, releasing one's personal affairs on social media (we are all guilty of this phenomena, in some way shape or form, even if we do mini FACEBOOK SERIES, LOL, WE ARE ALL GUILTY of being the REALITY SHOW TYPE, LOL). In this day and time, we (in general) are now proud to show our life to the world on social media, seems like now there are not- many secrets in the world today, everything is show cased, even the sacricy of sisterhood. The reality show type of sister clans, are "brassy, showy, newsy messy, and confronting, etc." Anything you want in a sister, when linked to a reality show is there. You can be a good sister, one minute, and then a bad one the next. You can be committed to each other, one day and lie or stir up confusion, the next. You can create an alliance with your Mom on the one sister, and make her the culprit, the next. You can all go on a sister trip one day, and fight and argue via text, Instagram, facebook the next. The reality show sisters have no boundaries, their lives are open books to the world and they use their "mantra" as being sisters to create wealth, power, and false fame. The reality show sisters lives are lived within the walls of their show. Sisterhood, in this regard, is based on what the show dictates.

The reality "ring (so-to-speak)" show can bring sisters closer or tear them apart, it can create scandal, conflict and demise and constant "riff/raff (as we used to say)" amongst sisters. The reality show sisters are what we all look for, it is what some of us wish to be, the reality show sisters has no regard for the integral bond of a sister, most of the time nor does It respect the true essence of what it means to be a sister (all they want is your show). I will say, although, I am sure that sisters that agree to portray their relational issues to the world, think that they are doing it, some good, to help the sister bond, they often times end up injuring it. Often with reality show sisters, it seems the fights have been ongoing for quite sometime. Even though they often say,they love each other on these type shows, and that we would go out for each other, we would do this or that with each other, but it is always a fuss, a fight, a "get back," "a let- down" a stab in the gut (in my own personal opinion) that these sisters endure. I love watching them, sometimes, as I want to see how far sisters will go to get noticed. It has given me a view and perspective, on what sisters are to the good,and the not so good. I talk to them via "(yelling, laughing and even crying), at my television, like they are right there with me, LOL)", during the show, I critique them, analyze them, talk about them, "turn the television off on them", and all of that! But what has penetrated my heart and soul in the midst of all of this, is the sisterhood bond, being "thrown around' like it is nothing, totally disrespected, disregarded and dismissed, as if it is nothing to be esteemed and exalted. I have seen sisterhood flaunt itself on reality shows as if it was an untrustworthy place of rest or connection. The reality show type is "all out there'. They can be "real bad" or they can be "real good". Let's not be this type! I am serious, some will be mad at me, but its okay, I move on.

Spiritual hard nosed type. The spiritual hardnosed type of sister group was raised in a strict upbringing, environment and religious type. This type lives and breathes their sisterhood bond through their religion. This type will have a big sister group normally that was reared in a specific religion. This religion determines, directs and guides how the sisters relate to each other. This type constantly criticizes the one sister that may fall out of line of the particular religion, The one that does so is scolded, put down and forced down, until "they come back up," based on the religions' articles. This type rebukes, scorns and constantly bashes each other with the religions decrees, statements and logic. This sister type can be educated, wealthy or not. The sister type has a pride that is unbreakable, snouted by their religion. They always say, "I am going to pray for you," "I will rebuke you," "The devil is a liar" or whatever religious jargon suits their style. They may be "nun" sisters that live in the covent that look down their nose at the other because she no longer chooses to live this way. The list and style of religious "brood of sisters" is endless. What is your religious type of sister group? This type is enduring and has rigid rules that must be followed. This sister type lacks intimacy and only uses the bond to "bind" and keep the sisters "under." They do not support much of anything outside of their religion. They are secretive and aloof. This type will force an emotion upon the group that will keep them all reveled in a catatonic state that can lead to various mental health symptoms and diagnoses'. This type can have touting's of disarray and tragedy. This sister type has a certain code of dress, language and demeanor. This sister type is the ultimate in rigidity. I will describe another- sister trait similar to this one later on in the book.

Betrayal Type. The betrayal type, this is the type of sister that you know will betray you. This is the type that you know will do you in, she has no reason to do you any other way. This type of sister is jealous and mean, uncaring, and has no boundaries, no-filter what-so-ever. You know this type and you expect her to do it every time. This type/ group of sisters, live to use their parents against one another, they are never satisfied and they are never full. They are always into something, keeping things going. Betrayal is their motivation and their drive, without it they have no identity. Their parents are the enabling type and they fuel their children's wrath against each other. They are not the strict type, they are the "non-schalant"-permissive type, that has sat back and allowed this sister type to "brew" all of their lives.

Being a sister can be a delightful instance or a traumatic instance. I know this all sounds really horrible and repetitive, but I want you all to get the point. Keep reading- I will get to other side of sisters, later in the book. I want to address this the way God gave it to me. I will say that growing up as a part of a trio of sisters, I thought that sisterhood was something that was deep and divine, yet as I begin to notice how I related to my sisters, I realized something else was missing between us at various times, something was greatly wrong often times. The connection was not always there, the trust was not always there. The backup was just not always there, the togetherness was not always there. So many untapped feelings were trapped inside of me and as I walked through life, I began to observe the relationship of sisters, this book is what I observed and kept bottled up inside of me, until God along with what he journeyed me through, life in order to experience- some with my sisters and some with other sisters. People, in whom I made and adopted as my sisters. Some were white, some were black (race wise). Some were other family members that I took on as my sister, some were not even related, but it all had the same affect.

I believed in my heart that whom ever it was, they were the person, at the time that God sent to be in that place to figure out, what a sister is. I walked and acted in the true place of a sister with individuals close and distant, near and far. I learned what it was like to have and not have a sister. I learned what it meant to be betrayed by a sister, I learned what it felt and looked like to endure what being jealous of a sister, and being the target of that emotion felt like. How many of you felt targeted by your sister's emotions, good or bad? I experienced people that I loved, dismiss my thoughts, my opinions and feelings as "crazy, non-important, and not respected". I experienced sister hood at its best and at its worst. I was a sister and I am a sister and I am now spilling what I have learned to the world, on what it feels like in the happiest of times as a sister and the worst of times of being a sister. I have experienced losing someone that I took as a sister to death. And also, what it means to gain life in a relationship with someone that you don't even share the same DNA as a sister. I have tried and tested various types of sister relationships with sisters, and I am still here to tell it. I hope and pray as we walk through my journey with sisters, that someone can find salvation in this memoir about what being a true sister is and what it is all about. Whether it is with a blood sister or not, and what being a sister or an enemy within this is truly all about.

Being a sister at 3, 4, and 5, is much different than being a sister at 30, 40, 50, and 60 (so on, and so on) and if there is a group of sister that made it to the 80 group, that are deeper and vetted. I will continue to observe and see, if he Lord allows me to witness this phenomemon and what the experiences are. I am still researching this particular sister set, but, hope by the time I finish this book, I will have been enlightened on what it means to be a sister at the age of 80 (or maybe not, I need to finish editing this book, it can be read and experienced). Lol!

In saying that, I will be the first to admit that I was insecure a lot growing up as a sister, about mine, other's people's sisters, you name it, that is why I am able to share this book with you, from God's lips to my heart (Yah)!. Growing up as a sister, with specific feelings of lack; in the area of physical beauty, I always felt that my sisters were a lot prettier than I. I was in a state of inner wonder, and at times, pain and disillusionment. Whenever we were out together in our early teens and 20s I thought that they got what I had- thought in my mixed up mind, was-- more attention than, I did, at the time. I will note though, I was not jealous, but, just insecure, more so. It seemed that the more attention they got the more less of a person, I was or felt, ever feel this way? Not knowing that I had all the attention in the world, from God. What I didn't realize was that, it was God keeping me covered, shielded, from an attention that could have turned my life upside down. The attention that I longed for, that was not good for me. The attention I wanted, would have led me down a very different path, one that would have not allowed me to be here to write this book. It was attention that I needed from my parents, that was displaced, but that is another whole story.

Sadly, I felt like I got pushed into a deeper hole, each time they (my sisters) got complimented or noted as being nice looking, by men at clubs, at church or wherever we were together as sisters. I felt fat and out of shape, and disproportioned it was always something, in my mind, that was just not right about me, this is my truth. What is yours? I want you to think about this, as you read more and get deeper into this book! Is there someone out there that feels that something is just not right with you, as it relates to your sister or sisters? Are you tormented by physical attributes, financial status and other menial issues that one sister may or may not have? Ask yourself, because if so, you are in for a long, tumultuous, wasteful journey of your life, because I had to learn who I was, in order to gain my own self confidence and assurance and when I did, it took me on flight!

Sisters, if you are reading, this book no matter if you are White, Black, Indian, Asian, Chinese, French, Jamaican, Italian or whatever race God entered you into, read it and weep, yes, weep, until you get it all out, that is what this book is about weeping! Weeping to bring on joy, weeping to bring on peace, weeping to bring on the newness of you and who God intended for you to be as sisters. Read on! So many of us, need this because we did not have support in areas of one parent or the other. I have noticed so and this may be biased, but it is a fact that girls that are not secured by their Dads have lots of inner issues. They tend to take longer to figure out who they are. Some mask it well with endeavors, yet I know it is so, that when a girl grow up without a Dad securing her inner person, she lacks a lot, a lot of confidence, a lot of drive to be empowered and sure of herself, she just lacks. Girls need to hear from their Dad's who they are. A girl needs to be protected a very young age, so that when she looks for a man in marriage, she can quickly identify what he is and what he is not to be in her life. Girls definitely need this. The Devil entered into our minds ideas that, girls don't need men. The devil has fooled girls in society to be so carefree until they hav begin to thwart the possibilities of fatherhood in their lives, only to become brutish, cold and non-caring. This is not God's plan for sisters or women at large. Explore who you are in this! Ask youselves "who am I, as a sister and individual"?

Special Note: At the younger ages of being a sister we did lots of fun things together, we watched television, we played, we laughed, we got with other sisters in our neighborhood (the Wrights and the Hampton Sisters) and walked down the streets of our little small town. We went to parties, we did a lot of hanging out in our neighborhoods, that was a lot more fun, back then- than being on Facebook! We had a ball as we were growing up. I can remember, that I was the head of the pack on lots of things we did, they may not remember a lot of it, but I do. I did it as a sister, as a friend, I did it as a protector. I did it to keep our connection alive. Little did I know I had a lot to learn! Furthermore, we would sit on the back side of the house and play jacks, jump rope, hope scotch, in the roads, before they turned paved (yes we had dirt roads in the city limits) or play hide and go seek. We would gather together as sisters and friends and do our things, we walked to church to-gether, vacation bible school, we would go to and walk from parties together as we got older, we went to clubs together, you name it we did it all as sisters and friends.

Being a sister as a teenage brings in lots of strange moods and feelings. It brings on personal hormonal issues that cause sisters to start looking at each other differently. It is when girls turn into what they think is womanhood, and when that time of the month introduces itself to you and your sisters, the once friendly sisterly bond that you have turns into a nightmare. The, "I am your sister atti-tude", turns into enemy ground and warfare. Sisters are at the emergence, of their identity, at these times. But as time progresses during these hormonial episodes, things begin to turn into- tumult and strife. We begin to see our sister like an opponent. Sisters start to develop in various ways to include, breasts, hips and thighs. We end up seeing and experiencing one being a bit more curvier than the other in certain areas, a bit more longer hair, a bit more "put together" than the other, not just in looks, it can vary from looks to intellect, athleticism, discipline, ability to make friends with others, creativity, skill, smarts, you name it. Sisters begin to take note of themselves and others outside of the sister circle, during these years, and this can sometimes create havoc. Being as though because sisters are often confused at the swift changes and lose cite of what sisterhood is. We experiment with the sister premise and sometimes we walk "straightway away from it, without even knowing we do so at these times".

During these years sisters tend to bond outside of the loop (so to speak) with other women that they begin to inwardly call their sisters, or deem as sisters.

My middle sister, bonded with our neighbor, Lynn Wright (of the Wright Sisters that I wrote about earlier), they were like sisters, knit together growing up, as one, at times, and still to this day, even though they are miles and miles apart. They are so much alike in so many ways, to themselves, walking their own paths, yet sisters, like I saw Lynn say, on several Facebooks posts "from another mother". Walking through life- in their own worlds and in their own way. Jenny and Lynn were always close to the core and heart, sisters weaved by another thread! Kinda like Oprah and Gayle, nothing will never separate their bond, no matter if they don't see each other for years, and years at the time- it is still the same. They somehow know each other, in a way that their real sisters don't they are two "peas in a pod". We always would use this phrase "two peas in a pod", but lets take look two peas in a pod. The descriptor in my mind, has shown me "two literal peas", like peas we shell when we were shelling peas with our mom or grandparents, two of them are in their together, look the same, feel the same and texture the same. That is how my sister, Jenny and Lynn were. Are you this way with your real, true sister, ask yourself? When I look at pictures of Lynn on Facebook with her other friends and Jenny, with us, it don't seem or feel the same, as seeing her with Lynn. We are blood of the same blood (me and Jenny), but when I see her and Lynn together, it is really different than what we have as sisters. I get this, and I appreciate seeing this, as it is rarity! If you have a sister that you are so connected with that you don't understand it and it never changes, go to her, if you have not been with her in a while, explore your sisterhood connection, don't let it waste away, in the time of COVID, we have to reach out to people that can reach us! Sometime flesh of our flesh aint it, sometims God has a sister, as LYNN says often from "another mother" to be there for you, the one that you can pour it all out to, the one that can sense your pain and understand it, in order to make you better, in order to help you function better, grab your sister, the one that is GOD sent! The one that you both were in your mother's womb at time of sameness that time cannot describe nor fathom. You know who she is, it does not forfeit your blood sisters, it only enhance it! I know some of you been waiting to hear this, as you may have felt guilty about this outer connection that you have with someone that was not pushed through the same womb, as you, or was she, but just in another dimension and time! Keep reading!

"My Cousins, The Martin Sisters"

Realize this-The highlight of sisterhood is the connection. The connection touts sisterhood, when we sometimes cannot get it from our biological sisters, God will always have a "ram in the bush (so-to-speak)". We all have that one sister that is not of blood that we just cannot let go of. She is that one that we are totally connected to, in a different way. This can be a everlasting and ongoing connection and commitment, when it happens. I look at my sister Jenny and Lynn, and I will forever see this bond and connection. We all saw their connecton growing up, 'ode to Lynn and Jenny' true sisters to the heart! Let's be this way! Lets learn of this connection! See the "Lynn and Jenny" in your lives!

More on sisters. In order to be a strong sister, in the sisterhood 'brood', one has to understand one's own strength and one's own power as a sister. Realizing what your link is- in the tie that binds is, what "makes a world of a difference" on how solid, a sister bond is. I remember when my oldest Aunt (Aunt Ann) lost her husband suddenly, all of her sisters rallied around her, they barely let her "foot touch (figure of speech)" the ground. They took my aunt's pain and bared in their own hearts. They stood very close to her physically, mentally and emotionally, they checked on her, they stayed with her, they cried with her, they even wanted her to leave what she knew as home to come to their dwelling places to monitor her more closely. Their sister signal was in full power. All of them were there for her and spared no expense, or time to be with her in her time of need. They jumped to my aunt's call the very same night and dove down a one way lane, secondary road (as I call it) during the middle of the night to serve my aunt in her darkest hour. It was something that we all would never forget the togetherness of the Sansbury Sisters, my aunts, when my Uncle Leo died suddenly, my oldest Aunt "Ann's" husband of over four decades!

Sisterhood was demonstrated throught this act of love with my aunts, they all used their ability to catch their sister's pain and hold it for her, as much as they could, while she traveled through this long dark path. This event, as awful of it was, repeated itself in my aunt, they call the "knee baby," Janice, when she lost her child Erica (her middle child). The same instance occurred, in the same manner, yet with even more intensity. The sisters had seen this before and was experienced in this, and stood even stronger with my Aunt Janice. I never saw such love, compassion and consistency, it was moving and touching, to show "even" more of the closeness of what a sister should be, in times such as these, the second time around. My aunts would drive back and forth from their homes to make sure, that My Aunt Janice in her time of suffereing, and loss of her daughter, be made strong. Even after the funeral was over, each one of the sisters that was able- made sure that my aunt was covered. They were so in tune with her grief they all tried to take a piece of her grief, onto themselves to help relieve her in her time of sorrow. They did this during both times of loss in our families, I applaud you Aunts! It was a devastating time for the family, as their loss, was everyone's loss. . They walked by each other's side until the very end (services, etc.). Yet, after it all ended, my aunts continued to be with each other,even up to the present day. This is what sisters are about, I shared this story,to help, direct, to guide and give an experience that was so divine, connected and pure, when it comes to sisterhood, it makes you want to cry. I am sure they would want this story to be passed on as an example to other sisters out there on how to love, and be there for one another. To be honest, in my opinion, My aunts are the perfected picture of what God created sisters to be, I am not saying they don't have their issues and are perfect, but they stand in the midst of it all and you would never really know it when they are together if they had a issue, because they never act as if anything is wrong. I highlight them because they were "one" of the closest pictures or observation of closeness and intimacy that I had of sisters. There are many other sisters that I have observed and will mention throughout this memoir. Continue to read this book in love. I hope you are enjoying, experiencing and increasing thus far!

I hope to promote more love, more togetherness, more "sticking with it power" that sisters should have. My Aunts are bonded at the soul and they stick it out with each other no matter what. I even believe when holidays come, although they have other family to attend to- on their husbands or children's sides, I personally think they feel funny about it inside, but just don't say it, because they have duties elsewhere with their children or spouses' families (just my opinion). Never did I know, I would be materializing their acts in this memoir. God is good! See a sister, be a sister!

Key Point 1. I think often times, we as individuals within the "sisterhood pack," we do not understand ourselves and the power we have in our role and position as a sister. One has to know where you were appointed as a sister in the line, that God created for you as a sister. If a sister can understand their role, she or she can come out shining in ways like never before. One can be triumphant in the relationship of a sister, no matter what position you play.

Key Point2. Holding on to insecure feelings of how, one sister looks, acts, projects, expounds or whatever it is, you have a "hang up over" can be toxic. Be careful at what you allow to enter into your heart and stay in your heart towards your sister. This is how the devil sets traps and "mounds" of complexities within your 'psyche'. Be very mindful of your feelings and express them to your sister immediately or if you are not open enough, and close enough or strong enough to express yourself, let another sister be the mediator. If one or the other of your sisters has a strong personality, then use that particular one to be the "go between". Don't allow yourself to be torn down anymore than you already are. Always move with caution, when you are weary or feeling under pressure by or with your sisters.

Often times, when one allows time to pass, and you wait too long to express how you feel, the other sister may not be in the right frame of mind to receive your templated thoughts towards her. Templates are already established and put together formats that we use in writing. A template is something set up that you can use "over and over." Be careful to pray often on this matter, if you cannot pray, have another sister to intervene. As noted earlier using another sister as your filter. One that can mediate the action with precision, caution and strength as to not create more distance and animosity. Remember the goal is always to bring the sister spirit together, not farther apart.

Another issue I noticed with sisters is influence. The group of sisters need to figure out which sister is most influential and in what designated areas. Not one sister has it all. Just because one sister is able to influence in one area, and you can't that does not make you less of a person (find out yours). Use each sister's gifts and talents to benefit the entire group, that is all what group work is about.

With being a sister, we all got to, work together to empower one another. We have to change our perspectives on sisterhood and note, if one sister has it in a area, then let her have it, let her get the job done and vice versa. It makes it easier for us all. We have to see ourselves as a tool, a working machine, if " you will". Using your sister's wealth, meaning her gift and talents given to her by God is something that can bless the sister group beyond measure if all pieces are working and acting properly when they need to. We need to learn how to apply the level of influence that a sister has in the appropriate places.

There are various ways to "apply" influence, it does not have to be one just one way. Always know, my dear sisters, if something is not for you, it's just not for you. Let your sister do her thing, let her practice who she is within the group. If it is your sister's thing, "let it be her thing". Don't let what your sister has, blind you from seeing who she is and who you are and what you all have. Don't allow the enemy to make you use the "blame" game or "I am a victim game" to under-mined or undercut the sister fold. See, it is ladies, that when one sister undercuts another sister, you may have had undercut them all. You are short circuiting the group. The "light' that you bring, is being dimmed, so the longer and the more time, you stay in this place of resistance (not complying or conforming) to the pact, the longer the sister group is short sided. This causes constant bickering, talking negatively, etc. And know this, that just because you may not be engag-ing with your sisters, don't think the atmosphere, does not know something is wrong. God gave us five senses and those senses are pulled into gear when there is a missing link or short circuit in the sister group. Don't think you are unim-portant or not special, God has a talent for you, that is necessary. I mean if you are for example, a silent type, that is a source, that is needed, some sisters that have this trait, bring in a security that is vital to the group. Silence is not always "deadly" as we suppose. It can bring forth solidarity and rigidness that can keep the group sane at times. Lets not get insecure because one of our sisters may not be as vocal as the others. What if a challenge comes up, where we don't need to speak on it and the one sister that has been exercising this gift for most of her life can stand the pressure, she can use her ability to pull the group together with her ability to say silent? The "art of silence" can be golden at times. She will then know when to come in and coach the other sisters how to "remain silent." I mean there are so many ways we can look at gifts, talents and abilities that are always apparent in the sister group. Just get to know who you are in the "sister group." Understand your traits and move forward. Knowing how to "fit" is vital to the sister connection. Lets learn and grow sisters. .

Key Point 3. It is very important to explore who you are as a sister, not doing so, drowns your voice. drowns your energies. drowns your image, whether you are quiet, loud, abrasive, charismatic, intelligent, and talented or the like. Analyzing your traits is as- vitally important as it shows- you and your sisters, how useful you are within the group of sisters. Understanding, yourself- helps "one's" confi-dence and engagement with the sister work. I have seen another sister group, let's call them the "The "D" sisters, it is three of them, one of the sisters have always taken charge, she is educated, "career stacked" and she is militant. She is the sister that has the birthright. She is the Eldest, the one that God created as the resource, the "filler and filter," this is the one that will give up and fight for her sisters- and the entire family. She will get up out her bed if need be, to conquer what needs to be done, she is assured of who she is in the sister group and moves on it constantly. Note: "Know your marching orders" as a sister. Understand who you are in marching and how "you are that" force to be reckoned with. The Eldest sister has the birth right, if she is in position 'That is key". She has to be in position,God will appoint the next in line- or the one that qualifies to take over, if she does not align with the role.

Let me explain what birth right is. Birth right is a particular right of possession or privilege one has from the day one is born. It is a natural or moral right, an inheritance, as noted by Merriam's online dictionary (September 15, 2018). The Eldest sister is entitled to certain benefits that is a reckoning force. This role sustains, lifts, keeps and restores all other sisters. I know some may have variances and that is okay. When the true Eldest sister is not in position, then there will always be a replacement. Some sisters allow the cares of life to strip them from their birth right. Some are tricked out of it, some are talked out of it, some "give it up or away", like Jacob did for selfish desires- it varies. I will discuss the "stripping" of a sister's role later. We have to be alert and equipped to maintain our position that God has granted us. I have always viewed "Sister D-1 (as I will call her, noted above) as a power within her sister TRIO, she is professional, dedicated, poised, she can "roll" with the best of them and the worst of them, she knows her stuff. That is what the Eldest sister does. She knows her stuff, sisters that are below the Eldest in birth order (alone), let her have her " just due," don't try to mock, ridicule or belittle your sister's role in being the Eldest/Oldest, she was birth there for a reason. She was chosen by God and pulled out of your mother's womb first, for a reason. She is the one that was appointed. Allow her to flow in the true essence of her sister power/role and watch how blessed the sister circle will be. I am an eldest sister, so I know this role, all so well. I will talk on other roles a bit later.

"The following is a real life example of a sister group. This is used to shed light on various scenarios that occur with sister"s.

"Sister D-1" as I will call her has always been the one that takes charge in the family and with her two other sisters, let's call them "Sister D-2" and " Sister D-3" the later sisters tend to get into line, with her orders or directions. Now, I know that may seem odd, but she has been known to take charge, take care of the family and settle disputes, face conflict, she is not afraid and she is equipped. I have noticed that her sisters never/ try to be her, they never side-step her or try to impose on who she is to the family. She has the qualities of superiority and leadership. She has lots of discipline, and her family takes her for every bit of who she is. A perfect example of a dynamic that has worked for the group for, decades. I wish I knew more, of them that I could share, but so far, what I observed they have the perfect roles and interconnectedness that sisters need. They are a perfect example of having an identity, a particular role, a skill, an ability and the proper level of action that needs to be taken and "by whom it should be taken by". Excellence, the D- sisters!

Sisters lets realize, that we all came out of the same womb, we have blood that is the same, why not let's act like it, take a few notes from the "D" sisters, they have allowed their oldest sister to be the oldest without persecution, dismay or animosity towards her, and they have grown because of it. She has guided the family, even her mother and father to a place of perfection. Their parents are well up in age (90s), and she cares for them emotionally, mentally and other ways needed. Not only does she make sure that her sisters are not taken advantage of, she makes sure her parents are well cared for as well. "Ode to ""The D Sisters (Create and assemble your own variations of the 'D'Sisters)."

Ultimately, It really should not matter which sister has the most of this, and/ or most of that, the less of this or the less of that (this is starting to- in all actuality, sound like a broken record isn't it, but I say it enough in the book to make you not want to hear or act in this manner ever again, get the point, yes, I am sure you do, read on ladies) because when it all boils down, if you are really sisters, the one sister or a few- will pull all the others up. I will give a great shout of applause to Toni Braxton, as she did just that, her fame, power and legacy bought her sisters up, even in the midst of what they seem to be going through now,this is my personal opinion, she has stood as the most influential of all the sisters.

No matter how you cut it, it was Toni's gift that endowed her sister group. Her sisters were granted- the open door to success- not dismissing their parents dedication to God that got them there, we know first and foremost it was the foundation they got, that caused Ms. Toni Braxton to get recognized at the gas station one day. Toni's gift got her noticed, it made room for the entire family! Lets acknowledge sisters which sister has the gift, that will endow or sharpen us all to make it, to achieve it to grab it! Let's not be jealous, lets not hold back, let's mate and bond with our sisters so that we can get what is due us, through that one or several sisters, --what God has granted us in and through his spirit! Let's not down play the gift of God that has come to take us where we need to be, through that special gifted sister or sisters! Let's do this! All these are my opinions and personal observation of sisters. Sisters, if one of your sisters has the power and the influence, "Let her have it," if you play your position as you should, you won't be far behind. Don't let jealousy and insecurity, blind you to what God has for you, just because one or two sisters, may have the "it" that can get you all there. Don't deny the very blessing that has been laid at your feet for redemption. Don't toss it to the side, pick it up, materialize it, manage it and be blessed by it. You see the world is so much smarter than us, I will say this again, as it was quoted by Jesus in Luke Chapter 16:8. The world knows how to take Godly principles and use them and then become wealthy (not just with money, but with stamina, class, strength and power, this is how it should be girls), emotionally, mentally and physically sound. Those of us that profess to know the Lord, we often fail to use what God gave us. Let's not do this any longer. Let's use all of what God has for us to prosper in our sister relationships and more.

Whether God created you to have a lots of this or lots of that, it should not matter when it comes to sisters. As I was reading in the book of Genesis, the bible noted the characteristics of Jacob and Esau (I will use men for these examples but the point is still on sisters), it noted that one brother, Esau, the oldest was one of the field and was a skillful hunter, while the other Jacob, was a plain man (Genesis 25:27). These traits were noted and the mother was fully aware of her son's traits. Sisters, know your traits, know your position, know what you are entitled to within your particular role. If you are a "plain sister" and you do not like to be in, or on the "showy" side of life then be-Just that, be what you are! God has made room for you. If he has made you to be the "quiet" out of the scenes type of person, be that person, stop mixing the roles and your identity, it will never work! Don't be afraid or ashamed to be who you are. If you desire to do something that fits within that trait, then do so, don't let the fact that you are the "quiet and plain type" deter you from your destiny. Don't let it side track you, or make you lazy and laid back. You have a gift too! Understand if you are a "half and half" kinda sister, you like a little bit of noise and ruckus, but you know how to be alone and enjoy yourself- to yourself, right in the midst of the chaos. You don't have to try to fit in or feel bad, because you don't fit in a certain area. Know your role and be who God created you to be, remember this sisters, whether you are loud, boisterous, humorous, or whatever have you, know that God created you, not we ourselves; so know that you can feel comfortable as such! I had a hard time, personally accepting who God created me to be, as I felt like the more I pushed outward, the more I was going to get ostracized and ridiculed. It took a lot of my lifetime to accept the "me" that I am. When I came into that place, it no longer matters what, anyone says. It is now, Who God says that I am and I have accepted the Pam, that I Am!

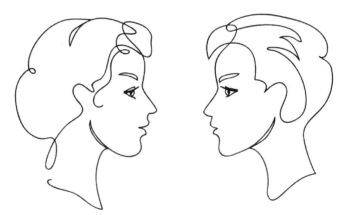

"The Pam that I am"

When you are before your sister, you are all at the lowest denominator of who you are, and as you all sit together in that spiritual place that connects you, there is no one that is better than the next. There is no sister that has anything that can make one feel better than or less than the other. There are no houses, cars, political status, material possession or any level of gain that one "_has or does not have_" that can deter the focus of the sister bond. Being open, upfront, during the times of sister "mating" is one of vitality. One of earthly significance, as one sister is lifted up, the other one is too (you will hear me say this often, in one way or the other, throughout).

Sister Mating is a process of coming together to process (in the literal sense, it is two animals of a different species coming together to produce). Let's look at it like sisters coming together to grow and evolve and learn of one another. When sisters come together, as I have seen my earthly neighbors from Clifford street, in the small town of Timmonsville, South Carolina, the town that I grew up in, The Wright Sisters: Lynn, Shoan, Cymp, Debbie and Angie, take their yearly sister trip. They come amongst each other's, with fun, gifts, love, laughter and excitement. They seem, to mix and mate- with each other in a place of love, joy, pain, and elevation. When I say "elevation", I mean that every trip brings about growth and a higher level of togetherness. They visit different cities, different cultures and ex-perience life beyond what they know, from the very small town of Timmonsville, South Carolina, that we all grew up in. They grow their sister machine as much as possible, while they have the chance to. By the stories and scenes depicted on Facebook, and what I experienced with them in life, as being our "down the street neighbors." I have seen them grow and connect day, by day and year by year. I watched them lose their mother, Mrs. Ernestine Wright, and continue to walk through life, in the way that she directed them to do, like she taught them to do, like she bred them to do! I remember Ms. Ernestine modeling what she wanted her girls to be, and I see a piece of her, in every one of them, I see her look in everyone of them, I see her actions in every one of them. They model what true sisterhood is all about! Furthermore, (I had to get this out because I want someone to see that real sisterhood still exists, and what it is about)! Cymp, Shoan, Debbie, Lynn and Angie allow themselves to come to the place of the "melting pot" of sisterhood, the place that sisters mold and mix, love and laugh, cry and release. Let's take a chance at sisterhood, like "the Wright sister do", the way it is supposed to be done! We can do this too, it may not be a yearly sister trip, it maybe something else, it may be a different setting of any kind, it may be on the telephone, it may be a prayer. Some sisters can meet in the realm of God's precious "Holy Spirit," his divine place of never-ending "connected" love, joy, peace and righteousness. There are many places that sisters can meet to stay close and unleash the powers that be, in order to have a great and inner connected sister experience, I mean it can be in the boardroom, it can be in a sister's den, it can be on ZOOM, it can be at your place of rest, place of business, in your car, in a park, wherever you as sisters deem it necessary and a place where you can connect. Let's get to the "drawing board" ladies, like the "Wright Sisters" have done. Lets figure out where, and how we can grow and develop as sisters, how we can spend time in some place and space in order to grow, it is never too late! Start thinking Sisters, Start Thinking! They take life by its storm and enjoy it at its finest. I marvel at what they have done with their sister group! Keep on doing it ladies!

Species of Matter. We are all are species of:,"matter (physical substance, one that occupies space,) " - that God put together, to be useful to one another, to strive for greatness to cry on one another's shoulder, to get together often, whether by phone, text email or whenever, or whatever. There may be times where you want nothing or times when you want everything! Sisters must have this type of connection, this type of "vibe" that lets the other know without words, I am there for you! Does your sister connection take root here? Is it engrafted in trust and deep inner attachment?God created a bond that sisters should hold on to for survival, and at times, dear life; but not negative and unclean usury. Now yes, we all will use our sisters in one way or the other, but we should learn "healthy usary" and realize when the usary gets bad and out of control. Strive to make the much needed and quick corrections. Don't allow what you need your sister for, to turn into to debauchery, cunningness and trickery.

Please don't use your sister to her demise, I ***am saying*** don't' take things from her, just to benefit yourself and not the entire group. Learn how to make your sister group resourceful and profitable. Make sure there is a mutual exchange when you are with your sister. You ask, how is that so, I will use this as an example. Say for instance one day, you are in need of some level of support. Well when your sister takes the time to endulge with your situation. In order to give you what you need, or process your issue, always let her know when it is over, your appreciation for what she has done, for you. Don't take your sister for granted. No dollar bill or loan can stop a sister from helping you if it is done in all fairness and love. She will excuse your mistakes quicker than you think, if you just acknowledge the truth that is always apparent. She knows you might not or will not pay her back. Let her know, it will work itself out, if you are as honest as possible with your sister or sisters at hand! Don't hold back- be, be truthful, if you know you don't have anything to give her back, say "Hey Sis, I need this, but I aint going to lie, I don't have it to give back, or I will give it back to you when I can." Or some will say, "Hey Sis, I owe you!" The acknowledgement is always appreciated! Try not to make your sister feel emotionally blackmailed, or drained, when you are done with her. Don't make her feel as if "that is all you want, is to "get from her." I mean it is noticeable and obvious, anyway, that is your sister (yes, she knows you, it is not hidden). I will say this, we all need as sisters yes there is always a need-, for one thing or the other, I promise you, this is not about promotion of one particular sister's role, and not the other, but it is about the various roles that are cited in a sister group and the deeds of sisters that need to be made know and conscious, so that change can come to the good.

I want to highlight, too- the not so popular, not so verbally inept sister, I want to highlight each and every sister in the group, after all we are all created equal and in the midst of our sisters we should be as an emptied vessel. An open sepulcher, a place of rest and ease, a place of peace and comfort. Is this where you are with your sister or do you have many miles to travel to get there? I wonder. Let's all wonder. Is there something I need to clear up? Is there an issue that has gone untalked about or touched because no one wants to address it? Is there a sore spot that needs healing? If so, let's begin today, to force this issue to the table, let's attack the "elephant in the room." When there is an issue that is pressing in the sister group, let's not all look away from it, in pride, shame, or dismay and say, "oh she will be alright."

Very Important: We should never cover up anything for our sisters! No act, word or deed! Let's be clear and accountable. If one owes a moral debt, lets let them pay for it, lets let our sister acknowledge it! Lets not make inner and outer excuses for her any more! Away with all of this "saving face," we need to face the issue head on and right now! Let's not wait, as tomorrow maybe too late (especially now, during COVID-19 times). Let's all come together and deal with the situation. Let's all pull together, if we need to and "ambush" the situation in our own sisterly way. I am sure there maybe resistance, but we just cannot continue to let our "little lost sister or sisters" get away, nor ourselves, because our identity is tied into the group, there is a "sister identity" that is set apart from the individual, that exists too, let's keep that in mind! I will talk on that later." Whom better to get it out in the open than a sister. Yes, there may be some controversy, meaning- yelling screaming, crying, speaking of not so nice words, or what have you, but at least you all have addressed it.

"Sisters during COVID-19 times"

Most importantly, don't leave your sister to the wolves, make all jointed and appointed efforts to help her and yourself, after all she is yours! After all our power comes from the home, from where we grew and were bred from, for the most part. The bible says that "charity" begins at home. Let's come together and deal with what needs to be dealt with no matter what the situation is. If you feel a sister has wronged you then tell her. If you feel "left out" or "looked over" tell your sisters. Don't just leave it hanging!

Have a meeting, have a session, have a cup of tea, have whatever it is you want to have to get it out! If you have a sister that is going down a "wrong path" and it becomes evident. Deal with it, have a family intervention. I love those shows. I love to see when families pull their family members together and then force them to receive help. Sometimes they are successful and sometimes not. But at least they try. Build a fortified wall and refuse to let your sister get out of it or around it, until the situation is faced. If there is some personal family crisis that your sister endured alone, as a sister, it will affect the family unit, so approach it as, if it is of utmost important. I know some may say, she is hard headed, she won't listen. Even still, anything is worth a try! Even if it does not go entirely the way you want it to go. Sisters, I admonish you- to then let it work, the way it will work. But get your strategy, get to your sister, that is in need. Let and make her deal with it. She may go off on you, and say things you don't like, I mean it maybe a travesty even, but at least it has been dealt with. I promise you with most certainty, it will get to her at some point, and a seed of correction will be planted. Eventually, she will come back home (in the most symbolic and physical sense). I remember a story where Juanita Bynum, a television Evangelist- talked/testified about her sister and how they had to lure her home. Juanita Bynum shared that her sister was on crack (a pressing issue) and she noted separate accounts when she or her mother would go looking for her as the spirit led them to. She made an overall point, that eventually after, they continued to go after her, that her sister finally came through, yet she said, that (in so many words) they had to lure her. She noted because of the bondage that she was in, she would often resist and would not come. Because they never stopped, no matter what she said or did, eventually they got her to yield. The fight is worth the yielding! Don't give up sisters on your sister!

Sisters we have to go after our sisters, no matter how bad it hurts, to pull them back in. You may have disputes, I mean serious ones. I mean you may be in an "all-out war" with your sister, in trying to bring her back to surface, but that is okay, we all know that sisters have battles. We all know that sisters disagree. That is what this book is about, when your sister is your enemy. I am taking you all down this spiritual, mental emotional and psychological journey, first then we will get to the "my sister (connected together)" part! I know you are 'so getting this" as the millennials say today! LOL!

Parent Relationships Amongst Sisters. Now let's look at another issue that I have observed in sister groups. The relationship that one sister or the other has with their parent or parents, and how all sisters relate to their parents collectively. There is a degree of separation amongst sisters, and there is a collaboraton when it comes to- interaction with sisters and their parents. Parents (mom or dad) of sisters- can cause, low circuits or high circuits, in the sister circle. Some sisters, in and at- some point and time, may have felt that one sister may have had a better connection with their parents and one may have not. Ask yourself sisters, is this true or not? Sure it is, at times, we all do. Is there a false sense of perspective when it comes to how each sister relates to their parent? Is there one that is feeling their connection is not as strong, with the parents or parent, Is there a reason why? Are there false perspectives being held in your mind? Or is there something deeper going on? I tread lightly, yet strongly here.

This section is for the parents, of a sister groups to read. Sisters, I honor respecting one's parent with all my heart, as I know that if you don't your life won't go so well. I believe in the scripture Honor thy mother and thy father, so that they days may go well (Exodus 20:12 King James Version). I believe that anybody that honors their parents, although one does not always agree, end up living quality lives even if at times the relationships are challenged. I believe and know that the essence and extension of who one is prospers, if one follows this command. So let's get this clear, we all must honor our parents, even if it is from a distance, and we will be able to conquer anything that we go through. I will add that is why I feel that my Aunts, the Original Sansbury Sisters mentioned earlier in the book, are so connected, as they have and had truly honored my grandmother, Mable K. Sansbury, growing up and even into adulthood, even beyond the grave. Because of this it has caused their bond to soar and roar throughout time, even when they don't feel like it has or is. I will say the same for the famous Braxton's sisters. I see a level of respect that they carry for their mom that keeps them knitted and close, even when they don't want to be! I will elaborate on this topic,. So let's move forward on relationships with parents. I wanted to add this because I have seen and heard sisters say constantly, oh 'momma or daddy loves her, or this one more," "She is momma or daddy's golden child" and that gets taken to the heart for some and not enough for others, get my drift, yes, I know you do, keep reading! I have seen some children develop pathologies because they get this into their head and it never leaves. They begin to see everything through one pair of "glasses". One has seen it as one--sister being advanced over the other through their parents! With this type of mind set, it always get's worse as time goes on.

Sisters we have to really grow up! Let's open our awareness on child/parent relationships. Sisters, first realize the value in having a parent that is loving and supportive and what they bring to you and what you bring to them, every child is different, and every parent's perspective of each child is different.This is true, no matter what people say! The myth of treating all children, the same is not totally true. Parents, NEXT- realize this, that being a parent is God ordained role, learn how to deal with each girl/child as you should. Understand what one needs and what the other does not. Study your children for the good and not always for the bad. Don't talk about and gossip with one child over the other, that's not relating, that's "baiting". If you learn how to process with your girl children, parent or parents your relationships with your "girl children" will go well. Just a side note- not only your girls kids- but all your kids, male or female (I thought I would add that to this story)! We have to sort through this process to increase one's self worth and know one's identity, parent and child. In knowing one's identity and your parents, thus you will begin to know and feel who you are as sisters, as well as the parent to your adult or even younger sibling girls. Parents of sister children, this thought is mainly for you.

In watching the celebrity families, the Braxton's and the Kardashians, I took noticed that the Mothers of the sister groups, Ms. Evelyn Braxton (Braxton Mother) and Kris Kardashian (Kardashian Mother), both try to manage their girls as best they can or as much as possible, by what, I can tell and observed, that they do love them dearly and they both have their own unique way of relating to each daughter, I watched and observed during the reality shows- the interaction among them all and with each one . Both cherrish each daughter and they share a uniqueness with each one of them, based on what I have observed. I have learned that when it seems a mother shows more of "proudness" towards one daughter, than the other, it is because she is only applauding that particular event or gift within her, daughter, and not just because she may be seeming to show favoritism. Just because there seems to be no applause for you presently, my dear sister, it is not because your mom is looking at you in a lesser sight, it is just that at the time, there is nothing, that warrants this particular praise, there maybe something else at a certain time that your mother will exalt you for, but when it is your sister's turn, its her turn and then when it comes to your turn, that it will be! Don't be dismayed, there are always seasons and it may not be your season, lets not take it personal when it is not. You may have had your season when you were a child, playing in the yard, your momma may have praised and pleasured you then and as time progressed, now it is your sisters turn, think about it has your turn come and gone or are you being gready for "turns", remember how we would argue over the front seat and your mom would say, girls, girls "take turns" or she would ask "who turn is it today or whose turn is it now", lets' know our "turns" lets know "our times". Do you know your season or time? Sisters has your turn been taken already think, long and hard, maybe you are "feening out of time". We all know what "feening means, it is when a person wants drugs, their system is calling for it because it is so addicted, but wrongly" are you feening for something that is not yours? Are you addicted to your sister's "turn" wanting to be her, wanting what she has, I know it hurts, but please, please know it is her time, and not yours. Your time will come or has already. God wants us free my dear sisters, I know this is hard to hear for some, but if we can "really and I mean really" get this we can be blessed. Take a seat and sit back and watch where God is taking your sister and watch how blessed you "too" can be because of it! This is by Godly inspiration, I been writing this book so long, until I myself am ready to release it to you, but as I am editing this book on September 12, 2020, God is giving me more! God is making me pour my heart and soul out, so that sisters can be healed. Not only am I re-reading and writing this book, I am living this book. Read on readers, read on!

Furthermore on parental relationships with mothers and daughters, I mean, let's be real, we as mothers can say all kinds of things to try to 'cover for one daughter' over the next,to make one feel just as valuable, when the other is doing something special, that is what mothers do, but I think we should learn as mothers to be open, honest and blunt with one's girls, so that you can "put fire under their feet of some in the right direction". Mom's let's stop trying to put one up and one down, because you feel one daughter may not be as much as the other! I know she is of your womb and whatever she does represents you, yes, I understand that, but stop the sneaky inner comparisons. No disrespect, but truthfully speaking, don't pull one up to say, she is "just as good'" in sneaky ways to make it seem that one is not less than the other, that is not God's way, all sisters are equal in the sight of God no matter what they have in the natural. Mothers I hope you are getting this! I know your daughter has been hurting over this for many years, but has taken it, to the respect of your honor and position, but it has been hurtful and painful to the one girl that is trying hard to do and be what she is purposed to be! I hope someone is getting deliverance from this!

Mother's be mothers when you need to, guides when you need to, but never be a biased tool, that causes rifts between your girls! You may not know that they realize it, but they do! The tricks and schemes that tries to balance them out, with your tongue- is not of God! Also It doesn't work, it only makes it worse and the one's you always make excuses for it, is not helping. Work and think on this maneuver, that you have been using. It seems that you are feeling it all accredits to you and in some cases it does, but at the same time, the words and strategies are not what will work to satisfy your inner guilt or feelings of what I didn't do for this one or what I didn't do for that one. This causes a lot of let downs and inner pain to take place! Please think deeply and soundly, on this my dear mothers! This is to help you, it will hurt, but you all that partake in this behavior, know it is deeply and profoundly true! Please realize, dear mothers, you are causing more damage than you know! I have had to stop and stop this book so many times, but in my starting and stopping, I get more and more inklings from God.

Special note (June 28, 2020, written earlier): I was listening at a sermon by Bishop T.D. Jakes and he talked about coming to God "empty". He said to come to God as if you know nothing! I am here in the middle of editing my book, as nothing! As I yield to emptiness, God is giving me more for this book! I don't know where we will end up sisters, but I forge on to see what God is giving me to say to you, to help you conquer this enemy that keeps sisters apart!

More on parent relationships Consequently, parents, It can be any situation or problem that your child is going through, it is not always what you think it is, it is not always finances, money or marital problems, girls have so many things, emotionally to deal with, and that they go through that needs to be addressed. A lot of times, the subtle things, are often missed, overlooked or bypassed. Moral, and emotional support are the bigger things that's often needed. Moms, of girls these issues need to be addressed. If you have a daughter that keeps over indulging in an area, to get the attention of you, the parent, then address it! Please do! Attack the situation upfront!This is for a mother that is reading this! Engage, and address the situation "hunt your daughter down," do what needs to be done, put all the cards on the table! Let your girls know, that you as a mom, want to conquer this mountain. Let them know that they all, are a team, yet individuals, and that is how it will be. Elaborate on closeness and togetherness and inform them of your place in their lives and the importance that it is- to them and to you, and on how each relationship can be different! You can do it!

Oddly, enough, I have noticed a lot of times the problems come in mostly with the "mother/daughter" relationship. I have seen "daddy/daughter" relationships mostly fair "really" well. It seems to me that men, have a knack for orchestrating relationships to each daughter differently and in a posied manner. It seems that women, mothers are more inclined to show or highlight what is special about one daughter and what is not. This is an inner thing, and I have observed this all my life when it comes to a band of sisters, and their mom, versus their dads. I have heard and visualized daughters that all get the same, exact vibe from their Dad, but not their Mom, I have heard during countless conversations, "momma treats me differently" than this one or that one! Some keep it a secret and act out on it. While others voice it constantly and it is a main source of confusion, when it comes to families. If the relationship ties with one's mom is not proper, it will cause constant chaos. Let this be an open topic of discussion and bring clarity to the union. Have constant talks about how one feels as a sister, as it relates to the mother of the sister group. The mother of the group of girls may have to constantly reassure each daughter of her love, and support (over time) by spending time, doing special things for the one daughter, that may have a problem with seeing herself in a certain light with her mom. The mom may have to use wisdom and strategic thinking in attacking this issue. Because it is a very sensitive issue, no one really wants to talk about this and it goes untouched or tapped into, for long periods of time. This issue may cause a lot of discomfort. Let's break those chains. Let's do it and bring in the liberty that being a sister group needs. The mother of the sister group, can be vital to securing the sister group or bond. It is okay, if your mother has passed on, explore it with your mother surrogate and face the issue head on.

All in all, let's not allow ourselves to despise the mother/daughter bond that we all share, let's all connect through our mother in order to enhance the sisterly affair. If there is a mother out there that is reading this book and you have a group of girls, that you birthed into the world. Be their "rock" be there foundation. Make and set them straight, always be the mother, don't be the sister. Stand in power and infuse your girls, let them know that they are all special. Don't choose one over the other, make sure that there is a healthy balance with all of your girls. The ones that are influential or special, make sure though, that whatever the other one does not have- that you make them feel, all as balanced and as important. Mother's don't make one of your girls feel like they are less or more, than the rest, based on their material achievement and accolades. This is very important, a mother's love can make a penniless person feel rich! I promise you that! I will elaborate more on the, mother of sister roles later.

Caption: "Mother/Daughter Love"

Key Point 4. Sisters make sure that you understand and know that parents relate to their children in different ways, on different days and in different states of being. We as sisters should not allow our selves to feel slighted just because a mother relates to each individual differently. This has happened in many of relations and in many of situations, where- we allow negative thoughts to build and, build and build because of our misinterprations of mother/daughter relationships. We end up allowing, a wall of hatred, anger, avoidance, and other negative feelings to erect within. I would like to emphasize that any mother that has several children, although it has been said throughout time, that, I love all my children the same. I know this will get me in trouble, but I will speak on it, so as to help those of you out there that have felt this way for a very long time I want to bring clarity and understanding, as loosen the bondage that has been holding us all down from time to time regarding this pressing issue.

There is a difference of love styles (hear me and hear me well readers), that a mother may have for each child, yet there maybe a level of sameness, but not quite. The difference is unique and fashioned to the child and who they are. A mother should not keep score with her daughters! If you are then, the scorekeeping card needs to be deleted and dropped. You have to work hard on ensuring each child of your special and crafted love, as it is due to them! God has granted a mother the skills to balance her love for each child, yet to engage with them in a way that her love flows to each, based on their, spiritual, natural and psychological make up. I am admonishing you mothers that have girls to--work on this- love thing hard. Aide your sister group of girls with feeling "inwardly" substantial on the level that they are on. A mother needs to know how to love each sister group, individually and collectively. Show them the balance and show them how it can be imbalanced (giving examples constantly).

Sometimes words and slips of the tongue can cause strongholds to stay, injected into the mind of a child. Mothers often, not knowing that this is being done, (to the defense of mothers -I am not trying to destroy mothers, and what you have built totally, just redesign it, ***if you will,*** a figure of speech used in preaching!). Don't allow other foreign elements to enter into the mind of your daughters, if they are still yet old enough to receive this. Sometimes children, but in the case of this book, girls, deal with Issues, that have been left untouched for many, many years and has caused- bitterness, pain and severe conflict towards one another. Additionally, Mothers, if this is the case- try to create a safe haven for each one of your daughters to be able to come into. A mother is supposed to make a child feel safe. Welcome your girl daughters home if you have not done this! You will be shocked at the results!

To further discuss the topic of relationships with mothers and daughters, I want to take this a little deeper, by noting how- being a mother to a child such as " child/daughter that abuses drugs", or "the successful leader/daughter of a Fortune 500 corporation". One needs to be able to handle either daughter, either situation, either attitude, either personality or either actions that the daughter reflects. A mother should esteem each child in their own place.

Let's say for instance, a mother has a daughter that is on crack, and then, one that is highly successful and productive. The one sister that seemingly "has it all" is more than likely going to take the position of "Momma you do too much for her (the daughter that is on crack)," let her go, leave her to her own devises," while the other daughter on drugs will say, "Momma you favored her (the highly successful daughter),all of our lives" and then because of these thoughts goes on to eat the drugs all the more (so to speak). Both sisters tend to blame the other-- but let's look at it, which is different? Which is better? Neither, both are in the same places of reckoning, they both feel their mother does more for the one than she does for the other. Both issues are the exact same, but in a different direction, the only thing that separates the plight of these two type of sisters, is material possession, in which ulitimately means nothing!

These two sisters have the same exact issue, they are looking "up and down" at each other, using their mother, as the rope that is to be tugged this way and that way. Imagine a tug of war type, or rope used for playful activities and one person on one side pulling and the other one on the other, trying their hardest to win! This is what this is! A total and out right "tug of war", if we use carnal eyes we will say the one with the money, success and power, is better, but is she? How many times do we make this major mistake thinking that because a person has money and power, they are better? It is always what is in the heart! Man looks at the outer, God looks onto a man's heart (I Samuel 16:7 New King James Version)! I will admit there will be times when a mother will respond and act differently, but it will all depend on the circumstances that present itself to her and her presentations to each child. Normally, situations of this sort, will be viewed as biased on the daughter's behalf. The key to this is can be done with prayer, petition and practice. Making sure to pray to God for your girls, for your thoughts, your actions and for the needs of your girls. Petition God for his way to handle and deal with your girls and then practice what is revealed regularly!

Key Point. Something that is very important in mother/daughter relationships is that -A mother should never talk about one child to the next in a negative way. I know that talking over situations will happen, but, telling one child the other's child's secrets needs to be kept. This happens in families all the time and we all know it, but learning how to master this skill, will probably take some time, but it can be done.

Examples of these behaviors happen frequently, an consistent example is when one sister does something that is not the norm or possibly disruptive to the circle or family, the one sister or sisters get on the phone with the other sister or the Momma to discuss the issue. The conversation can go from one thing to the next, causing more confusion and mayhem. Caution! Don't let the conversation go "AWOL" mothers of daughters, learn to facilitate a healthy conversation unto your girls, when the other one is not around. Now this is the "catch" when you all are having a family meeting that is different, those that want to confront and "deal," do so. If you want your mother to stay out, then you all find a facilitator to take notes or monitor the groups' interactions to prevent fights and serious arguments. Let's get it all out and through! I am being for real, let's do what we have to do to settle and hammer out what needs to be! Let's not get violent and vulgar towards one another and if it does, please, please try to make amends of some sort before you leave one another's prescense . Please!

We all have had our "momma complexes" at some point and time in life, but let's deal with them before they are too late! Mom's you too, need to air out your stuff before it's too late! A example of this, that I am about to share is that, I had this friend of mine, let's call her Betty, she told me that her Momma treated her different for most of her life and that on her death bed, she was the one that ended up taking care of her until her last breath! She said to me, that her Mom uttered to her, on her death bed, that "Betty, you were one the strongest one of all, and that is why I treated you the way I did!" But she didn't know this throughout her life! She was left feeling abandoned and estranged. See those of us that are often seen as the strongest are often the weakest, even though we don't realize or admit it at the time, we feel used, abused, inundated with thoughts of impurity, insecurity and at times the lowest on the "todem pole"! The Lord spoke to me last night and said that "Good is not always good and bad is not always bad". I told my husband of this revelation and as I was editing this portion of the book, the Lord gave me the revelation that what- we always deem as being good, can have a lot of "BAD" in it and what we deem as 'BAD" can have some hidden good in it. There were some men or people in the bible that greeted Jesus and he didn't' respond as they thought- he should, he said "I know the heart of man", I am saying this to say, our human hearts can perceive often times something that we think as good, that is not so good. For the purpose of this book, "Sisters, just because it seems that your older sister has it going on, it may not be all what you think". It has been researched that women that are successful, have battled with self-esteem, self-worth, depression and other serious mental and emotional issues. Don't think of your sister as one way, it might not be what you think- the good you think she has over you (so-to speak, it can be all, all bad)!

Going onward, I think that if we understand 'ourselves', as we are supposed, it can prove for making our sisterly bond a lot better, don't try to make one sister be like you, or grow like you! Also, don't try to make her relationship with your mother's mirror yours, ask God for your own special place with your mother, don't make her try to do the things that you do, nor you do what she does, don't try to be like her, you are hindering the process trying to do this. Whatever you lost in life, as a sister, don't be embarrassed about it, don't beat yourself up about, it and most definitely, don't feel like you are a failure. If it is that bad and she is that good, go find a place of safety with your sisters, help yourself feel secure about yourself, and your sister, don't keep this stuff inside. ! Yes do it! Just a little side-note.

Key Pont 5. Sisters if one of your parents have passed on and you feel a void or deep hole,use your family bond, as sisters to fill in the gaps of love. The love that you know your parent would have wanted passed on to each one of you in the way that it should be. I know it may be difficult at times, but use what you have left of your parent or parents that have "gone on" to keep your bond secure and tight! The Wright Sisters that I mentioned early are really good at this! You all should try it! Your parent raised you close and left an inheritance of love, for you to use when they are gone, some of us, live in despair, not realizing this, but if you must know, you have been doing so incorrectly, go back and read what I said about the Wright Sister and see their example of their Mom's love walking itself out in their lives right now and prosper!

Growth

Key Point 6. Growth is something that we all need as indivdiuals and sisters. If there is a sister that is underdeveloped, let her grow, don't stunt her growth or hinder it in anyway. Allow and let your sister, that needs-the-- growth to- learn on her own, and grow on her own. Don't deprive one another of the space to evolve into the best "you and sister you can be". It can all benefit your sister group. Sisters when a sister is in need, It is okay to help her, when she needs it, if the help you are giving adds value to her life. Just don't- allow yourself to enable your sister! Because, what will happen is that you will be taking away from her value. Let her learn and grow into the person who God wants her to be as a part of the group. Let her grow on her own, even if it hurts, even if you have to go to the bed and cry for her and call out to God for her every night, do so. Leave your sister's soul to God at certain times (even when it hurts, even when you have to deny her time, and space). Understand this sisters, there is a confrontational aspect of being a sister, that we must "fess up to". If we stop avoiding this part of being sisters, we can really grow into something big. At some point and time and in life, we have to and need to have"these talks." We must avoid the behaviors that cause emotional and spiritual laziness. When we enable our sisters, we make them lazy. We make them forfeit the valuable work, that they--, 'themselves' need to make -their own priority. The work that they need to perform of themselves, in order to help them achieve and grow - their own processes. I hope you all are enjoying this book, it took a life time of experiences, knowledge, research and sitting with God to get this out of my spirit, soul, and mind and onto these papers! Smile!.

On the other side of that sisters, is- if you have a sister that you tend to, constantly make attempts to try and make her "your way- meaning take on your thoughts, take on your actions or your behaviors" -it will not work on either side, because, for one, no one can change a person or make them be what you want them to be. I say this to the good, in all aspects. We have to realize sisters, that a sister that is seemingly in a hole or in a place where she feels stuck, that we cannot totally pull her out, there has to be a place of self-awareness of self consciousness, where a person needs to learn of their selves and make the much needed changes.

Growing is a process and we all need it, sometimes one sister may have a "growth spurt". When this happens, work on identifying when the growth spurts occur with you or your sister. I remember with one of my sons, Gavin, his knees and legs would hurt at certain ages and stages of his life, I would take him to the doctor and the doctor always said that they were "growth spurts". He explained how, when the body expounds pain often times come through. This is what we have to be able to notice sisters, is when we are having "growth" spurts and allow for the change to occur, so that we can work as we should, grow as we should and evolve as we should. Eventually with my son, his growth spurts stopped. The pain will stop and you will open your eyes and see what "God was trying to do"! Stop fighting the change, let it work it self through- and out of the sister circle! You will be happy that you did!

Example. Sisters, if you have a sister that wants to reach the sky and work hard, play hard, and live hard, don't get mad or upset in your hearts at what she does, in order to ascertain her destined elements. Let her cravings be fulfilled, let her eat the devine cup of fulfillment and appetite, while fulfilling her every desire and objective! it will ultimately benefit everyone. Let what she desires, be just- that for her (she will come around, and back to he sisters, eventually) ! Let's not resist our sisters with attitudes, faulty break-ups, back-biting, evil chatter, delusional perceptions and the like- just because you envy her process. Be mindful of sister invoked sabotage towards another, it is traumatic to the sister group and sometimes it cannot be revived! When one sister does subtle- secret things to bring about chaos among the sisters. Furthermore on excellence and sisters- if one sisters goes out, becomes prosperous internally and outwardly, remember that is her 'plight in life, her focus'. Don't try to take it from her, ruin it for her or sabotage it for her. If, on the otherside of that, a sister wants to- NOT- be as popular, and not live a lavish lifestyle (I am using this for an example, yours may vary, but the principle is all the same), then I urge you (as my husband says "leave her", in other words, let her be, let her live her life the way she chooses, as long as it is safe and productive In "her own way")." I have experienced, allowing people to let life, change them or move them as it should. I have learned that people, in the case of 'sisters', sometimes- don't want help from the other, sometimes. I have learned to allow my sisters to learn their own life lessons, without me trying to 'bully' or "force" them into it. These are just a few that I have seen, but ask yourself "What is my issue with my sister"? What is it that I need to clear my heart of? Am I satisfied with the sister that I am? Some of you may say, yes and some of you may say, no, this book is to allow you to explore both. Call it out and rebuke it! Read On.

The bible clearly tells us, "to get understanding" and he tells us with all that you "get; get understanding,"! You see, as sisters, we often fail to get and gain understanding of each other. We want everything we do, say and feel to be "the way we want it to be," but it will not always be that way. Yet, if we strive to understand what one sister is, her plight, and what she is trying to master in life, we can learn a lot about life, just from her. Finding out, particulary what she means and what she does to herself and for herself, and unto the sister group. We can then, be joined, connected, and bonded, and enjoy our sister life! We can get along a lot better to produce much fruits of our labor as sisters!.

Name Calling & Labeling. Why do I refer to the very person that I have shared the same body with, as "a her"? I indicate this because truthfully in the deep - depths of our hearts some of us, have- referred to our sister as a "her" at times in our life and relationship (may have been worse than that). We develop these

Dr. Pamela Renee Applewhite, PhD

theories about our sister and take them entirely "too far." We may have secretly or openly called our sister the "B" word and meant it. Let's deal with name calling.

Some of us, have referred to, inferred to, or even stated, if not verbally, or mentally, that our sister was this, or that. Names like "Crazy as h---", "Stupid" " Ignorant," "Jealous," "A nobody," "A low life," "Inhuman," "Insolent, "Child please", "Girl, Momma thinks this child's stuff don't stink", 'Humph (a few of the favorites, what are the favorites that you call your sister, you know them one's that you don't want to say, yup)? I mean the list goes on, we have said even more things like " You ungrateful so and so, Unloyal, Dis-inherited fiend, Traitor, Disenchanted, insolent! Somewhere throughout life, you have referred to, or thought this of your sister, and don't forget the "Who does she think she is," phrase! I have seen so many talk shows, reality shows and real life occurrences where sisters have done or said the most horrible things to, or about each other.

Shocking, but it is true and if we did not call her the infamous "B" word, we have surely alluded to the fact that "my sister is crazy," or "off her rocker". And we have said the infamous- "I don't have time for that," because of the hurt and pain she may have caused . Because you thought that it was "shameful" to utter such thoughts and images regarding someone that you are supposed to love, as a sister, as a cherished being in your life (it gets deeper)"!We all hurt in relationships, why should sisterhood be any different? Why is getting "stabbed "in the back by a sister any different? We all have had these conversations, with everyone, except the one we offend or the one that we- are "offended by." I am speaking on personal experiences, that maybe, just maybe, being a sister is an intimidating thing. Let's take this further.

Intimidation is defined as, generally the feeling of being threatened or frightful. Let's admit sometimes our sister's might, prowess, and power, may do this to us and we never really come out and say it. We just act on it, causing us to battle with each other, more times than we should. The false perception that one can have about one's,sister and what you think she is doing to you. She (meaning all of us, as sisters) can see the, actions or non-actions that manifest, and most of the time it is always interpreted, as jealousy or envy (in any event, versus just misconception, misguidance or confusion), this is a common practice. I have seen sisters with millions of dollars say "Oh I am this and I am that, and it's my millions, that she is jealous of," This is ridiculous, even though it happens. I mean to get a "thrill out of the fact" that your sister is jealous of you is warped, self-centered and ill-fated. Nothing good can come out of this, no matter how "you look at it (figure of speech)".Using this is as triump or a trump card- should not be, because, in any case or event—one's sister should be a millionaire right up there with you! Pitting' your "Papers (slang word for money, as the kids say it)" against your own sister is ludacris, (not the rapper Ludacris), but crazy and insane. I know some of you are saying well you don't know, my sister, and what she has tried to do to me. She has done things I don't think that my own enemy would do to me. I will get into the "high collar crime sin-filled- sister later on in this book."

NEWS FLASH!!

Since the writing of this book, things have happened in the Sister World, the Braxton's have aired a show with Iyanla Vanzant where one of the sisters, "Traci, has made a comment that she was numb of her sisterhood group (in so many words)." Iyanla tried her hardest to get her to say what she felt, but in my opinion, she avoided the truth of the matter, and skimmed the surface. We have to share who we are and what we are, we cannot hide our true feelings, it is the only way we can get healed. I will say though as the story continued with the Braxton's, Toni Braxton, when interviewed separately, said that she did not like her family and then said it later in front of them, that they would not be her friends if they were not her family, yes, it seemed harsh to hear,but it was her truth. This is often how some sisters feel that have had disruptions in their circle. WE all need to acknowledge our truth, no matter how old it is or cold it is. We need to get it to the fertile place! Iyanla, in my view, was trying to do just that, get not only the sisters, but the family In the fertile place! She wanted to open the place that was damaged and repair it. The sisters on the Braxton Family Values is and always will be at the root of the show, but the bond should be the highlight, in my opinion and sometimes it was there and sometimes it was not there (my opinion). The show depicts sisterhood, but it almost never really makes it to the depth that it could, due to one fallacy or the other, one mishap on the other. Braxton's don't get upset with me. I am giving my opinion (especially, Ms. E)!

I think that we as sisters fear being frank and saying our true expressions to each other in our sister group. We often let years pass by, being silent on what should be said to each other, as sisters. We often- allow one sister to have the voice, and that is good in its proper place, this is what Toni Braxton did, although the atmosphere was quite intimidating. I give Toni Braxton, her props for speaking up, when she could. We should all speak up, as Toni did when it comes to vital issues that we need to die out, in our souls. We need to rid ourselves of the inadequacies and dysfunction of the sister brood.

**Key Point 7.** Have sister meetings regularly to settle issues, disputes, or any problems. Work on bonding, and find out who needs what; emotionally, physically,etc. Not all meetings will call for one thing over the other, let the "vibe" determine what is needed at your gatherings. I met a sister group that I am working with, currently in the Adoption process, let's call them the "Boston Girls"! I have only met them a few times, but what I have learned in my observations about them, is that they are really close. They all traveled together to Alabama to visit with a child that I am to place in one sister's home. The entire time throughout the planning phases of the trip, the one that I am working with continuously mentioned, "It's my sisters' this or my sister's that," She made sure that I understood it was a "sister thing" and that they had already made their "t-Shirts," with different comments, like "I am the youngest", "I get by with everything" OR "I am the oldest, what I say goes," . The shirts all had something to say regarding their personalities and how they relate to each other. This showed me that when it came to their sister group there are "no holds barred." Are we truly sisters or do we pretend to be sisters?. Real sisters, get down in the dirt together, when one has the other has, when the other does not, we all chip in, and try to make it work and not talk behind one another's back. Is that what we are doing as sisters?

NOTE: I am dealing with sister issues mainly from what I have seen observed, experienced, and researched. I will elaborate on cultural norms when it comes to how sisters relate, as you read further on in the book.

"Black and Brown Sisters".

We often act like we are "so close" intimately, but we fear saying certain things to our sisters, in fear of "what"? We hang up in our sister's face, we mock each other, but for what reason? I mean I can think of a lot of things, we do unto our sisters that we wouldn't not even think of doing to our friends. Let's ask ourselves, what are we really afraid of, when it comes to letting our flesh and blood sister, or any other form of a "sister, we may have," know how we feel, and what is it that "bars" us from doing so? Why do we run behind each other's back, when the sister is right there at your disposal? You can call her and say these things, but, instead, we don't! We talk to others about our sister or sisters, and this most definitely should not be! We need to work on correcting our interactions with our sister or sisters, if this is something you need to do, go to the counselor about it, then do so! Make sure to tell them that, "I am here because I am having a problem with my relationship with you, my sister, and I want it healed."

Care Plans. Let that be on your plan of care (goals and objectives). A plan of care is a method/strategy that is used for treatment and care for patients-at hospitals, mental health facilities, doctors' offices and nursing homes, just to name a few. Develop a plan of care, by setting goals and objectives to meet at certain times within your group or for yourselves. Work on obtaining a positive goal for you and your sister's relationship/group. Purge yourself- with hyssop. Hyssop used in the Bible, is a shrub that is used for purification. Use care planning in order to purge and cleanse the sister inner circle. Rid yourself of all the "sister clutter", this is so you can live a blessed life, a good life, an endearing life!

His Prescense! I sense there is someone that may – not have made your peace with your sister and she is gone, on to "Glory,"! God is saying it is okay, you have time, if you betrayed your sister or if she betrayed you, and you all never really got to the point of letting it go- so much until it led her and you down a path of- brokenheartedness. The Lord is saying, you, can be healed from that issue, even though your sister has gone on! Your sister, if she was alive, she would have forgiven you (I feel him saying this to me). She would not have wanted you to suffer in this manner, so in the name of the Lord Jesus Christ, be healed, be released, and set free from the guilt, hurt and the agony!

Get on your knees and release this by confessing the truth of what you did to your sister or even, if your deceased sister wronged you. I know that you feel really horrible about it, because the situation was never really settled! Reveal and confess- to yourself and God- how bad you feel about it and you will be forgiven! " You will feel the release, immediately, if you do it now"! After you confess your sins to God (_this is the prophetic, coming out of me, as I write, please don't consider this as robbery, in other words something being put there to take from you, but something that has come to expose the enemy and set you free from within_) … the time is now, sister. For someone out there reading this book or for someone you know - in this situation, alert them, it is their time. If someone is reading this book in whom, you have offended your sister (and you want to get it right) and you know it in your heart, and she is still yet alive (and she maybe on the verge of death), go to her, she will be waiting, it does not matter, if you have not spoken in years, time has healed her pain and she wants the reconciliation, as much as you ! As, Gladys Hamlin says, one of my favorite "play aunts" says, "To God be the Glory"!

I am sure for some of you, as current readers; being able to see what your soul is speaking is an experience that is warranted. A instance that is liberating. Yes, your soul, has been crying out for years to release this agonizing thing into the atmosphere. For some it maybe just "confirming' what you thought or already felt. I am sure the feeling is an overwhelming and "a mixed feeling, "kind of bag". I am sure you all are wondering, where on earth this came from? It came from the depth of me, my heart, soul and my spirit- it came from God's lips to my spiritual ears and fingertips (typing in) inorder-- to bring deliverance and freedom to those that are bound, by this secret dilemma that has been lived out for years. Let's continue. Let's explore how sisterhood has changed, how it has delved into "territory" that no one ever thought or believed it would ever come to. Believing that this person you lived with, shared with, cried with, devised with, ate dinner with, and fought with," has- actually seem to have grown to now dislike you. Your very own sister seems to have a vendetta against you, seems to want the worse for you. Let's further look at what has transpired over time into one feeling in their heart that *Your Sister is Your Enemy*". WE are going to 'Walk this thing out' and pull all of one's emotions, feelings and thought into the light, so that you can be healed. The part of you that has a sister and wants your sister back, close and near to your heart, inorder- to be close to you again! "Just like that". Read on.

Consciousness-I want to inject something about the conscious into this writing, that I shared with my husband just this week, while editing my book (10/07/2020). I tell you everytime I think that I am done, writing or editing, my spirit slows and I have to put something else in, anyway ladies, the Lord revealed to me that the consciousness is where relationships dwell and when the consciousness is not dealt with from both sides, meaning all individuals that were in the relation-ship, one person is left tormented or antagonized, as one may have moved on, had counseling, had spiritual impartations, experience, epiphanys, etc and the other person may not have--, but, and this is a "big" but if the other party has not forgiven you or moved on, it stays "latched" to your soul and it seems like a person, or being is just there sitting--in your conscious. God is saying for one to be completely healed of a bad relationship one must confront or deal with the individual, to explain this phenomen more, say for instance you and your sister had a big blow up and you are really mad at each other and one is healed and the other one is not, but at times, you get images in your head, you feel sick on the stomache and sometimes you feel like someone or something is just lingering around in your soul, that is because the other person has not dealt with it or they are holding on to you or the grudge, that was created. Grudges and unresolved entangled relationships keep you attached to the person, especially if one does not want to let go. If this is you or your sister relationship, one may have to contact your sister to say, hey, "this is enough", lets settle this, I don't feel free. I promise you if you settle it, even if you don't end up as closely bonded as before--, you will feel a sense of freedom deep down in your spirit, and you will be able to function a whole lot better, this much I can promise! Read on.

Sister Examples.

Let's look a little bit deeper into what Sisters are . Sisters have been long ago- dating back in time, all the way back to the bible. Sisters such as Ruth and Orpah have been real, alive and functioning, and had differences in perspectives. For those of you that know the story of Ruth and Orpah, (not Oprah), great, but if not, read in the Bible, the entire Chapter of Ruth 1, King James Version. In this passage of scripture- one wanted to stay and follow her mother-in-law after both their husbands died and the other one, said 'forget this (in so many words)", I am moving on! The one that left was gone out of the picture, but the one that stayed gained her inheritance and blessings, after staying with what she know and held dear, her ability to stay led her to - her Kinsman Redeemer,(Note) Read the entire book of Ruth Chapters 1-4 King James Version! This will show you how each sister had their own individual ideas on their destiny and where they wanted to be in life, this is very important for sisters to know their own individual desitinies, and where God ordained for you to be. Ruth decided to suffer with her former mother in-law, but only to get her blessing. She became a woman of stature, wealth and power, after her suffering. How many times sisters do we forfeit our blessing because we do not want to suffer. Sisters, this is a powerful point, here that I want you all to get, we must suffer as sisters, if we want to reign as Christ did (I Timothy 2:12, NKJV)! He is all powerful! If we want to be all powerful, we must suffer and then we REIGN!!

A few other biblical examples are Leah and Rachel, Mary and Martha, present world, sisters include": Janet Jackson, Latoya, Rebie, The Lohan sisters, Brittany and Jami Lynn, Penelope and Monica Cruz, The Gospel duo-Erica and Tina Campbell of Mary, Mary (and their other sibling sisters), The Braxton's and of course- the reality sisters the Kardashians, and not to mention Beyoncé and Solange, I spoke on them some earlier. Imagine sisters, having a life such, as the above mentioned sisters (celebrity sisters). The sisters mentioned are iconic in the eyes of some or at least the most of us. These historical, legendary, and world re-nowned women - have stepped forth and allowed themselves to be seen as sisters that are connected and not so connected (good and bad). Showing themselves as sisters that fight, sisters that hate, sisters that destroy, sisters that hide who they really are, sisters that support, sisters, that lift up and tear down, no matter how much they try to hide it their lives are a reflection of our lives (no matter what or how much they have, we all are some how the same, no matter how secretive they try to be, a glimmer of who they are resonates with who we are in some way, shape or form). We have to touch all basis of sister hood in order to grow and change out patterns of destruction. The sistesr mentoned above have gone through all of this and more, yet while the world watches. A recent episode (2020) of the Kardashians that is currently going viral is showing Kim and Kourtney fighting. I have yet to view the clip, but as it seems, it is nothing that we should boast about, but it proves my point! Sister examples, activities, personalities and behavior never "really" changes from rich to poor the cup is the same. We often view celebrity status as void of problems and issues. We have to realize that celebrity sisters are just as human as anybody else!We all are supposed to be bonded to the heart, yet we can be totally ripped apart by the atrocities of life. Can I get a amen! I say this, before I move on-- lets look at my two little- grandbabies Chrissy Chanel Thomas and Meliana Thomas's love for each other, it is so pure, so sweet, so gentle, when I look at them interact, I have said to myself during times of babysitting, why can't sisters be that way. When Chrissy see's Meliana, her eyes glimmer and she jumps, scuffles and moves around and kicks her little legs and arms with excitement, and when Meliana can be of help the oldest, she is always quick and eager to do what she can for what she calls "baby"! She is only two years old and Chrissy is only 7 months old, this is a shame that two little beings that know nothing about life can examply what sisterhood really means! I think

I want cry (the Bible does not lie and it says, "And a child shall lead them -latter sentence of Isaiah 11:6, King James Version)"! Lets move on!

The sister mantle crosses over into dispensations and times that no man can change. The sisters in the Bible Rachel and Leah were two living, breathing human beings like us, they had real life dilemmas, they had real live conflict and strife. There story begins to unfold in the book of Genesis 29 and 30, King James Version. They both desired one thing and that was acceptance, but in different ways. Rachel, had it all, but needed acceptance in another way. She needed children, she needed to feel validated as a woman. At the time she did not have the ability to bear a child. Child bearing was a sign of acceptance back in Biblical times. It was one's identity. If a woman was barren back then, it was seen in a negative way and it made a woman feel less than. How many of us, don't have identify, even in physical beauty and we are depressed. Back in biblical times, women didn't get implants to make themselves beautiful, they relied on God's attributes and natural earthly things. Rachel, was noted as so very- beautiful until Jacob worked 14 years just to have her, but that was not enough for her, even in her desired state she was still lost. How many of us are still lost and carry a beauty that is infallible, inside and out, but that is still not enough? How many of us have gifts that are million dollar rich, and we are focused on other stuff about ourselves and others, until we cannot see the true essence of who we are? The same goes for Leah (the oldest sister of the group), she was so demeaned by her issues of not being desired by her husband, until she kept having babies thinking it would prove for acceptance (although we know God was building the Children of Israel) even in her distress, she didn't know she was the bearer of the Kingdom of God, she was so focused on her "lack thereof." How many of us do this sisters? Let's get past this and explore our hearts and desires,to first know who we are! Identify is important, first from above and then within! Seek the Lord! Seek the one and only God! He will identify you!

_Destruction!_I will start with discussing further, "when a sister destroys," I am sure there are people out there that have been in relationships with people that you consider your sister that you felt has destroyed you or at least tried to. You have felt that their presences in some instances was set for that very purpose. If that is you, then read on. We need to first figure out, how it all started. I need for those of you that have a secret hatred or vendetta against your sister, whether she is a blood sister, or a sister that you grew up with and she ended up in a place in your heart like a sister (surrogate). I want you to dig down to the depth of your soul and make an attempt to find out, where did this all start. We never forget transitional moments, so I want you, as you read this book to get a piece of paper, or if you and all of your sisters, play or real-- are reading this book, all of you to get a piece of paper and ask yourself, where did this come from, was I a little girl, outside playing with my sister or play sister, and she took my candy, my special doll baby, my special friend, my special dress, my special pair of shoes or anything of value that broke me to pieces. With that being said, was this the day that changed my life? Was this the time that I could no longer shake what was done to me by my sister or play sister? Was it that, I could not shake this act of thievery? Or did I feel robbed of my very own consciousness? Always looking back, in your mind seeing your sister or play/surrogate sister in a- taken state, meaning she took from you every chance that she could? If so, it is time to let it go. It is time to deal with this issue, before it eats you alive! The surrogate sisters is no different than the real sister, she is always there and so any person that you have been connected to for so long and you see or saw her as a sister, this is for that relationship too! Read on.

I have seen and heard the most mysterious things that has caused "sister turmoil". Things that can dwell in the atmosphere for decades, and generations, due to it being unresolved. I wonder did she steal your childhood sweetheart/ boyfriend or a BFF that you cherished, and then you- yourself was ousted,"? Did she steal your parents heart and you never felt "as accepted" by your parents? Did your parents spoil her more so than you (in your eyes) and make you feel insecure, overlooked or avoided, (this happens too). Were you the sister that never felt accomplished and no one ever pushed you, applauded you or serenaded you? Did you just plain old feel like "the black sheep sister of the family" or was it something else so sinister, that you created in your own "mind's eye"? Are you ashamed to think on it, or even mention it to anybody? It has been so soul wrenching, that the mention of your sister, causes you to draw a blank, to become paralyzed in space and time, at the mention of her name or citing of her physically?

I mean it could be a number of things that halted you or hindered you from connecting with your sister. Something that came and took your relationship down a dark path that you somehow cannot seem to "let a loose," only you and your heart knows what it is. If you want to get rid of it now and once- and for all it is the time to do so, now! You can do it, if you try! If you are afraid and ashamed, the alternative is to get on your knees and ask God for assistance and guidance so that you can move forward and take this awful burden from your heart. Help is on the way, if you desire it! Don't let whatever happened or why it happened destroy you! Pick up the pieces, attack it and take back what the Devil and all his imps stole! I am going to talk about the "play/surrogate sister' specifically - later on, so hold on! I have not forgotten this importance piece of the puzzle! Read on!

Sister More ...

Now in reflecting on the sisters mentioned, I am sure much comes to mind, naming just those few instances. We have watched, read and understood about how sisters act, feel, and relate to each other. It can be downright awful at times, when sisters "brawl." Sisters at times can say the craziest things to each other, it can come out of nowhere and ultimately "shock" the soul that you reside in.

Saying mean and hurtful things to one's sister is unacceptable. Blocking your sister's opinions, and thoughts during a conversation or sister time, is totally wrong and obtrusive. Sister's that have dominace as a personality trait, don't block your sister from speaking her truths, don't be so self-centered and insecure, that you cannot stand to hear your flaws and weaknesses, someone else see's yours as you see theres! Let's all be fair at this!

The Braxton's legend, Toni (celebrity and singer, for those of you who don't know who she is) said that she felt responsible for her sisters and that hindered her (in so many words) from soaring. She said in an interview, that she could have gone a lot further if she did not feel that she was responsible for them. Some sisters can grow up this way, wanting to be away from it all. The very thing that we struggle - with is what Toni Braxton confessed. Toni obviously did not have the "guts" to say this to her family, in the past, but came "all out with it in the interview". Seems like she - was burdened with this for a while. I am sure after she confessed this and got it out in the open, she felt a lot better! We have to be honest with one another even if it hurts us to say it- and hurts us to deliver it. As long as it is not mean, cruel and disrespectful it can, eventually- be a bad thing turned good.

On another note, I can say that when one is the oldest (speaking from experience) there is a sense of responsibility (**_Note_**: not all **_ELDEST_** sisters by age- act as the oldest or end up holding the eldest position, elder sistership is ordained and appointed by God). I will address that later, but the one that is the true Eldest always tend to have this thing in their heart towards protecting and making sure the rest of the sisters are okay. Being a elder sister is one being in a kind of surrogate mother's role. "Surely, I know there are those of you out there, that carry this title that can relate." This role causes the eldest sister to always "look back" at the other sisters and try to make sure they are okay, socially, emotionally and in some cases financially. I have observed sisters, real and imagined (in the arts) that have bought things for their sisters, paid them salaries, bought them cars, bought them houses, found them boyfriends. I mean the list goes on. I because, I am an elder sister, do not see anything wrong with that, just so long as it is done in good faith, good merit and honor; not as an enabler or as the product of usary. The eldest sister is entitled to the birth rite. The birth rite of passage is a role that carries entitlement.

It carries insight and boldness amongst the sisters. This role carries "A" type personality individuals that are always, and I mean always taken to be "snooty, stuck up and think she know it all and got it all"! Know this, that the eldest sister comes as a three (3) way package (maybe more), she has it all and she thinks it all. She does, it all. Let's admit it, I am talking true, "pure" elder sisters okay, not the forfeit 3 dollar bill kind (LOL)! This type of sister, she is resourceful, she is full of some of everything! She is like the Oprah Winfreys, the Toni Braxtons, Jodie Fosters, and the Dolly Pardons in the family. She is the one that God has sent to bless you and she doesn't care that you come to her. She is a open sepulcher, she is set up to sell you her philosophy her propaganda, and her story. When she really feels that she is privileged to be your sister, she begins to carry that thing, like a banner. She is the eldest, she is special, but she is special for you! Sisters don't forget this, I remember a picture that I saw on Facebook, where my cousin

Sonya, noted that she loved going into her big sister, Nicole's closet! She knew that her sister had the goodies! Girls, if you can get this, you will be blessed for life, your eldest sister has the goods, whether it is good story telling, good advice, good finances, good examples of mothering, good education, good insight, good ability to attract, good ability to win at a- thing. The list goes on and on. But I say to you if you have a problem with your eldest sister, if for the most part, she has been there for you (not talking the exceptions), then you need to regroup, take a step back and see her for who she is, she is your blessing, your "Walmart, Your Target, your online shopping vender, she is the eldest, brightest, smartest, girl you know, she is your oldest -sister! And how about that!!! Know that she will always tell you, warn you, keep you, and hold you even when you don't want to be helped. No matter how mad she is at you, or you at her, she will never turn you down when you are in need. She is a straight line, but can be a jack of all trades, and she can be a ferocious "she lion (even if she is not the oldest)", if need be for the sister cause, if you allow her in the "right way", ask a certain celebrity in the elevator (oops, did I say that, my opinion). Furthermore, if she doesn''t have the answer, she knows someone that does, she is the 'eldest' love her, keep her and applaud her! Read below.

Key Point 8 . The eldest sister, has the tools to act in an executive manner, that is because God gave her the ability and the insight to act in this manner, let's look back at the "Boston Sisters" that I referred to previously (true story) the one sister took charge of the conversation, when I called to check on them when they visited with a child that was to be adopted, the one that was actually doing the adoption was not the one that was "heading up" the trip, she allowed each one of her sisters to play their role and she did too. We as sisters, if we can sit back and access "the who is who in the sister regime" we can process through lot easier.'

What do you mean when you say "process" the functioning of the sister bond and actions involved in being sisters can go a lot easier, and each piece can operate or function as it should . The Bible speaks of "parts of the body" when discussing how the church is to function as a whole and together- in the book of I Corinthians 12:12-27, New Living Translation, "One body with many parts," sisters, we are all "one body" functioning with many parts. The Scripture says this, (New Living Translation). The human body has many parts, but the many parts make up one whole body. Yes the body has many different parts, not just one part … You see sisters each one of us, has a part, not just one. The bible further reads, If the foot says "I am not a part of the body, because I am not a hand, that does not make me any less part of the body" … see sisters just because you may not have a certain character trait, a certain skill, a certain look, a certain house, a certain husband, a certain child, a certain title, a certain inheritance, a certain dowry, a certain traditional passage, it does not mean that you are less of a sister. Your function in the body of Sisters (is just as important). Find out which part you play in the body of sisters and begin to act on it. If you are not a vocal sister, then don't try to be vocal, if you are not a sister that loves to cook, then don 't try to cook.

Pay attention to what you are, and not what you are not. If you are a sister that makes the group of sisters laugh then do so, if you are the sister that has class, and style and is creative, then be that, stop trying to be part of a mold that you are not (hear me and hear me well), be the one that God has created you to be in the sister group and watch your self soar! I encourage you right now in his name! I need for those sisters reading this book to stop and take the time to realize who you are. Realize that you are special, realize that you do not have to compete for nothing; not one bit or lessen or "dumb down, a figure of speech" for any sister or anybody for that matter. Not amongst each other, or with and amongst your parents, your friends, your family, no one. Negative challenges should not be put in the front of your relationship! If there are negative instances that continue to creep up, then take that negative instances and create positives out of it. Let the bad energy go, when it comes to sisterhood. I know that there has been a lot of competiveness that has caused strife and distance among you all as sisters, but lets get rid of it and get rid of it now. Let go of- competing for parental love, let go of it all. It is not worth it! There is enough of everything and everyone to share. There is also a sister that has been a part of a sister's groups that tries to "avoid" the sister group all together! You cannot sit on the outskirts of the sister relationship for too much longer! Read on! Furthermore, There are some sisters out there that tend to avoid getting involved with their sisters, they are the "lost sheeps of the sister groups,". Somewhere along the lines, you felt lost and you decided that you were going to do some "subtle rebelling, subtle isolations" to teach them all a lesson, you used this as your mantra, your ability to hide and not be seen in order to stay away from them all. But nope, that is not at all how it is supposed to be, you are supposed to be upfront (*you are not hidden, you are even seen a lot brighter, in the light than you think*) and personal in the way that God wants it to be! You my sister, fell by the wayside because of your insecurities and because of what you felt deep down in your heart, you felt that you needed to step down, step away from them all. The inner space of what you felt as rejection, for who you were as a person was too much! God is saying "not so", it is now time for you to pick up the pieces and get ready to get back in the "game' of sisterhood.

God is calling you up, now and forever; to be what he called you to be! Realize, though what your calling is about and know that - if he called you to be silent, in your stance as a sister, and your silence, gives strength to the group, then that's okay! Be who you are and have wanted to be! Don't try to amount to no- one else. Explore yourself in order to make sure you are operating in the fruit of your gift in the sister group. Are you a silent partner or a rebellious renegade?

Ask yourself, because I want to see you flourish. Ask yourself the question, and if you know in your heart that you have been the "rebellious renegade " for all of your life, when it comes to your sisters, it is time to let it go and drop the feelings, the complexed thoughts towards your sisters and come home. Call the sister that you trust and let her know the deep secrets of your heart and begin the process of healing. Get back into sync with your sisters and to the place where you belong and identify with. I know that being a sister is not always what is 'seems to be'. I know this all well, but we want to "crack this case (so-to-speak)" wide open and get to the root cause of one's sister being one's enemy. '? Do we wish we could get more out of sister relationships? Is our sister relationship a "surfaced one" or a "deep one ?

Ask yourself, all of these deep rooted questions, mentioned above, and take your time with the questions, do not "rush through" the questions. Work on this so that you can be done with it! I want you to take as much time, as you need, but not a lifetime, that has already taken place, so in essence only take a reasonable amount of time to ponder what caused this to happened and then let's get the work done! Further think on the following: 1) Do I feel comfortable sharing my hurts, pains and fears with my sisters, or do I keep a lot of it in? 2) Is my heart safe with my sister? 3) What is it that gnaws at my soul ?4) How can I release these thoughts? 5) What is my personality trait when I am with my sisters? Ask yourself these questions and then begin to heal. Begin to meet with your sisters to discuss each and every fiber of the questions and thoughts mentioned above.

Serious Limits. Now, I do realize there are limits with one's personal (person) when it comes to our sister bond. For sisters that are married. Some of you may not want to share your marital information with your sister or sisters, and that is perfectly okay, that is your right as a sister. I know some sisters that "draw the line" when it comes to their sisters knowing intimate details that go on, in their bedroom, home, life, or children. Yet there are some that do not, it all depends on how you "all set it up." Even if you do set the serious limits, that should not hinder your sisterhood bond. I heard Solange, say that she doesn't not "spank Beyoncé's child" and that "Beyoncé does not spank hers." She says they would make the call to each other, if either one of their children got out of control, is what I interpreted from her interview as. That is perfectly alright, as we have to learn to respect our sister's space and "serious limits" although I spoke earlier on this to the "opposite,". This is reasonable and fair, yet- I do think and still will say, that we as sisters, should have certain passages of rights if we are engaged with our sister's children, not to abuse them, but to engage them and keep the sister connection going. I will not change my thoughts on that. Yet I know the exceptions, in instances of one sister or the other having serious emotional, mental of physical challenges, that is a different story, I am only speaking to the average in this instance. Also having clear understandings among sisters is always valuable, whether directly or indirectly, is important in rearing of one's kids. It causes our children to grow up respectfully among the sister group. Think on this!

Rights of Privacy. "Sisters don't fret if your sister has a private side, just because she does not tell you certain intimate details that occurs within her home or with her spouse, don't see that as a violation.

If a sister allows all "access," then "you are good (as they say now-a days)," if not respect her space in that manner, it will make you closer in the long run. Only you know your sister to the core, what you can share and what you cannot share, it' s her choice, it's her life, don't get upset, just learn to respect it. Some of us know what is good and what is not good to share when it comes to our intimacies with our spouses or partners. If you as a sister, have reservations about how much your sister shares, with you, you will have to get over it. We are close and bonded at points of intimacy as sisters, but when it comes to one's significant other, spouse, lover or friend, it is our right of passage to privacy on how far we go with disclosing every little detail.

A past thought. Remember those days when we were young girls playing in the yard and we could say and do almost anything to our sisters, and it was taken as a "grain of salt," now it's different, times have changed, sometimes, in some sister relationships, you are total oblivious as to what you can say to a sister or your sister. There is a lot of uncertaintity and we don't know if we can have the same tell alls with our sisters that we have had in the past. This is because life has changed and a lot of what used to connect sisters and keep us grounded has reversed. Sisters have grown jealous and rigid towards each other, non trusting, non-loving. This is sad! In the past, the way our grandmothers were raised has been thrown out of the window! The fight to stay close and relevant with one's sister has changed dramatically.

Exceptions to the Rule. Now sisters along with mothers of sisters, if there is a situation that is dangerous or has the potential for danger, in any form, such as extortion, lies, thievery, or even death, somebody that has the "guts' to do so, needs to step up to the plate and let the other sister know, how the issues should be handled. "I don't trust you with my children", if these are your thoughts. Be upfront honest and transparent. Don't sneak around in it. Tell your sister why, you feel this way. I am forewarning you though, that you, will be faced with terrible blacklash, but that's okay. Your honesty will prevail in the long run! It may even let your sister see the reason why trust is lacking in that area. Don't back down from this sister! Someone needs to be the arrow that is shot into the camp! Remember when the Indians in "cowboy and indian shows" would shoot arrows for warnings. Do this, send out a signal, let your sister know this is coming and do it! This is what needs to be done, some type of signal needs to be sent that "we are coming In," whether you want us to or not. This is because this issue needs to be settled, sooner than later. When you see that your sister needs help and she is isolating herself or she is in a 'tight spot", go to her, and I mean fast, don't let a sister in need suffer from lack of care, compassion or understanding. If she denies you entrance, then all of the sisters that can, need to begin to pray that God opens a door for you to have access to your sister's heart, home or whatever it is you need to gain access to- in order to help her come back to her place of balance .

Exception Number 2. Now with that being said, there is a person in all of this that is the bearer of the seeds planted in her womb, and that is the mother of the sister siblings. This role is vital to the group in tackling any situation! Whether the mother of the group is here or she has passed on, all of us-know that a mother plays a vital role in linking sister hood and keeping sisters bonded. I often hear my Aunts say, "Now you know Momma wouldn't go for that." A comment as simple as that is a connector of the seed of sisters. Sisters, there is a place that's in all of you, whether It Is only two sisters or ten- that a knows that a -mother keeps the rope connected. Without a mother, or a caregiver, there often times is not a solid connection. There is someone though--, whether by birth or not, that has connected you all (living or dead) into sisterhood. You all have to realize that a mother, caregiver or surrogate mother's role is very important. The mother role or person in that role- fuels, pushes and tries to keep the love lucid (for the sisters). Even those of you that are not getting along right now, you all say and know that "If It were not for your mother or caregiver", you probably would not be where you are today; nor would you be involved with the sister relationship.

Sister's remember this- there is a piece of the sister make up that requires a mother or someone like a mother, to be involved or acknowledged as a part of this group. A mother has the power to exert her motherly power or influence in the group in all areas (she can make the group or break the group). A mother's legendary quotes and love languages- aid the sisters throughout! We as sisters must pay attention to those sayings that are connectors to the blood line of sisters.

I know with my Aunts, that what my Grandmother Mable, said is always in the back of their minds, no matter how far apart they drift!

Sometimes, I know, though- that girls sometimes- do "lock outs (keeping them clueless as to what is going on)" or - even their mother, during - times that " juicy sister secret stuff is brewing (whether intimately or outwardly)". We often don't admit it, but it's true, some sisters that have a living Mom, surmise to saying things, like "Don't tell Momma, or you know how this is going to turn out if you do", some don't say anything at all, they just move and groove around in secret, because they know the tiniest hint of movement, will alert the mother of the group of some sisterly disconnect or indiscretions. We all know that in most cases, when the serious stuff hits, the momma has the power to execute, dispatch and disband anything outside of her approval, if she is the exceptional kind of mother. This happens all the time, and even though we as sisters do not like it, we should all respect her role as the mother. We should always find tactful ways to garner a situation when it comes to one's mother. Sometimes things maybe best kept a secret until things are pulled together fashionably (so-to-speak), but cold hearted isolation of one's mom, is not proper or accept-able in times of crisis.

**Mother of Sisters (More).** That leads me to the other- mother part of this. Sisters, know that the woman that God has chosen to be your mother, is the womb he wanted you to enter into the earth through. Yes it gets hard sometimes, and God will send surrogate mothers along the way, but still yet through it all, try your best to honor that vessel that pushed you into the atmosphere. It was very hard work. Moms of sisters, know that you are very much important, don't' get this "book wrong,". A mother's love, guidance and affection is important to keep the girls together. A mother's position is often times in some sister situations the only way that things are kept together. Mothers, moving forward- If you lose "the special mother's grip (so-to-speak)" with your daughters, then they lose their grip often times as sister's too. I encourage a mother of girls, to stay engaged and stay on top of the issues that a mother needs to. I am not saying to "but in to" all of their affairs, but try to keep your motherly stance in tow. Know that- you as a mother, have your own life, too, so set boundaries, so that you will have your individualized life styles, as well as a family oriented life style. Know that this piece of information that is being released is to help the sister group, and to keep you as a mother- "sane, secure and sound", when it comes to dealing with your daughters. Breathing the breath of life back into one's daughters is always necessary from time to time.

Additional Motherly Examples.On another episode of the filming of the Braxton's with Iyanla Vanzant (2018, same episode that I have been referring to this far), the mother, Ms. Evelyn, did a "loud yell" that stopped you, (if you were watching), in your tracks! She told her daughter, "Tamar, this is not how I raised you (Tamar was twitching in her seat, personal observation), she was referring to respect! Ms. Evelyn's comments and reactions were totally strong and message filled, but seemingly- much needed at that moment (my opinion)! You see a mother can do that! She can use her influence, that may seem bad at the time inorder to take things to other levels that they need to be taken to! It maybe a yell, a shout, it maybe any power tool that she needs to get the job done (speaking metaphorically).

Key note.—I know mothers some of you have been burdened with carrying your girls all throughout life, and that is okay, just revert to the healthy balance, especially if you are "talking, full grown adult daughters." Allow your girls the time to grow and breathe. Let your daughters learn how to function as individuals, as well as a group. You stay at a distance, yet be there when they need you, when it comes to sister problems. Keep natural, spiritual and emotional arms around them. I am sure those of you that are mothers, know this is needed from both ends of the spectrum. I ask you to pray for your girl's connection to stay fluid, active and connected, as you allow them to become themselves!

Sisters, it is time to grow up. It Is time to stop putting up fronts. It is time to take a real look at where we are and how we need to proceed. Sisters show love to each other and mend. Let's drop all the facades and move into life. Totally in abundance for sisters. Let's walk into our blessings. Let's not hide anymore, let's get it together, it is time now to do so! Let's do it! A few words of sister encouragement that you can use below:

Sister Words of Encouragement.

"Sister, I love you"!

"Sister how can I help you"?

"Sister I need you"!

"Sister without you I am incomplete."

"Girl Go-On"!

"Girl, you are crazy"!

"Girl, you better stop"!

"Girl you better get it together"!

"Girl, you are a beautiful flower, that I love to see"!

"Girl Momma gonna get you"!

"Momma get her"!

"My Sister, My Friend"!

"My Sister, My Enemy (Lol)"

Point of Meditation (Think on these below) in Prayer.

Pray over these issues, my dear sisters and, let's no longer hide secret feelings of envy, jealousy, fallacy, spite, guilt, hate, inadequacy towards one's sister? Let's not hide our truths from each other anymore! Let's speak to one another in the way that we should. Let's act, think, and feel the way we should towards one another, even if we have to walk alone sometimes. I want you sisters to think on the hard, deep things that needs to be said to one's sister. Think on these - What are the secrets we hide and live with just because we are sisters? Does one sister bear the burden of all the other sisters' indiscretions. Does one sister think she is better, and we allow this complex to tear into our thread of "a connection" because we all at some point have believed this? We all have talents and gifts that are distinct and separate and may carry one different and higher in the wordly, financial and tangible sense, yet we are all the same, get this! I hope you all are understanding what I mean. We are all the same, even though one may have this or that, it doesn't mean that one is no less, even if they have a bit more items, we are all the same! I pray you all are getting this! We are one and we are different, we are sisters, we are one blood! We are the same, repeat this in your mind!

Deep thoughts ... take it further, in order to get to the bottom of the issues ... Do we feel that the oldest think she's the better, acts the better, always bragging on this issue or that? Do we think the middle sister is the weakest, most internally dependent on the other sisters and yet further- do we think the baby sister of the bunch is always the one that gets away with everything and is never called to the carpet for it? We have all thought things such as this, when it comes to our sisters. Or maybe there are some lucky ones out there, that have not had these thoughts or feelings. But back to the heart of the matter, we as sisters are supposed to- at some point and time acknowledge how we feel. We as sisters, are supposed to go to the "deep place" in order to feel the most richest and succulent feelings of sister- hood, before we leave this earth to travel unto glory to that distant place in the sky. I guess some people are wondering how is this so? How can I be close to my sister when she is full of deceit, hatred, jealousy, envy, evil and all other else (figure of speech)? If there are sisters that refuses to intertwine or interact like the symbolism of the visual of rope that is twisted together rightly, then there are answers for them as well in this memoir. If you have troubling thoughts and feelings and emotions that co-exist within your sister group, then there is something here for you, keep reading.

Let's keep moving! I have learned as being the eldest sister, that when situations arise and you do all that you can to aid, one sister, and this is after the entire council of sisters have been hailed together, then you all have to let it be. You continue to love, care and protect (internally, if that is all the space you have left to hold her in) in order to care for her, but if arguing, pleading and begging continues, you have no other choice but to stop and release her. Don't continue to make matters worse. So sisters, when there is a problem sister in the group. Learn to strategize, work towards helping, but when the objective is complete. Stop, evaluate and move to the next step, no matter what it is.

Sisters, I spoke to the role of the mother inorder to allow your sister to grow, on her own or suffer on her own, now you all as sisters, have to do the same for the weaker sister, and that is to love and leave. Let her grow on her own. This will prove for a better relationships with all sisters in the long run. Sister's keep the understanding though! Keep the compassion! When the time for the wayward sister to return she and you all will know. Always keep a "look-out" person in the group, if there are more than two sisters, one is always to keep their "eyes" on the other one that is rebellious. There will always be a sister that Is rebellious, or one that will not fall in line with the agenda of sisters, whether internally or outwardly, but that is okay, you have to allow time and the flow to take control. Don't fight when fighting is harmful, whether, verbally internally, through electronic means, or whatever- know when enough is enough! When a sister group is faced with turbulent times, always follow your steps to solutions, and if they don't work, then take the next step available Always determine, as a group through talk and wise council, when there is severe conflict in the midst that you- your selves (sisters) cannot solve alone. Getting advice from the mother of the group, as she can be the first choice or the last choice, if your mother is too emotionally connected to each of her daughters, then outside help would be wisest!

Further Key Points.This book is written to help sisters heal (I will repeat this a lot throughout the book), come to reality, move forward, confront, acknowledge and share. This book will hurt us all, as I write it I myself feel, feelings of pain and pressure that makes my heart feel- like I want to weep, cry, yell and scream(sometimes I do), but as I am writing this memoir on sisters, I am growing too. As my heart and soul speaks and my fingers type, I heal, I rise, and I die (to myself, my will and my ways in order to be a better sister, and I hope you do to, as you read through).Sisters, so- let's get it all out front! I guarantee you will feel better. Since the initial writing of this book, I have had to change certain phrases, words, comments and thoughts- previously said, because throughout the journey of this book, a lot of my inner experiences and personal observations of life grew and developed. A lot of circumstances changed as I have changed, I had to make major modifications to this book. I could have finished this book years ago, yet God allowed me to procrastinate in order to grow and add a lot more insight in order to make this book speak to the vast types and kinds of races, colors, breeds and voices, of sisters that are out in the world today. God wants this message to impact sisters in the universe, now and throughout the annals of time!

Special Note:-Sisters, as I speak this book into a state of being, "into existence" I want - to say that, this book is not to detrimentally- accuse or blame, but to be honest there is no "way around it"! Sometimes, you just cannot "save face (as we say in the African American culture)"! We all know, if we all had to write a book on our story with our sisters, we would have so much to say, that we hate to say or don't say at all, or say it to someone we know it won't get back to our sisters! So guess what, I am saying it for you! Let's continue! Read on readers. -- I have set various pictures in the inset of this book to show different expressions of sisterhood, I pray as you turn to every 10 pages or so, you see a reflection of who you and your sisters are or at least hope to what this will be! Keep reading......

This book, is to help us get out all of the modes of despair, to help us come out of the "accusational" or "feeling accused" mode. This book is to help us to drop off the dead weight that holds us back (Hebrews 12:1 King James Version). We need to face what we have done, whether good or bad so that we can secure our relationships with one another as sisters. We need to ditch the imprisoned mind sets that have keep us bounded for years and years. We need to get to the bottom of the indiscretions that have held us up for years and years. We need to know and understand what is really going on with each one of us, then- we can come to places of understanding so that we can function a lot better together, as one and as many (sisters). Lets get to know our sister's perceptions, her mind on matters, lets stop assuming. Lets talk! We listen to everyone else do it, let's get together and do it ourselves! No matter how much we like it or not! No matter how much it hurts! Let's explore strongholds!

**Strong Holds**, What is a stronghold-a stronghold is defined as a thought or be-lief or way of thinking that we strongly uphold, even if it is wrong inappropriate or impacts our life negatively. Some of us are walking with strong holds in our minds. We are having thoughts that we have developed from childhood, because of some-thing- one- or the other sister has achieved, gained, did or said. Let's say for instance one sister (middle, older, younger, in-between, it doesn't matter which one) is excited about a major accomplishment, let's say she get a new house, a new car, heard of her new pregnancy, got a promotion, was able to make a major purchase for one's parents, or any other issue that was seen as important and this comes out, "Oh she makes me sick for her bragging ways or the most famous one of all, "who does she think she is". Other thoughts pertrude such as, "I am so sick of her", "I am too full of her",or " I am going home,,"! Pay attention to the things that the enemy takes to create strongholds in the mind. Some of us have a strong hold in our minds (that just sit there and won't leave, like a christmas ornament of the sort), unto our sister or because of our sister. This should not be so! It is not always what you think it is.

This memoir is geared to bring all of us "sisters" to balance. In love and in hopes to save some sister relationships. Relationships are the way we are connected. We as sisters need to understand our connections, and what they mean to us and how we can use them to succeed in life. God wants us to understand our inner workings and functions so that we can use our sisterhood as means for growth, renewal and projection. That is for --projection for us all to grow and expand. This is needed for our individual and collective lives. Let's not continue to live in a mode of accusation. Lets stop doing this to one another so that we can expand and live good decent lives.

The words says that "satan is the accuser" and the Bible does not lie, so if you are in a place of accusation towards your sister (Revelation 12:10, King James Version). Lets' dissect this place and "walk it right on up out of you"! Let's dig up that accusational moment that hit your soul, that you held onto for several years that you have never let go. Let's deal with the issue of the heart when it comes to one's sister connection. Let's let the feeling out! Let's destroy the feeling so that you no longer look or act this part! Let's ex-communicate these voices or ongoing messages that the devil has planted in your mind! Let's attack the delusions that have managed to compile itself on the clean place given to us by God. Lets purify our hearts and mind towards our sister, so we can see clearly. Lets go way back to that, pure place that God gave sisters to dwell in, like my granddaugthers have, Chrissy and Meliana! Lets rebuke the devil out of our circle, so we can live together freely the way God intended in peace and for the most part harmony. Let's try imagining going back to that place of purity. Let's get there by "doing the work' and I quote, Ms. Iyanla Vanzant. Sisters don't emasculate those thoughts and images any longer. Let's bring them out! Let's work on getting them in the right place, let's interpret what you are seeing and hearing so that you can get back to the connected spot, you once held with your sisters. Let's do it girls, we fight and conquer everything else, so let's do this! Let's get it and let's go! Lets do this to help sisters face and deal with their issues.

Key Point 9. Jealousy is a very high and common feeling that manifests itself in, or between sisters. Jealousy is defined as the desire to have what someone else has or it's the act of wanting what some one else wants. The act of envy or covetousness also falls in line with jealousy. We all have had a feelings like this whether it was towards our sisters or someone else that we deemed as a sister. The thoughts or actions of wanting to have something that is not yours, or the sick inner feelings that lunge a big lump in the pit of your belly is jealously, yep that feeling right there, is it! We want it gone! We want it diminished and destroyed! Now for those of you that have had the "green eyed monster (a figure of speech, a little bit deeper than envy and jealousy)" towards your sister, let's eradicate it, and explore where it came from. Sometimes jealousy comes from one sister feeling that the other sister is not being as talented as the other, but the less talented one ends up getting the part, getting the contract, ending up the celebrity, it happens all the time.

When one wants to become a winner in sisterhood or life, the winner is always the one with the greatest attitude, the greatest strength and greatest ability to challenge, be challenged and overcome adversity! I have noticed that with-some celebrity sisters that- they have hidden their heart and true feelings because they were afraid to speak up! Now is your time, too (speaking straight to you sister, in a celebrity family). You have always felt that your talent was better, but you did not get chosen! It is okay, God had your time to shine and it's now, it was not then! You were not ready, but your sister was. The inheritance was not left to you, my dear sister, because you were not the one at the time (I say this lightly), you would not have done the proper things with it, your sister had something you didn't have that would allow her to protect the family name! It is not you, it was her this time! But your time has come, but before it comes, God wants you to grow up and accept what God has allowed her, my dear sister, and when you do, it will immediately transfer over to you, yes it is yours! Now in Coronavirus, mask wearing times, things have been giving to those that thought they were not. You see when times like this manifest, we have to know for sure who we are, and what our sister is all at the same time, this is because all in all, we all win if we are tight knit sisters that can accept the giftings and callings of another sister! We can all mesh and win,when we can "take it just like that!" Don't be jealous! If you are the jealous type, I ask you now, to sit in your jealousy, explore why you have felt this way, go all the way back to the beginning ! Sit in it, let it rack through your entire body! Let it pass through so you can be healed. Sometimes getting to know deep within what a, vice or emotion can do, is liberating. Many times I engaged a feeling that had negatively impacted my life, so that I could rid myself of it and be healed. I have heard that when the common flu shot is given it gives you the very virus that you are trying to get rid of and somehow It combats itself to help you to become well. Use this strategy to win! It can and will happen, if you are willing!

More Sister Stuff. Now let's change the subject, a bit- and look into the Bible, Genesis 37:1-36 King James Version:, and explore a brother situation from centuries ago, that reflects this very topic. Joseph's brothers, hated him and the Bible clearly and explicitly says that his brothers wanted him dead because he had a dream of his sheaf standing, while his brothers sheaf's bowed down to him. At that very moment jealousy struck his brothers' heart, because they were looking at him saying to each other "Who do you think you are"? Why is he so special (in so many words)? Why is he having such strong dreams and ambitions? Why does he think he is going to rule over us? Malarkey (is what they said in so many words, we got an answer for that)! And isn't that how some sisters are? Isn't that how we view one another when one sister is deemed as "the one"? Joseph was ultimately chosen to do a work, a job, carry and hold a position, that his siblings could not. It is obvious, that Joseph had what it took to hold the part. Joseph had what it took to take the persecution, to withstand betrayal and to show compassion in the end that his other siblings may not have extended. You see, Joseph became the Prime Minister, a position that is similar to a modern day Governor, and had to end up rescuing his family, from famine. Joseph's many gifts afforded him the opportunity to suffer, yet to only reign and lift his siblings up, in the end. He was their life source. I pointed this out so that, sisters you will realize that not all are chosen to take the lead.

God only chooses certain ones to carry the lead, not all sisters are made to carry the lead or load for that "fact," and then there are some sisters in other families where several sisters, if not all are made in a way that's powerful and unique and carry the lead, but in a different ways. I will use the Simmons Sisters (Vanessa and Angela Joseph, RUN DMC's daughters, legendary rapper, for those of you who are not familiar with rap music legends), they are both powerful and ambitious. They both carry the torch and seem to hold it horizontally with, out too much noticeable jealousy or enviousness. I said that to say, that not all sisters have just one leader, some have several, the key to this portion of the writing is to know who you are and in knowing this - jealousy will be alleviated amongst sisters. One will vouch for what the other lacks and vice versa. Additionally, the feelings of jealousy are inordinate and should be immediately eradicated when found out. Don't let jealousy be your ground, your purpose or your goal!

**Prophetic**. In the realm of the Spirit, God has shown me for the purpose of this book, several women that are sitting at the "thrown of jealousy," you have dwelt there for a very long time and it is because of what you think "is" when it comes to a particular "sister," God is telling you to allow his spirit to deter the demonic force and cleanse your soul. He wants you to let go of the thoughts, the illusions, the delusions, that the enemy has put in your mind regarding your sister and how you view her. Let it go, give it up, it has been burdening you for most of your life, to the point of "death wishes," God says it is not so, he wants to relieve you, ask for forgiveness and go get help. Go to one of your sisters that you are not having the issue with and confess, if it is not another sister, you want to release to, then go to someone you trust, it can be a parent, a co-worker, a close friend, someone you just met, but release it, the time Is here, it was not you, it was the ENEMY, he dragged your soul for all this time to pass an assault onto you, to your sibling. The time is now, take your deliverance!

Cultural Differences/Sisters. There are other cultural sisters that engage differently than I do, or my particular culture- such as, Asian Sisters, Jamaican Sisters, Islamic Sisters, and Arabic Sisters. All different types of sisters and cultures tend to experience the bond or disbandment of sisterhood, because of one reason or the other. Jealousy has been cited with much research, as a main reason for controversy among sisters from all cultures! I have viewed countless videos and stories on sisters of various cultures, styles, types, means or kinds- that fight over inheritances, honor and positions. It seems there are different levels and kinds of jealousies within different cultures.

One thing I know for certain, sisters, is that jealousy can destroy a family connection in any facet. I have seen it destroy, the best of relationships. I have seen people be stabbed in the back, imprisoned, blocked, or hindered due to jealousy, all done by sisters.

Me, my sister Jenny, younger days

Me and My Sister Jenny, Today,
plus Melianna and Chrissy
(Sister/Grandbabies), plus
one Jonathan (my son)

Jealousy is the "rage of a man (Proverbs 6:34 KJV)." So let's look at how the rage of a feeling affects sisters. I plan to take a look at sister hood in terms of one's cultural dictates, but first lets' look at the Hebrew Sisters Leah and Rachel noted in the bible, that I spoke on earlier. As it was written, Leah was jealous of Rachel and Rachel was jealous of Leah, both had something desirable, one had the husband, and one had the children. Both seemingly- jealous of what the other one had, not realizing the bond that they shared as sisters. Each sister ignored their bond in order to hang onto the band wagon of jealousy.

Both sisters were blinded by the arousal of an emotion that espouses rage, competitiveness and lack of compassion for who they are or were as sisters. Neither acknowledged their sisterhood, they only focused on what they wanted. The possession that each had, that the other one didn't. Leah wanted the very love that Rachel had from her husband. Rachel wanted the children that Leah had, neither was focused, as they were so, in want of each other's stuff, sound familiar? One thing in particular that I noted, that was, what the other failed to realize what they had, what they held, the power in each, neither came to a realization of that! Both women had purpose (although they didn't know it), they both had a gift given to them by God, to use for his purpose, Both forfeited their prizes to focus on the "loss or the missing piece" that both thought they had, when all in all they were both prized and honored in the sight of God. They were both tricked, by the enemy's hand into believing something internally negative about themselves. Sisters is that you, today? Do you focus so much on what your sister has and she on you, until you cannot see what you have? I would ask that you read this story about Rachel and Leah and see, if you see yourself or your sister in this story (Genesis 30:1-22 King James Version)?

More on Culture. On cultural biases, customs and traditions when it comes to sisters, If you are birthed into a culture where you were not allowed to express your feelings, but somehow one of your sisters has found that door to openness, and jealousy has crept in because you are bond to your cultural perspectives, let it go! Release it, plain and simple. Take what your bolder sister has done to receive the same level of freedom! Don't be jealous of her ambition and riskier side, tied to her freedom. Make an attempt to connect with your one and only supporter and igniter of strength, yes your sister, she is there for you! Don't think otherwise, she has been waiting! Don't hold you sister that is bolder and enlightened, don't reverse her plight, by psychologically blinding or binding her anymore. Don't envy her ability to step outside of customs, give her-her own chance! I think you understand what I mean.

Key Note 10. When I copy wrote this book, I called into The Library of Congress in order to complete the process on line and I spoke to a particular representative, I told him the title of this book, and his first words were, "Wow, that should resonate with a lot of people and he went on to tell me about his wife and her sister and how they were in a major dispute (at the time)" regarding heir property! Often times sisters end up states of battle due to executor issues and the like. God wants me to talk to the group of sisters that are in the population of people that have issues with heir property being stolen. The guy on the phone, briefly shared with me, how one sister 'stole' the other sister's inheritance or did not equally divide it. He expounded on how this has always been a problem for his wife. He told me he could not wait to read this book. Furthermore the story that was told to me, indicated that the inheritance dispute caused war among the sisters. This was where, two sister- siblings hated each other, over their family's trust and inheritance. This story is a common one. The story was further revealed, to me, as one sister's, act of telling lies, deception and thievery, while the other sister, sat back and took the brunt of the other sister's manipulation. The one sister that "sat back" was his wife. He noted that one sister wanted it all and was not willing to be fair and share what they both had inherited! Does this story sound familiar?

Sisters, if you are now having a dispute over parental assignment of funds, this is something that will cause major estrangement and conflict. Be fair to each other, listen to each other and disperse what is rightfully yours to one or the other! Let's not be selfish anymore! Money is always at the root of all evil! Sisters when there are issues of inheritance various levels of conflict, can involve and can include millions of dollars, lands, entitlements, etc. This should always be handled by attorneys and estate managers, not by handwritten documents by your elderly grandparents (although this was frequented in the past). I am sure though by now, your story is past this process. If this is the case for you, my dear sister, let it go. The money will not profit, if there is constant strife and mayheim "railing above it, the money will be held in hostage", until you all do it righteously! Let God work the process out, you will gain more in the long run and be blessed in other ways. I know losing what is rightfully yours is criminal and warrants punishment, but God is telling me to tell you today, as you read these words, that, "He will reward you and repay"! Money is always at the core of evil,my dear sister! Money cuts a relationship in two. If we are not rooted and grounded in Christ's love, it is very easy for the enemy to use money as a barrier to distance sisters from each other. I have watched and observed in real life and television shows from "Law and Order," to " Life Time" to other "TV Specials" that have shown sisters at odds, - when it came to money or inheritance. In most cases, real life and television, both stories end up the same in trauma, turmoil and hurt. No one wins fighting the enemy of money! Let it go, you will and can gain in other ways. I promise you my dear sister, if you are broken hearted because of this issue, let it go. No longer give into what the enemy is using to keep you confused, hurt and dismayed. No longer play into the scheme of lies, let yourself go, once you give up the fight, you will see with the sister that you are fighting with, it was probably not about the money anyway, once you give in there will no longer be this ineffective bond between you two and as my grandma used to say, one person cannot fight alone!

Lets' move on and discuss this issue a bit more. But why jealousy, all the time, why is this how we often function as sisters? Why is it, when this emotion or feeling rise, up, why don't we just delete it or deal with it, why is it so prevalent among sisters? I have found and researched that - jealousy has been in the earth from the beginning of time. Jealousy has stirred the minds and souls of many sisters! Jealousy has destroyed homes, jealousy had aroused anger, jealousy has clouded the minds and streams of connection, jealousy had been the food of thought of lots of people, all of the time. But now is the time for us to get rid of this monster of life! We now have to beat and destroy- this thing that destroys the sisterhood bond . Stop letting the enemy replay in and through your mind- the very thing you hate about your sister, her stance, her position - her friends, your parents, the way she talks, the ways she walks. Let it go, its all deception. Jealousy is- the rottenest of the bones (Proverbs 14:30, KJV). It eats away at one sister's soul to the other, making one think she needs what the other one has! Not so! Stop feeling the lack, that the enemy places in your soul and, immediately turn to feeling your own sense of[1] self, your own confidence! Don't let the enemy have your sisterly pos-session, your sisterly gift, your sisterly connection, he has had it in the palm of his hands for too long. It is a trick and hijacker of one's soul! It is a negative image in one's mind of one self and one's sister, combined. If you are jealous of your sister, there has to be a negative issue that you personally are facing, or something you feel you, personally- lack? Ask yourself what is it? Go back in your mind, track it down! Don't allow the devil's twisted-impeded thoughts to continue to linger in your mind with tauntings of failure. Don't allow the devil to make you think you failed because of some minor mishap that occurred in your childhood that makes you feel like you are being judged by your sister or sisters. Remove his voice out of your hearing, get it out of your head, the very thing that constantly repeats to you and your mind- "that you are not as good enough", it is his trick. Don't allow the enemy from within make you think, that you are being mocked, or ridiculed. It is within you, stop blaming others, for what you have allowed. Take up your own battle gear and fight for your soul. Sister, If you want to be the person God has destined, stop blaming your sisters, and take a look at your "own-self (as my grandbaby-Memphis says)". Take on your own responsibility! This my dear sister, is not your sister's fault, it's your own issue-, because you have allowed it to go on too long with out a fight, internal and mental fight that is! You are keeping yourself in your own prison. It is the same old trick all the time, it is his plan to maintain and keep your sister as your enemy! Lets do this (figure of speech)!

Your sisters have been waiting on you and they know this spirit "all" well. They know that this spirit has grappled you for many many years. Your sisters have been waiting on you to come up out of it (figure of speech), but to no avail. But it is time now! Know this my dear, that your sisters, can and have been feeling the trajectory of this spirit for a very long time. They have longed for it to "come up off (figure of speech)" of you! My dear sister, the sooner you acknowledge it, the better off you will be! Yes, my dear, I will say this in my Iyanla Vanzant voice, "yes beloved" accept it, come out of it, press in, then breathe in and out! This type of acknowledgment, in the long run will help you and set you free. Work on the exploration of the feelings inside, instead of suppressing the feelings and burying them in your heart. One needs to explore one's heart to determine it's origin. Ask yourself, where did it start and why. The heart is at the seat of our emotions, the heart is the core of our being, it takes in joy and pain. It takes in peace and chaos. The heart is like waves in the ocean, they move around, backwards, forwards and with force! We have to, at some point in life learn how to manage what comes into, goes and leaves out of our heart! The heart is the important part of our human make up, without it nothing else works, all else fails, when nothing flows to the heart and the blood does not circulate to the heart, what happens, we all know, a heart attack! Don't give yourself a "sister attack" by not letting it all go, by not cleansing your arteries! Clogged arteries are dangerous ! Manage the distance, by stopping the furtherance of it! Let the mirage in your mind go!

Caution. The heart of your "sistership" is at risk, if you are not constantly cleaning and keeping the heart clear of 'muck' and other unclean thoughts, acts and anxieties, nothing will change, it will only get worse. Often times we as humans, don't realize what it takes to keep a relationship going. Yes there will be stress involved in the maintenance and upkeep of a sister relationship. Sister or Sisters, if we don't build, we lose. Sisters, we don't realize when relational compasses are off beat, especially with sisters, the damaging effects that it has. Sometimes, our whole entire being can tend to be off, if we don't apply the act of maintenance.

Cleanse your heart of the jealous rage and other inuendos. Don't let the evil stare, that presses through your vision, evidently take control of your heart,as the eyes are the windows to our soul (Proverbs 30:17, KJV). Jealousy is the enemy's voice, his tool to keep sisters apart. Stop using this inordinate speech- that lingers in your head and hearing- to evolve through and in the life of you, first and foremost and then your sisters! Don't let the in- opportuness of jealousy manifest itself in your life and the life of your sisters, over and over again. Time is running out for the anchor's extension, some are tired of waiting, so sister, that's reading this, lets take that leap of rescue- before it is too late. Don't let the shame of jealousy keep you from coming aboard. Don't let it overrule who you are to- yourself, and your sister group. It is time to kick jealousy off deck. There are some sisters though, I caution you that have become embittered, and will refuse take extension of rescue from the other sisters-- and I am sorry to say,but the act of spiritual drowning in what they think is normality (the enemies voice) will forever be their anchor's hold! I ask those of you that can receive this do so, and those that cannot I will continue my cry out to God, for you to come, yes come back into the fold! I pray that your destiny as sister, yes, you the other sister- comes forward and "on board" in Jesus Name!

__Sisters, Look, Explore and Find__ Find out sisters as your move forward and on, how you- as sisters stimulate each other. Find out how your role fits in the total scheme of sister companionship. Figure out what it is that you "do" like about each other, figure out your strengths, your weaknesses and how it all works together. I know that my baby sister makes me laugh a lot and my other sister, Jenny is always supportive for the good to the both of us and she tends to be laid back but will without a doubt speak her mind when she needs to. Jenny, my middle sister seems to always want what is best for us all no matter what, in any circumstance! Yes look for the good in your sister's personality and use it to your advantage, not to your bad. Remember early on, I noted that a sister needs to find who she is in the midst of it all (in so many words). Having an identity is very important when you have large or small sister groups. One should quickly get to know who one is, within the sister group, as to have a relationship with one's self. . Find you and not your sister. Once you find you, you will then find her (or them, your sisters that is)!

"Sister Brides"

**Finding myself as a sister**. How do I do that, you ask yourself, "who am I"? What are my likes and dislikes, what is it that is different, for me or about me- than it is for my sister, and even if she is, or has something that I don't have; whether outwardly or inwardly, how can I learn from her? How can I discuss how she makes me feel with her, when I am around her? How can I do this if it continues to nag and "gnaw" at my soul? How can I separate who we were as kids, into who we are as adults? How do I see myself now? How does my sister see herself? Is the way she see herself different than how I see myself? Does that cause her personality to move and engage in 'time' in a way that is a lot bigger than or less than I? What is my self-perception of me? What makes me tick? What are my deeper, subtle or unseen personality traits? Sisters, those are a few questions that you can ask yourselves. A little side note, and reminder(as I have said this before and will say it through out, as sisters, we often battle with this- issue more often than not) No matter how much you have, or don't have, this is still your sister! Know and keep this in your head, mind and heart, that whatever one has, it does not make anyone any better (_this has always been the major issue with sisters, the "who has what issue and who does not have"_)! Sisters get a grip on who you are! Sisters, if you can answer, process and explore most of those questions, in order to find the deep rooted answers., then you are well on your way to discovering who you are as a sister, and created being. Forge on to create your profile in the midst of the sister group. Don't let another moment pass you by without developing your own identity, you will be so glad that you did, you will figure out the jewels, of your heart, that you have been missing out on. Try to have a sister meeting on self-identity, if this is as problem amongst you, to help you all come to terms with your inner self. When identities are revealed and discovered, it is the road to solid connections, improved building, and massive productivity of one's sister group.

**Key Point 11**- Sisters, after you find out who you are! Get to know yourself. Take your time to do this. Know that your Identity is key in a sister group, so take you time in getting to know the new you. I keep saying this over and over for a reason, as it is at the core of sister problems, lack of self-identity, know yourself, explore you!. Get to the point of understanding the sister direction, create a sister vision and motto for the group, and yourself as part of the group. Understand how your sibling sister's companionship influences your life, versus you feeling that she has been "taking away" from your life or even "overshadowing your life". Know that sisterhood adds to your life, if you play the sister game correctly! Let's put this all in reverse, to make the ultimate life correction, so to not stay in a neutral or parked mode!

More on Sister Identity. Know who you are and your sister is! Remember that you all are a team! Know that as a group that you all can make it and not the other way around. Use this vechicle to make it happen. ***Example 1.*** I have a friend, let's call her Andrea, she and her sisters were like a team and with Andrea being the oldest, she was always in "lead mode"! Andrea was always trying to make things work for her and her sisters! This is how it is supposed to be.Andrea,was like a fire cracker, she was always excited to share her knowledge, wisdom and love to her sisters! She was a true elder sister! Andrea knew who she was, even though she was often times misunderstood. Know my sisters your role and position as a sister! ***Example 2***. Andrea is the oldest of them all and she never, put a wedge between her and her sisters, no matter what they went through, she cried for them, prayed for them, rescued them, fought for them, wept for them, the list goes on, she was a true warrior, for her sisters, this is what sisters do! Normally elder sisters fall into this category! I say normally,there are exceptions! Let's be clear! ***Example 3***. Andrea and her sisters are a lot older than me, but what I loved was how they flowed as sisters. I met Andrea, the oldest, at a church function. It was not long after that they took me in as their little sister (a topic I will touch later on, "sisters, but not by blood"). I will say that although, Andrea was the leader of the pact, she fully respected her sisters and allowed them to be who they were at the time. Showing respect for your sister is so, so important. Sisters, sometimes we lose our sisters, because we do not know how to respect them. Respect is the act of regarding one's wishes, feelings, emotions, etc. I saw Andrea show high regard and respect for Tommie and Mitzy! Andrea lost one of her sisters, the middle one Mitzy. I saw how deeply, this touched Andrea! I saw Andrea's hurt and sadness! The response of a true sister!. (I will reveal a poem/excerpt on the loss of a sister a little further in the book). I applaud you Andrea, for being the true example of a elder sister!

Taking it backwards.Going back is always good for our souls. When we have ill feelings towards our sister or sisters. Exploring the day and the hour the dreadful dart -struck one's heart always helps relieve feelings that carry us for a life time, when it comes to our sisters. This happens all the time. Now it is time for one of us to "take a stand" so that we "all can be helped." I think, what happens is when sisters harbor feelngs contrary to what it should be, we stay in a fixed, stuck place. Feelings are harbored from times past, which can some time turn into shame and pride, mixed together. Shame and pride are terrible combinations- when it comes to one's relationship bond with one's sister.When a person is ashamed, they will use pride to mask it. Often times this type of feeling will afford you a lot of fury and rage. I have seen sisters harbor something really petty and then something really big and obscure, becomes of it. It is because, fury dashed it's face and shadow into the lives of the sister group in a harsh and devastating way! Let's talk about these things before it comes to this! Sisters stop defending this ill that is trapped inside of you. Release it now! This theory is not just for sisters, this happens to all of us. But for the purposes of this book hiding how one feels and putting it on something or someone else makes it become the pathway to "hell". Sisters when we attack each other with our emotions and things held inside for long periods of time, it turns into something different. Remember, when we were little and we took dirt and water and made "mud pies," prior to "patting the cake into whatever shape it was" it was another texture, and another form, but after a day or two the once soft "what we thought was our best cake" turned into "hard, unbreakable dirt and sand" that we couldn't do anything with the next day. That is how shame, guilt and pride works when it comes to our sister bond, after a few days, weeks, months and years, it becomes hard and unyielding, and you cannot do much with it, but throw it away or avoid it! We need to be more open to talking while things are soft and pliable, because once it's hardened, there is not much one can do with it. Just like cement, it takes major tools to break up hardened cement, after several years (something to think about, sisters). Dealing with conflict amongst sisters can be a traumatic thing, if left undone for several years. If we allow the "thing" to go through cycle after cycle of relationships, it is a tough task. We as sisters, must handle the situation and handle it quickly. Sisters, let's make the attempt to put the first foot forward. This must be the first step, if not, the bond will forever be severed.

We must realize what is happening, or what has happened that has kept us distant from our sisters for extended amounts of time. I heard a sister story where some sisters are in a place of total disillusionment, in regards to what has been done to them by their sister and how they were held in an emotional hostage situation. One sister held a grudge above the others in which caused a halt in time of their lives. Due to this hidden secret, all were confused, thought stopped and held at a stand still.

The story unfolds like this, a group of sisters were isolated from their sister's life for a very long time. The case- of denial of the sister's love and affection caused the sisters opposite of this particular- sister to feel inwardly tormented by the denial of communication and connection. The sisters always felt like they were to blame and was always- at odds with one another. They did not know what had occurred. The process eventually tore the sisters apart, because of the lack of understanding through communicating the "real problem". When things came to light, they realized, that it was not them at all, but the voice of the enemy in their sister's head, based on her on personal issue that she herself kept concealed.

Sister's please pay attention to the false allegations made by the Devil, yes the "enemy" himself of one's soul and one's sister's soul. Taking one's sister's soul and leaving it there, is not proper protocol for sister relationships. Allowing that to be the ruse for a deep inner concealed issues is always something that the devil uses to keep sisters apart. A past, emotional feeling one may have had for a very long time, for one reason or the other, is a mask that satan uses to keep sister's at naught with each other., when it may not even be the "group's problem.

Knowing what is underneath the entire scheme of things is always essential for breaking ground among Sisters in regards to the conflict or any-issue at hand. Sisters beware, of the enemy's trap. Don't let yourself get caught in this horrendous web. This will tear at your consciousness, if you feel that your sister is doing this to you, put a stop to it! Go straight to it! Address, confront or deal with the issue. And deal with it in the way that will suit the situation. For instance, you can only deal with it a few ways, set up an appointment, time, or place to talk or process the issue, if the issue is too tense, due to the time passed or the enemy's set ups, then you may need a third party involved. If you goal is to truly make amends, then do so, but If you are not at that point, where you tried and tried and feel that there is no more to do, then don't do anything. I have learned in life, that if a person is not committed to the process of reparation then you cannot force it. No one can change a person's will. Don't allow yourself to be belittled or mocked. Let it go. If there is no dedication to the process, let it stay where it is. Don't allow the sibling bond to keep you tied to scorn or sin, that God didn't intend to be so. God wants us without doubt, to bond with each other, but not at the expense of our souls been twisted, tied and manipulated, so if the timing is bad or there is not equal participation, then it is best to leave it alone and let it go. Don't be the intended target. – Don't let the devil "reverse or curse the very thing that God is trying to Bless"!

Another issue that sisters face is classcism. Don't allow this poison of classcism to be- to your detriment- when it comes to sisters. It is okay for one to hold a positions in businesses, corporations, non-profits, churches, communities, or what have you. Yet classcism, should not separate you all, by no means what so ever- in your role as sisters, don't allow this to binder, means-- to "blind" your connection. Sister's should be a "unit." Sisters should all function and sit as one "whole, and not several parts," when it comes to your connection. I am not speaking to your role right now, just your connection! Sisters we all have our positions that we must play. Yet, never should outside forces meaning titles, status, influence, or money come between one's connection to one's sister. None of these things should be at the precipice of who you and your sisters are. None of these things are even questionable or should be when it comes to how you relate and mate with your sister. Anything that is intangible is not, or should not be in with the sister bond. Things that are material, should not take priority or place, over, who you are as sisters. Those things should only be seen as resources, not weapons. We as sisters, should not allow what we achieve in life to be our weapon against our sisters, nor should a sister accuse you of doing so, if you are not. One should be fully aware of one's status and one's place. If you get accused of being "this or that," simply confront the issue, if you know that it is not true. Don't let the lies "fly"! Stop the enemy from using you as his crutch against your sister, confront the enemy where he stands!

Furthermore, don't allow the fact that one particular sister has more material or influential success to make you feel less than. Your sister is your sister. She is the same person that you knew years ago, with a lot of influence, matter and power, attached to her, she is down in there some where, just search for her! Things are nothing in the sight of God, and they should not be for us as sisters! Know that consequently, none of this is important, when it comes to being with your sister, none of this matters. If you cherish your sister relationship, then those of you are, guilty of such behaviors-deal with it!, "Open your eyes," make the changes that need to be made to correct this fallacy that the enemy has wedged between you and your sister. I am sure your sister does not feel the way you think she does. The thoughts of her thinking that she is any better is really not what should go through the head of one's sister, no matter where she is positioned in the sister order. None of it really means anything, yet the bond should mean everything. Relationship is superlative to materialism. A sister relationship should never enter into rounds (as in a boxing match) with material positions, status and titles. This is the devil's ploy. Take heed, pay attention and listen to his tricks. I know you all may think, well, where this all is coming from. I am wondering myself, I am typing and my heart and spirit is speaking to my fingers. Please, please sisters as we journey through this book, even if you have to stop, take a break, cry scream, call your sister, do it, get this thing straight, get It right, when you come through, you are not going to believe the places that God will take you as sisters.

Take a lesson from Oprah, famous talk show celebrity "queen" and her sister. Oprah's sister because of her dedication to their bond, made a decision. I am sure she never believed she would be where she is today, I am sure she had no idea her life would turn out the way it has, a lot of it in my opinion was because when she found out she was linked to a celebrity- decided to not take advantage of her blood connection. You see some sisters take advantage of their blood sister connection,, but Oprah's sister did not. You see when we understand where the bond and connection lies, we benefit more. A sister is a sister and if one is a true sister, she will love unconditionally and give of herself to her sister unconditionally, tangibly or not.

Let's learn how to get in alignment with our sisters, in spirit not in materialism. Once we align, all else will come and be added in all shapes and forms. Sisterhood has a devine, supernatural ability to sustain, invoke production, love and movement!

Sister Power-Let me add that all sisters have strengths and weaknesses. One or all sisters, maybe consciously aware of these areas. Whomever it is—that is aware of this within the sister circle- make useful attempts to fair things, meaning some of you that are strong, may have to become weak and some of you that are weak may have to become strong! Furthermore, let's not use or make attempts to take devilish advantages, when this level of awareness is ephiphanized! Stop this, let's not - do this. Because, just because your sister, may not have - that which you have, or you may have, that which she don't. Let's not shoot one another in the foot (an expression) because of it, take the links that God has blessed you with and connect them to make your life and your family's life better, after all SISTERS do- make it happen, when we are connected, when we are disconnected, things fall part.

I have some cousins, that are great examples of what I am trying to portray, they are Krystle, Candace and Traci, I have watched, them grow into one of the best team of sisters, that I know. My cousins, if I must say, have yielded some of the crops from their mother's sister group- the Sansbury Sisters, my Aunt Gloria, their mother--part of the Sansbury Sisters' labor with her sisters (my aunts), they are so connected and bonded. I can tell they cherish their bond and would not allow nothing to come between them, no matter what goes on amongst them. Their sister connection is their secret weapon and their power. I have noticed how dedicated they are to each other and how they stand by each other no matter what. Nothing that goes on between them becomes a spectacle, they keep it private and they keep flowing in their "sister power"! This is how it should be. For instance, when one is connected to one's sister, the power that God gives you is enormous, because each sister knows their place and they respect it even, if they don't like it. My cousin Krystle, is the oldest and the leader, I have watched her advise and lead, her sisters, always with their best interest at heart. Krystle, is self-less and she gives to her sisters with a kind and loving heart, she protects them, even when it is hard to do so, by giving them hard, truths Krystle knocks on the doors of their heart, (metaphorically speaking) so that in the long run they are strong, guarded and in step with life and sisterhood. Krystle is the mother hen, and she tries really hard to aid her sisters in their development and walk with God. I have seen Krystle watch her sister's make mistakes, when they do, she does not mock them or make them feel ashamed, she loves them straight through it. I have watched, observed and felt the vibe. Yes my cousins, they are perfect examples of what sisters should be, I commend them, you are one of the most commendable sister groups that I know! The Graham Sisters!

__Personalities.__ Appearances, looks and shows (or fronts, terms used in the African American culture to mean, "being fake or not real)" can and will deceive you. Sisters have various personalities, "some exact and some not so exact", true or to the point. So I am going to say it bluntly, sisters, lets put the fakeness away, let's "squash it", it is time to stop playing sister games! Starting out with sisters personalities, I want to look at the eldest first, this I know is not uncommon to some of you reading this book. The oldest sister is most of the time, the "A" type personality. A trait of the eldest sister, is normally, the strong and unyielding types. Elder sisters are large vessels that pour spiritual strength into the younger minded, or younger aged sister- siblings, while sometimes forgetting themselves. A Types, sisters, have their strengths coupled with their weaknesses, too, as they can be super- sensitive, inwhich often times lends it's hand to emotional weakness. A example of this would show itself in her personality that manifests and lends itself to being an- enabler, which accounts to one of her weakest, weakest signatures, of her sister portfolio. They tend to forget themselves, while always thinking about their sisters, helping to the point of pain and mostly forgetting theirselves in the process, as mentioned earlier. When this type of behavior occurs, they (The "A type-eldest") tends to weaken their younger sisters, by giving them too much and not leading them to their own power, they give them all of their power; thus spoiling, and giving them the right to "not" do a thing! This is not good,my dear Elder sister. A type Elder Sisters, this one is for you. Know that you cannot do it all. Know that you cannot "be it all"! Know when to take a break and stop. This is something, I think all Elder sister's need to absorb, process and take in! It will take time, this is not a demand, only a recommendation. It will cause you less pain in the years to come.

__Next Personality__-Pay attention to what you may like, as you, for instance, you may not be the same person that your sister is. She maybe an upfront 'person type' and you may not be. If your sister or sisters have a knack for handling certain things in a certain way, that may not be "your cup of tea", don't sweat it or fret about it. It is just that God didn't create you the same, or to do the same things. First, and foremost don't get jealous, figure out what your niche is and "run with it'. It is "so time out" for jealousy in the days of "COVID-19". God delayed my book for this time, for me to bring in a perspective that aligns with the "shut in" that we are now going through. We all now should be taking the time to realize who we are, and what we can become as sisters as the doors are "shut" 'in all of our lives as sisters. We will never be the same as sisters after COVID-19. Now is the time to take total inventory of your mind, your soul, and personality as a sister to see where God created you to fit in the scheme of all of this. If you have a sister still here after COVID-19, then you should be totally grateful and thankful for her! I want to add here, sisters that we need to learn how to exert some level of self-control (whether inwardly or outwardly), this is the reason for so much jealousy and enviousness, we don't know how to manage our emotions. We don't know how to manage, stabilize or disband certain emotions. Emotions that take you down and keep you in an upheaval, need to be dealt with or dismissed, emotions that bring joy, peace and inspiration need to be attended, to learned and applied as you grow and mature! We as not only sisters, but as human beings at some point need to learn how to manage our emotions, our thoughts and our spirits. Some of us don't realize this and we act and think the same way we did when we are babies, even today as adults, and most definitely as sisters, it is "so time for us to grow up"! Read on!

Accept that this is, as the mode that God created for your personality, as well as her personality. There may be other modes that you can fit in with your sisters, inwardly and outwardly. Look to see if you are the one in the sister group that is needed in the group that brings in morale support. Just start evaluating, while we all have this time on our hands to now, and see who we are as a individuals and sisters. I want to continuously point you to the direction of who you are and your role in sisterhood. Evaluate it and do it now- if it is upfront, then be that, if it is not upfront then be that- find your place in the back, in the front, the middle or wherever it is that you belong in the sister group. Don't let insecurity be your guide. BE strong "my sisters", be strong and let's get it together! Sisters, find out what you like? Are you introverted, extroverted? What is your personality style?

Knowing personality styles and types can help you to know where you fit, and why you have been a particular way all of your life. If you are an introvert, then maybe you like being alone and not in the crowd. Yet if one of your sisters does, let it be and accept it, stop allowing the enemy within tell you otherwise. Be who you were meant to be and pick up the success that come's with that role, if you are who I am, then there are no variances in our descriptions. There will always be variances in who we all are. Stop bickering within and among the sisterhood group. Stop wasting your time and talents. God has something totally different that is truly a blessing, that correlates with your personality, your style and your look, it is not your sister's look, don't try to compare it. Don't consider her stuff, consider your own! Consider who you are and what righteousness is inside of you and not your sister, for the purpose of defining your own individuality.

SPECIAL NOTE: Inferior complexes. Inferior complexes were coined into psychological theories in the earlier years. This theory speaks to the thought of one having all kinds of thoughts and feelings being, of just that, "inferior (feeling less than)". One having the mindset to thinking one is less, feeling one is less, walking in fear of one's ability to act or do. Having all kinds of thoughts of being incapable. Inferiority complexes rage and ravage our souls, clouds our minds and mobilizes us in one place. As we continue to look through the eyes of comparisons, thoughts of being left out, being not up to "par" or standards (for the purposes of this book), when it comes to measuring ourself to one's sister or the other. Explore your inferior complexes in order to rid yourself of them, face them and grow. Deal with the fears of feeling that some physical, mental or social stance is not being measured up "to," according to what you see in your sister".

Special Definition: Introversion-Is a personality trait where the individual is more "inwardly stimulated", examples would be a person that is normally "to themselves in a crowd", does not talk as much as others, is not excited about outward stimuli, but more connected to isolation within and without.

Extroversion refers to a person being stimulated by outward tangibles. A person that is stimulated by exciting or moving stimuli. A person that evolves from large crowds, excitement and strong arousal of events, relationships or things.

**Key Point 11 (More on traits).** In keeping in alignment with sisterhood and the application and usage of introversion and extroversion- Not all introverts are shy people nor do all introverts like being behind the scenes or vice versa these traits can be isolated of itself used "independently as in what we learned in school that applies to independent and dependant variables or it can be used dependently". They are extroverts, consequently, that like certain atmospheres and are not always up front type "of" people it varies, just learn your type and who you are as a sister. Explore your introverted or extroverted side, so that you can add to the sister relationship! Understand what you entered into the earth for! Explore, Explore, Explore! Introversion and Extroversion are key underlying traits that affect the sisterhood brood greatly! Learn of this.

**Moving forward.** Christ redeemed us from the curse of the law (Galatians 3:13). Cursed is every one that "hangeth on a tree." We are cursed if we continuously put ourselves in a position that warrants contempt towards our sister or sisters. In biblical times, when someone died by a hanging, the body had to be removed the same day or else it would be seen as a curse. Let the cursed behaviors go, let the thing that is binding you be loosed in Jesus name. A cross reference to this scripture is in Deuteronomy 21:23. God does not want us to lose out on what he gave us as sisters or misuse the endowment involved in being partnered together as sisters. Being a sister is an inherited position. There are many blessings that come with being wrapped in the bonds of sisterhood. There are many benefits, although it is not often seen that way. Some of us, think that because you are close that is, all there is to being a sister, which is, by no means, all it is. What is the usefulness of being close if you are not creating, dev- eloping, and building? That means there is work! There is work in sisterhood! Keep and know this! We as sisters should be creative mode, in innovative mode, furthermore in a mode of defining our bond and using our bond to gain in the world, that God has given us, not the other way around. God wants sisterhood to be a source, a resource, an option for us all. He wants being a sister to not be a vice, but an invite! Yes an invite for some to know that we all stand and we all fight, not with our fists, but for our God, ourselves, our bond, our connection, our families, society, etc or at large. We as sisters should be a force to be reckoned with. We are sisters, let's not be enemies! Let's stop, as sisters, the fighting, the bickering, the "Facebook" wars. I see some sisters that post one thing or the other on Facebook, and then the other sister posts something, and it becomes a back and forth battle. I am telling you all the truth. I have seen things tear sisters apart that is useless, petty and miniscule. Let's move away from this, and move forward. God is calling your names sisters, "march to the beat of God's drum and what he has in store for you as a sister, not an enemy." If we want our relationships to get better, we need to accept the truth of the 'evil' sin that follows us as sisters to only end up erupting like a volcano (the negative traits of the enemy). Let's not allow our feelings and complexes to destroy what God has for us as sisters, and our ability to bond. Let's not isolate ourselves any longer from each other, if we are true sisters, let's not miss a life time of pleasure, creation and development- and enjoyment as sisters.

Let's show the world and others that believe negatively, into the demise of sister-hood, something better. Let's go in the opposite direction. Let's show the world that we can come out on top. Let's work on being the best sisters possible! Let's carry on the name sake (family name) of_____ (you fill in the blanks) to be the best! Let's do this thing, sisters! Making your heart clean and pure unto your sisterhood and namesake. Do not allow the curse of distractions take you away from your sister group. Let's not allow acts through the "green eyed monster (slang for jealousy)" or any other psychological issues -deter "us all" from being a really good sister (to one another). As I am writing the Lord is showing me that there are sisters that want to love their sisters to the fullest, but they have been seen as an outcast, because they either have the same mother and not the same father or vice versa. God is saying half is okay, you can fit in. God wants you to yield to his will and his way, seek him and he will guide you or send an angel your way to help you bond with the sisters you so long for! This memoir is for you today!

Special Note: Other important topics that are relevant and vital to sisterhood mating and bonding!

More on Mothering Sisters This one is MORE, for the mothers of girls that are sisters. Mothers, when you have several daughters that are linked through the bond of sisterhood. Don't get in the way! Now, I am talking adult sisters, here, not the younger minor sisters. Let me be clear to all mothers of "sister groups". You hold a special positon. This position is to manage and aid your daughters when it is necessary, vital and needed, but not to be used to distance your girls by talking with one, about the other or taking inappropriate or "sneaky" sides. I have seen mothers take "sneaky sides", meaning they side with one daughter over the other, but they do it in a way that is somewhat sneaky or hidden (Due to some inner feeling that one daughter is better than the other)! Let's not do this, mothers, be upfront and honest, tell you children when they call you in some level of distress about a situation that may have occurred with them and a sister-that, "You need to talk it over with your sister"! I am staying out of this one! Allow get involved if you need to or if it is a dire situation! Furthermore, mother's don't allow your girls to pull you into the middle of their sister battles- I urge you to "Don't do this", it breeds strife and discontentment, because when the girls do come together, that is all that enters into their mind; whatever you put or discussed at the time-with the one daughter over other. It will cause your child or children to start looking at their sister in a oppositional or aloof (not friendly, not cool or distant) way!

Mother's you are often seen as somewhat of the "releaser stimulant," this is a term described, as a place where a child can release their issues, a place where all that occurs is stimulated in to your presence, a comfort level for your child or children, in other words. When your child or children come to you, stay as neutral as possible and if it gets too intense, you will have to call a meeting with your girls to let them hash it out, with you only- being the facilitator in your own special way! This keeps the heat off of you! Furthermore mothers, as a person that holds this position, often times the daughters or children will come expecting this. This can often be a challenge, I know, as you have to be "on the side" of all your girls (in a sense), to make them feel as if they can undoubtedly come to you and "release" or feel comforted. Be encouraged and EXAlLTED in THAT, mothers! Yet work your process right! You have to manage and maneuver the process carefully, gently and firmly, when called for. I think that as mothers, certain aspects of being a mother to girls, falls short, because one wants each girl to be right in her plight, but we all know that this is not always so! Mother's I understand the stress involved in this, but I say this to the good and perfection of your daughter's circle. Work on this and watch your daughters be strengthened in who they are as individuals and as a group, as a whole! On and on, mothers, I will continue to- hit this one straight-t forwardly, because sometimes, I see mothers use their positions incorrectly. So in saying that-mothers first, when God blesses your womb with more than one daughter, child, immediate preparation should take place. One should first learn your daughters apart from the love you have for them, so that you will know "how to love them, how to hold them and their individual hearts." Sometimes mothers do not have the line drawn and identified when it comes to relating to their daughters the way it should be. First one needs to be aware from a very early age, the various aspects of the "girl child."

The "girl child" is a unique speciman, with many different wants, needs and desires. A mother that knows how to, "pan it all out (so-to-speak)" when it comes to "her girls" is important. You just cannot give each one of your girls, the same portions (destiny or lot). One has to learn which portion (destiny or lot) is which, for each one of your girls. One girl, for instance, may require a lot of support (not control), while the other one may not, where one may require a bit more attention than the other, and then the next one may not, one may require a little more of toughness, while the other may not. It is a mother's duty to understand this and know where it applies, if you give the portions incorrectly, you will have a mess on your hands. If you try to steal one of your daughter's portions by motherly thievery, and give it to another to try to make your daughter-- that you feel is not meeting certain standards and guidelines, important, you will inevitably mess the portion disbursement up!

These things happen all the time, but God has come to you today, to let you know that this is not his way or his plan for your life a a mother of girls (or any child for that fact, but keeping in line with the subject) ! He is compelling you "mothers of girls" to get rid of the thoughts that you have, that have crept up in your mind that one daughter deserves this and one deserves that, that is God's job, you just manage it and endow them with your mother love in order to undergird your children with your love, support, compassion, understanding and motherly advise, not gossip, lies, schemes and inopportune intrusions!j Please do not apply your mother power improperly. Use your motherly-girl/daughter- power, that

God gave you in order to help groom, grow, facilitate and monitor your girls lives and situations. I am sure you understand! Read on!

Mothers-thoughts of you comparing one daughter to the next causes lots of emotional damage, deception and acts of disbarment. What do I mean by disbarment, the sister that sees you stealing the portion (destiny or lot) is going to get spiteful, vengeful and hateful. She will realize what you are trying to take that- which is hers (internally or outwardly), in order to give it to the other sister illegally. Yes, your daughter will know and she will sense it, feel it and take it in and become psychologically estranged and damaged! Please "mother of girls", don't take one child' s portion and give it to the other, it will never, ever work! My dear, "mother" (speaking in general), you may think they or that particular daughter may need it, but God may not, you may change a lifetime of inheritant gifts and destinies by altering God's plan for the portions that you daughters are due (individually and collectively). Mothers if you have acted and walked in this manner, it is okay, but now- it is time, for you to get it right, to make it right and repent! You can do it unto God and if you are strong enough you can do it unto your girls! It is totally up to you how you approach this situation, but do it. Mothers, if you have inheritantly made a mess of natural and physical allotments, this can be corrected to. Do it! Pray and ask God for guidance, he will show you how to handle your own unique "daughterly" situation! If you know you have made a mess of your girls. Get it right and get it right, while you still have time! Tomorrow, may be too late, especially in uncertain COVID-19 times, that we are in! Mothers, out there understand the bond!. Be successful with your girls, be a mother of truth and not a mother of lies and trickery (I know I will get in trouble for this, but it's okay, this one is for God's power to show forth in your life), don't be one that manipulates and pulls tricks that always shows- itself up later on. Jacob and Esau's mother, Rebekah (Genesis 27:1-46), manipulated God's plan for her sons, she told he youngest what to do to deceive his Dad into blessing him with his brother's birthrite. Rebekah, had no concern about God's plan, she made her own plans! She favored Esau over Jacob, for some reason, the bible does not clearly say why, but it is not hard to understand that mothers sometimes show favoritism with one child over the other and this is what Rebekah displayed. Don't rob one girl's gift for the other, don't do illegal "swip-swaps." We cannot reverse or replace God's portions that he has already assigned. Mothers don't do this, this can be a dangerous act. Give each daughter what they deserve, even If it is a small portion (but give them more as they need and deserve it), you will be doing them an in-service. Think on this Mother, what God has for the one that you think deserves more, God himself, can definately blow on it and make it a lot! His ways are not our ways, A thousand years is like a day and a day, as a thousand years unto the Lord (2 Peter 3:8) don't short change your "girl child", give her the proper portion and tell her, that is all you have, whether it is a lot or a little bit let her know that "God has the rest"! He will never fail! Nor will you, if you follow his plans for your girl child or children!

Lastly, God is calling for changes in these type of scenarios! I know this book is for sisters, but I am throwing one in their for all children, this should not be! Let go of the favortism and come correct! You maybe handing a child over something that they were not built to handle and will never be effective in! Don't feel like one child deserves this or that, because they are not as motivated as the next child! You can damage a child by giving them a mantle (important role or responsibility, in biblical terms, it was a cloak or shawl, worn symbolically to represent one's title or position) that's not theres! Mother's let's not do this anymore! It is time for a change! A little side note, mother's we know that sometimes one of your girl daughters may allow you to invoke your motherly power "over her" more than others, but don't take sides in that! Don't try to make her come up to the level of your other daughter, this is where the problems come in at! Let your daughter be who she Is ordained to be! Let her traits come out naturally, guidance is vital to your children, yes, but not manipulation, trickery and control! Realize this and stop trying to make up the slack, between your girls! Realize that one or some of your girls may be naturally more independent than others. Realize that one may not be as astute as the other one, realize that one may not have the character to take risks as the other one does, just open your eyes! You will be a success when it come to mothering girl daugthers, if you can grab a hold of this concept! Don't be like Rebekah (Genesis 27:1-46), by feeling that your daughter deserves this because you "feel" she is your favorite, feelings often get in the way of God's true devine plan! Let God arrive in your daughter's life!

Mothers plan conversations with your girls, when needed mothers, facilitate truth, not lies. Have confessionals. Be assured that adding confessionals to the group dynamic is vital to the functioning of girl children. I think that if this is adhered to, this is the lifeline of the sister's bloodline I think that If we teach our girl/daughters how to confess to each other as children, it won't be so hard when they get older. The bible talks about "confession " being good for the soul (Psalm 32, entire passage of scripture). I think that we have fallen short in that area. I say that because it is very hard for "us (as humans and sisters)" to confess or say when we are wrong. There is nothing wrong with saying that you are wrong, neither is there anything wrong with one being vulnerable around "supposed (I say supposed, because we often fail to realize this)" people that you love. I think that if we teach our children how to confess their faults to each other at very young ages, that the relationships amongst, not only among sisters, but children as well -will blossom and change in ways we could not imagine. But what is confession? Confession is defined as "a state of admitting one is guilty." A state of telling the truth, releasing, dumping, acknowledging. It is a state of renewal, this is why when people are on the stand and in court, those that dare to tell the truth, and when and after they do, they almost always speak of the relief it brings after holding the lie so long, even criminals, if it has been years, always speak to the burden that they carry for committing crimes that they had never told the truth about. Work on this mothers, watch the glow of your love sprout upon your daughters!

Confessing. Think on this, plainly admitting one's guilt is confession. I have watched television shows where investigators on now, current shows like "The Next 48 or Criminal Minds" interrogate their suspects, they seem to play on the fact that there is some "good" or "home" training "deep down in their sub-conscious and that with "softness" they can take that person back to that place where they were "TAUGHT" to be honest, fair, and of value. Most of the times, it works and the ones that do have that "training that comes from home" end up confessing. I elaborated in order to declare that "mothers old and young" if we teach our "girls" the art of "confessing, sharing their inner thoughts, feel-ings and emotions, this can alleviate much conflict and stress amongst sisters. Additionally, for mothers that are reading this book- that have daughters that are in constant conflict, try teaching them the "art of confession" it will prove for great healing, and bonding in the long run. As if they continue to hold "stuff" in, they will only damage themselves and their connections, or-- "what is left of a sister relationship that they have."

Feelings. Sisters, I know some of you are crying right now, I cried when the Lord revealed this to me, but was happy at the same time! Lets engage our feelings so that we can all be delivered and set free! Let's not carry these loads forever, life is just too short! Let's do this thing, no matter how hard or much it hurts! Now is the time to release those deep inner feelings and thoughts that were held in for so long, sisters to sisters, mothers to daugthers (girl children)!

Key Point (Other type of sisters) 12. Remember back in the days we heard the commercial, "Is it live or Memorex"! To ask if the sound of what we were seeing or experiencing was the "real thing" or not, in so many words, I want to use this analogy to compare the real sister versus the sister that is not birth or born of the same womb or flesh. Some of us in life will meet people over the course of life, that are not our birth sisters, God may send us someone in lieu of our birth sister for various reasons, the one that we have for instance, may not be walking in his perfect will, for one or the other sisters life. Furthermore, some type of estrangement may have crept up over the years, where one sister needed some-one they could allow themselves to be transparent within a relationship. Various other situations of life circumstances may have separated you, estranged you or removed you far from the connection that sisters would normally have such as foster care, adoptions, parental decisions, and many other life circumstances that may limit or hinder the normal sister bond. God will then place other sisters that often times that are often, put there by him. God will use this relationship to fill in the gap or sister that is missing or distant, to be just that for us, when our real, blood related sister or sisters just don't or won't do right!

As I talk about non-related sisters, that "just become"! This type of situation can cause the inner connection with a real or birth sisters to be broken or non-mendable oftentimes! This does not happen all the time, yet it does hap-pen! God will send you somewhere, " along the line a sister surrogate"! We all have them, some are just seen as passers-by, while there are others that stay and stay for a long time. There are some that we take in our hearts and deem them, as close as we would a blood tied sister or even closer! Let's address this type of sister! The surrogate sister is someone that you encounter in your life that is there for you! She helps you, she listens to you and she in some cases molds you! This is the one that listens to your dirt and doesn't look down on you (like a birth sister does sometimes or at least should be doing, if in the case it is not. Keep in mind-this particular portion of writing is ONLY deemed for those that it designed for)!We all have encountered them at some point and time in our lives that- surrogate sister, yes her! Sometimes we have them, even when we have biological sisters, and everything is going just fine, and there is simply nothing wrong! It can go in that direction, too, yes, "just like that"!

God will send you that someone, that is so inner connected to you, that she feels like you were birth from the same womb! She is"the" someone that understands you, the one that just "gets you" that connects to the depths of your soul the way a sister should. She is the person that has your back, the person that holds you when you need to be held from within, she is the one that wakes up in the middle of the night to hear of a disagreement, fight or issue that you have had with your spouse or significant other, she is that sister that they all say is from "another mother" She is like none other, she is your cheerleader and your warrior, she vows to be there from the start to the very end, this is the Gail to the Oprah, the Patricia to the Pam, the Nicole Ritchie to the Paris Hilton, you fill in the blank as to who is your God given surrogate sister!

There is often no explanation, as to how you got or became so connected, it is like you just know this person is special, and that you are soul tied and bonded like nothing you can explain, sometimes it feels better than a sister, yes, this can happen too ! God sends them to us all the time, that need them, and you don't have to feel bad about this sister, nor do you have to hide her from your real sisters! She is the one that you can ask her for money and she doesn't mind it, or hold it to you, and if she does, she is bold enough to ask you for it back without talking behind your back, she is the one you love, the one you send shout outs on Facebook,she is the one that you trust at all times, with your life, she is that soul sister, that "gold sister', she is the one that is not jealous of you and is proud of you! She is the one that would not take the money back if you did owe it to her, she has different personalties and different styles, she is that one that is made just for you! She is your surrogate sister! She is that one that you connect with like none other at times, yes, that is her. Sister surrogates are set in your life, as one that's there to fill a void. God sends us replacements for various reasons! Jesus when he ascended, said to his very own mother and a male figure that, "She is now your mother, and he is now your son, as to give his mother a replacement for the void, that she would have felt, because of his leaving (John 19:25-27, King James Version)". God allows this and it is perfectly alright for those of you that have struggled with this issue for a very long time!

God lets us know that it is okay to have sister surrogates when it comes to relationships. God will send us people that we bond with so closely that we feel that there is a deep inner connection that occurred from the foundation of the earth! A spiritual tie that goes so deep, you often wonder,how it came to be.Sometimes if you are too close, your bio sister, will get a little mad and a little jealous (in a

good way though, for the mature ones) It happens all the time and those of you that have surrogate sisters, because of some deficiency that caused you and your birth sister to not bond, it's still okay! So yes it is real, and it is "live"! God has ordained certain people for us, in this manner that add the spark that we need, or someone that enhances the bond that we already have with a functioning sister or sister group. This person 's spirit, can take us places that often times our birth siblings cannot. This surrogate is a substitute that infuses life in a different way. God allows us to connect to a person in a deep place of security and "I got your back" type of place in order to aid us in our aspirations, goals, and our daily walk and it is perfectly okay. Sometimes we find people that we connect with so, deep, until we think the same, act the same, and we see things the same! It can sometimes be a total out of body and inner body experience, with the surrogate sister that God connects you to!

There are some surrogate sisters that end up messy! Yes, there are those too! They come to tear a wedge between you and your birth sisters, to steal your place and throw the deep connection of your sister group into a wedge! Know the difference, you will know them by their fruit (Matthew 7:16, King James Version), by their authencity! We all know when something is true and real, and in the same token, false and fake! For those of you that know diamond classes or grades, there are classed with alphabets from D to Z with classes of clarity being at its highest at "D" meaning it is a colorless diamond! We should all know the class of a person, by paying attention to what they are bearing! The evidence of their actions, the sincerity in their eyes, the responses that they give, the reactions that are apparent! Yes pay attention to the themes of behaviors and you can and will be able to tell if this surrogate sister was a "tare" that came to evade the wheat! Confusion, controversy, tale bearing, nosiness, false-support, false concern, you name it, this will be the characteristics of a false, or opportunistic sister that came in posing as a true sister surrogate. Be on alert and aware of a true colorless sister surrogate (best quality diamond) versus a fake surrogate with no clarity (low quality/graded diamond) there are always tell-tale signs! Learn them and then boot the "fake surrogate out". Life is short, no time to waste! Let's do this thing! It's all in the name of sisters!

Special Note: More on Sister Relationships _Sisters_ when you are burdened with the inner issues of sisterhood begin to seek peace. Seek solitude, seek the presence of God. Rachel and Leah (Genesis 29:1-35, King James Version), as I mentioned earlier, from the Bible, didn't understand their purpose. God had a purpose for Leah, but she was so blindsided by her sister's life, that she could not see what was going on in hers. We have to stay focused on what is ahead and current in our individuals lives, and not worry about what you see going on in your sister's life.

More on Leah and Rachel In exploring the lives of Rachel and Leah (Genesis 29:1-35, King James Version), Leah was chosen first, but later "put behind the scenes," based on customs required at that time. Leah felt like (in my view) like someone was playing with her life, consequently Leah was not aware of the circumstances surrounding her "God given" position, or she would not have been so jealous or insecure. Rachel on the other hand was feeling the same insecurity and jealousy towards her sister because she too was envious of her sister's abiiity to have children . Both desired what the other had and were not thankful for what God had given them! How many times are we both looking at each other, wishing and desiring secretly "that something", our sister has! This is a travesty! We should know what we have and what has been given to us to enhance God's kingdom! Sister's lets not continue to fall prey to the 'enemies' traps, schemes and tricks, and ultimately- begin to secretly feel insecure or eye our sister's lot! Let's be thankful with the lot that God has granted us! I just woke up from my nap, today on November 1, 2020 while editing my book. I was awakened by Bishop T.D. Jakes, a famous world renowned preacher, nationally acclaimed man of the cloth, dispatcher of God's word, via my phone repeating the words "Know your role". In the sermon he spoke of John the Baptist and how Jesus referred to him as the greatest. The explanation and total summation of that awesome word, as I lay half awake, but came to total consciousness after I heard these words were, that "John the Baptist was referred to as the greatest, as he knew who he was, he didn't compare him to no other disciple, apostle, minister or anyone else, he simply was John the one that was the forerunner, the one that came before Jesus, the one that presented Jesus (Matthew chapter 11:9-11, King James Version)! But, - the thing that got to me, was when Bishop Jakes said that, "How many times do we secretly compare or measure ourselves up to others" and for how many years have we been tormented by this"? God is saying to us all as, sisters, stop comparing yourselves, I have said this throughout the book, but it came to light even more so by the hearing of this message. It is time to be the best you and sister that you, yourself, can be! Stop looking at your sister's ability to do this or do that and say within yourself, "why wasn't it me, that had this instead of her". Don't do this to yourselves any longer my dear sisters! Read on!

More Rachel and Leah examples (sister roles and birthorder).Elder sister roles, such as Leah and Rachel can sometimes pose problems. Because it seems that, Leah didn't understand her role and how powerful it was. Leah, didn't realize that she had power, authority and a nature that elicited being the one, yes the first! How many times do we as a sisters forget the unspoken rule, the eldest is normally first! That is normally how it goes, that is how the order is built. The first one out of the womb, has the privilege, as well as the responsibility (don't forget that) Leah, didn't know, this though, or realize- her worth. I want you all to be patient, as you read this part of the book. I know some may feel this is totally wrong, because some "baby, middle or whichever position you hold in the birth order" you may feel you were first in situational circumstances. But, let me elaborate first before you get upset. Alfred Adler, a psychologist talks on the eldest position, in his book on birth order, he describes their role as somewhat being "in the highest" position, in other words, he talks about how the eldest child, is normally the "first", in most things, as research has proven, yet he goes on at some point to explain how the eldest can sometimes forfeit their position. Additionally, some articles point out, "too," that the "firstborn (of any gender)" do amazing things. The reports point to "first born children being A-Type, ex-troverts (in most cases)." I read that a lot of Astronauts are first born's. Presidents where first born's, CEO's were first born, so on and so on. Some people believe that "first borns" are more intelligent, wiser, head strong, resilient, unyielding, focused, self-centered, and self-motivated and the list goes on," and this is okay. If your oldest sister has the goods, it is okay, don't fret, because whatever she has, you have- somewhat in your blood, but just not in the same way. Don't worry about your sister having something that you think you want or should have, like Leah did, focus on "Your own self (like my grandbaby Memphis says)," in so many words! Because without a doubt being the Eldest child comes with a price!

Special note parental problems.At times, sisters, we are put in situations by our parents, loved ones, or caregivers when we are a child that tend to provoke certain warped inner emotions, feelings and dispositions! Sin visits us down to the third and fourth generations (Exodus 34:7 King James Version). Due to this happening often times we are faced with scenarios that cause us to end up low in areas of communication, honesty, integrity and more. Sometimes sisters, the problems that your sister group is facing, maybe a figment of something that was passed down to you from your forefathers! It may not be something that just sprung up. It maybe a family curse that needs to be dealt with! Explore it! Deal with problems that were invoked upon you as sisters, that was outside of your control!

Now going back to Rachel and Leah. I want to note that my purpose in highlight-ing this is because, Leah, did not understand her position, nor did she under-stand her sisters position, in God's plan for their lives. God had a plan for both, although we do not live in "several wife marriages" in the United States, this was customary in those times. Leah, was so focused on what her sister was getting and not focused on what she had, and what God used her for, the phenomenal "her" that she was at that time because, she was drowned and submerged into her feelings of displacement and disdain about herself and who her sister was. You see, that is what is wrong with we sisters, we do not understand our role, our strengths and our weaknesses as being a firstborn sister, a middle born sister and a baby sister or "somewhere in there or in between sister." I say, again, knowing your purpose, and having confidence in your purposed objective, stretches your self-esteem and confidence to levels from within that you forget about what is all the confusion that the enemy tries to invoke in the the sister group.

A primary example, is with the Braxton family values show (my opinion and interpretation) was that at the time of crisis prior to the visit to Iyanla Vanzant, Traci (one of the middle sisters), was too focused on what her sisters had and not so much what God had purposed for her. It was not until later in the seasons that she realized that she had purpose, a call an objective that she could use for herself, her life and for her family. She always projected herself as being "numb" and would always point to, what her sisters did or didn't do unto her. She would often bring up, how she had to step aside, during the initial phases of the Braxton Sister's career- due to her personal life. Her down trodden state always showed up in her actions or sullen outlook towards the sister group (my opinion). There was a lot of rage that would creep up with Traci, because in my opinion she seemed to feel as if she was left behind or missed her opportunity. I mean no harm my dear Braxton sisters, that rage will often times show it's ugly head, if a sister does not find herself. Sisters, lets' get this point, if nothing else, that we need to deal with our inner issues and grow, stop holding on to something that happened years and years ago. I realized this though, that forgetting the past is something that we all have to grow into. Lets take the time to process one's hurt in order to be able to grow out of the holding cell of pain, hurt and misunderstanding into growth, power and strength! Sisters lets work on the remedies that we need to in order to heal. Lets' begin to pray, fast, and seek your own counseling apart from your sisters to first deal with ourselves, if you are indeed are in this particular place. Know yourself, don't be like Leah (Genesis 27, King James Version, the entire chapter) and worry yourself to death (so-to-speak) because of your focusing on your sister and not yourself. Let your sister be your sister and let you be you!

Let's try to understand these things, in order to expand and empower ourselves. Ask yourselves, "Why am I the oldest, why did God make me the the baby" what is my purpose in being the oldest or the youngest, or middle child for that fact? How can I add to being a good sister, how can I add to being a valuable sister. How can I stand strong and "hold onto" the position that I was born into, and not worry about my sister's so much? What is my purpose for being born into this family at this particular time? If we understood these things, we would make for great service not only to our sister, but to society as well. You see Leah, the youngest sister had a purpose, she birthed the tribes of Judah, her sister had the same purpose and was a part of delivering children that were to be used for God's glory and purpose. You will hear more on this throughout. Now what is your sisterly purpose?

Realizing you importance as a sister (Dissecting Leah)Let's take a deeper look at Leah. Leah had seven sons from the Patriarch Jacob (Genesis 29:31-35, King James Version). Leah yet, did not realize the importance of who she was. Leah did not know, nor did she value her worth. Leah, if she knew this, I am sure things maybe would have been different for her, personally and internally. Leah didn't realize that she was not any less of a person, because she felt, that she was not loved, as her sister was. The relationship that she got put in was by choosing of the "father (Leah's and Rachel's Dad)" and she was not Joseph's first choice, although it was God's choice. You see, we have to understand what God is purposing in our lives, and when we miss that, we miss our identify and calling. Leah, was used for purpose, but she didn't realize it. She had a powerful role in birthing God's chosen people into the earth. Often times, when we lack the ability to see God's purpose, we end up depressed, lonely, feeling rejected, and dejected. That is not how God wants it to be. Let's all take a lesson from Leah, and realize what our purpose is, let's not let an insecurity set us back for a lifetime. With that being said, How many times do we, as sisters, see one little narrow eyed insecurity, and allow it to be the actual "apple" of our eye and then it becomes "sour," because we are so focused, "only on this one little thing" regarding what our sister's issue meant to us, and not to the situation that was occurring. We miss out on so much love and life, when we allow our hearts to turn "inside out"- towards our sister, because of lack of understanding or perspective, in who we are as individuals and then how we are as sisters. We need to learn this principle and learn it fast! It will make a world of a difference!

Why did Leah not focus on her blessings that God gave her in which were her sons? Why did Leah not realize that she was 'just as chosen' as Rachel by being able to birth her husband's sons, the very men that would carry the tribes of Judah. The importance of what she represented was diminished (in her very own eyes) and she lived a seemingly depressed, sad, and burdensome life, being more concerned with what was going on with her sister's blessing and not her blessings. How many of us, as sisters, take our whole lives to focus on what our sister has and what we do not have, instead of being thankful to God for who he made us to be. Leah, failed to realize that her sister was indirectly envying her ability to have children (more on that later). Rachel was not able to conceive and she herself, was burdened because of this. Her sister and she were caught in the crossfire of wanting what the other one had, and not realizing the individual/unique gift that God had given and purposed in each one their lives.

Now let's look at Rachel, the other sister described as "beautiful in the eyes of Jacob (in so many words Genesis 20:17-18 King James Version)." Let's look at Rachel's issues, because she had them too! As beautiful as she was, as attractive as she was, she had some serious issues too, that were not so obvious! Often times beautiful women or women seen as highly attractive have problems like any other woman. The world is often blindsided with outer appearance and this can happen in sisterhood too! We can feel that because one sister my have certain features that are a bit more attractive, whether it is "outer or inner"; as a threat!. We can secretly look at our sister's ability as something that is "side-swipping us (a figure of speech)". We can go all of our lives holding in the thought of "who does she think she is" ! These thoughts can come from things that happened and were highlighted long, long, ago! Rachel was described as being one way and her sister the other, both in opposing places internally and psychologically! Is this you? Are you being spell bound, by something that you sister holds, no matter what it is and what you think you don't have or are incapable of doing or being? Ask yourself, dig deep down inside. Know this my dear sisters, the decriptions that both these women held, were just that 'descriptors'! What is your descriptor, as a sister? Identify yourself! Speak now or forever hold your peace! Know yourself sisters!

Sisters realize that all of us have a "vice or achilles heal"! Sisters let's learn from Rachel and Leah's examples, by "not" down playing what we have. Both felt they had nothing, when they both had it all.

Think on times, sisters when we feel, think and act like Rachel having it all, but in our own eyes really having nothing, Rachel felt nothing towards how she looked and how she was adored, she worried her husband for something that he could not give her, she asked for something that had to be approved by God, something that God had to deliver to her, and it was not her husband . (Ask yourself -what is it that God has to deliver to you that you have yet to realize)? Sisters, listen carefully, no one can deliver to you, what God has for you, not your sister, not your mother, not anyone in this earth, can set your soul or your "identity," in a place that is to be "set" by God. No matter who you are or what you are in or out of when it comes to your sister bond, know that God is the first and the last to sustain you. Grab ahold of your confidence, of your esteem, of your drive! Read on!

How many of us, are already gifted and "got it going on" and are down on ourselves because we "don't really think so (so to speak)." Keep this in your heart, souls and mind sisters that are reading this book that, just because your sister was always the favored one (in your mind), don't think she does not have problems, weaknesses, and tears. God planned for your sister to be born on the day and hour that she was to be born on and you the same! Be proud, be happy about the day your mother bore you into this earth, let the torment of your soul aloose!

Just a little joke! The scriptures gives some insight on the rivalry that occurred between two sisters 'married' to the same man, can you imagine, can you (LOL)? It is one thing when, I am sure women had to be married to one man, at the time and they are blood sisters, but imagine being married to a man and that you had to share him with your "own" blood sister (*some of you already know*, even though this was intended as a joke)!.

Don't be like Leah and Rachel, "fighting the wind," striving for something that was a hindrance and not their purpose, how many times do we miss out because of one not having the knowledge. Leah was the mother of a good portion of the birthing of the 12 tribes of Israel (what an honor), and she could not focus on her position and role, because she was internally not satisfied with who she was, and who God created her to be. What if God is trying to "birth" a nation out of you and you are blind-sided by your sister's stuff or your stuff to be exact, something you lost, something you missed or think you have missed, something you are desiring, 'painstakingly' and it is just not happening for you. Stop antagonizing yourself the way these two sisters did and take a look at yourself and what God is trying to get into you and through you! Be reminded that God CHOSE both of these women and their issues! God closed Rachel's womb until he was ready for it to happen, is it that your womb is closed because God has it closed, (speaking metaphorically, and for some it maybe literally), something Rachel had longed for, but could not, because God had 'closed her womb'. What you are feeling, my dear sister, is a closed womb in a certain area of your sisters life and a open womb in your sister's life, believe me, it is for a reason!

Sisters, don't straggle along in life, thinking secretly to yourself, if I only had what she had, my life would be so much better, nonsense! You have what you have, and she has what she has to be a blessing! Don't think these thoughts any longer, such as, " If she would have not been so prized in Momma's or Daddy's eyes, my life and hers would be different". Please, Please Cast down those vain images (I Corinthians 10:5-7, King James Version) Let it go.! Anything that is exalting itself against God's knowledge is to be left, to be forgotten, is to be fought hard for removal! This "part" is not intended to be humorous, this is serious, it is to help some of you sisters out there that's focused so intensely on what your sister has, until you cannot focus on what you have, this is what happened to Rachel and Leah.

Satisfaction.Women, learn to be satisfied (fulfilled) with who you are and not who your sister is and vice versa. Work on your problems and stop trying to get a PhD in your sister's affairs (the air she breathes and 'everything else)'. Pay attention to what is common and customary in your life. Satisfaction is feeling the fulfillment of one's expectations. Feel your deep rooted desires and what is important to you. Find your place of rest, your place of satisfaction, and watch what God does for you and your sister group!

Robbery! Sisters don't rob one another of their devices. Don't sit back and mimick or overlord a place that is not yours! It will always be apparent who the thief is! Don't allow yourself to continue to try to imitate your sister or her things, be your true, "authentic" self. Robbery is against main's law and it is against God's law. Be who you were created to be!

Insight! Know this, there is always one sister that sets the stage in a family, it was Toni Braxton for the Braxton's, it was Beyoncé for the Knowles family, Although we don't hear much about this, it was Rebbie Jackson for the Jackson girls (Michael Jackson's sisters). Excel in your gift girls! Move on and upward! Don't hold back, hide back or pull back! Be the first! Do and act out your purpose! Bring the family of sisters where they need to be! Other sisters, stand in support and watch you all be blessed because of her one single gift that God gave one particular sister or it maybe several if, of a larger sister group, there are many possibilities, the goal in this memoir is to understand what your individual and group possibilities are!

More on- Special EXCEPTIONAL Mothers of Sisters (Positions). Our mothers are normally our source of strength and power. A good mother has the ability to be there for her children, no matter how many in number. A good mother is able to maneuver through the conflict, the trials and ills of sibling rivalry. This mother knows what to say to each one of her children and what "not" to say to the other (and she doesn't stir the pot in between, if you know what I mean). This mother knows and identifies which one of her children needs more affection than the other, and she has the ability to apply her special touch where it needs to be to enhance it, give it or take some of the pain away, as the order it appears in. This mother gives valuable information to her mature daughters to empower them to be stronger, while she tends to the weaker of her daughters. She is not the type of mother that takes sides for favoritism, but she takes sides to promote growth and development for each one of her children. This mother is concerned about what her daughters act and feel and she is totally gifted at making them all feel special. She also knows when her daughters do not need to be made to feel special, and starves them in order to solicit growth. The special mother knows "what is what", and can decipher through the problem exceptionally well when it comes to her girls. Sometimes she will sit and let it all pass over her head, until her girls fix it themselves. She is a wise mother and knows when silence is the best remedy for girl children controversy (from her perspective).

A mother that gives nothing is always giving something, even though it may not feel that way at the time, A wise mother floods her bed with tears when she is not able to give, when God tells her not, to, but she recognizes the need for suffering and allows her daughter to do so, for the will of God to come forth. A good mother knows and recognizes the hand of God on her daughters and allows them to walk their own path, even when it hurts. A wise mother will know when God says to "Snatch her out" or when "that is enough". A wise mother of sister groups (her daughters), will be very attentive and if "nothing" is what she has to give to her daughters, she lets them know, as to communicate God's plan to them, even if it is her removing her hand and let God's hands work instead. This Is a very special mother. She will spend lots of time on the road to make sure that all of her daughters have support, when they are happy, when they are sad, when they are sick. She will be there to support, back- up and even fight for her daughters if she has to. A wise mother will not fight for her girls, when she knows that they are wrong, she will gently, yet firmly let her daughters know when the time is not right for her to be involved and will gently and lovingly- bow out. A wise mother will intervene when God's voice tells her so and then alone, will she fight with all her might in prayer and supplication on her girls behalf. A wise and good mother of sibling sisters, knows her plight and knows how to manage and maneuver being accused of favoritism, as she is not afraid to say, "Yes, I favor her, as she is to be favored at this point and time," You work on your favor and leave your sister's alone, this is done properly, not with malice, but with grace, truth and intregrity! She is a special mother, she truly understands how to "mother manage" her girls. This mother does not fall short of standing up for herself and not allow her daughters to use her callously, although she spoils them "just a little (smile)."

The opposite. But what about the mother that does not know how to? She some-times gets confused in the acts of one sibling, daughter- to the next. What should a mother do? How should a mother behave when her children, mainly her "girls" are always at "each other's throats"? Should she, side with one over the other, when there are brutal combative wars amongst her children/girls? Even though she may know who is right and who is wrong. Or should she blatantly, choose sides no matter what, or should she remain neutral? What if at times she cannot remain neutral, what should a mother do? Read on. Some mothers are pulled in several different directions when she has more than one daughter, because she sees some of her in each one of them, and sometimes she wants to expand the extension of her within her girls. She also wants to love, and hold them dear and wants them all protected, but at times it cannot be done, and a mother is pulled into the middle of a big "spat" of some sort with her daughters. A wise mother can maneuver this, but lots of mothers cannot, causing increased pain amongst sisters, as well as the mother themselves. Mothers don't be the source of your daughter's pain, if you are confused on how to parent 'adult daughters' seek guidance through prayer or professional help. Don't; allow the smart alec, daughter that is bold enough to accuse you of hi- jacked biases get away with it! Choose wisely and seek Godly advice and outside professional help as warranted. You will find your answer there.

Mothers don't!Mothers, this section is for you. I have seen some mothers take the side of one daughter over the next and, cause great grief, in a bad way, not in contradiction to my words a few paragraphs above. Don't do this, unless it is totally unfathomed, and full of God's indignance towards wrong behavior.If one of your daughters is causing great grief to the group, this must be addressed. Don't take a side because you feel sorry for a daughters situation or plight. You have to dissect the reason she is there, the reason she got there and deal with it, not take her side, in pitty and cause it to grow worse.

Mothers, be one hundred percent assured and ready to deal with your girls. I have seen some mothers degrade, belittle, and gossip about their daughters to the next daughter and cause resentment to show up because there is always a sense of "de-tection there" where the sister can actually sense being talked about by her mother and sisters, some do not even have to use their "sensing abilities," some get told by the other sisters that Momma said this or Momma said that, this should not be so! For those sisters that are strong don't hurt your sister, by telling her this, pray and ask the Lord to allow your "tongue to cleave to the roof of your mouth" if it is a dire situation that your sister cannot handle. Be mature, be strong save your sister the hurt and pain, don't do this to her, if you know she is already bruised by, and within the sister bond and the motherly relationship. Don't "get stimulated " by thinking you are getting ahead, because in the end we all lose!

Now I am sure I will get highly criticized by now, for saying this, but I must a lot of mother-daughter relationships have been a total mess and mothers of girls, you must take the blame. I want this memoir to be a book of healing, so I must address it all. All that has affected the sisterly bond! READ on!

"Mom's this message is for you, it is time for you to mature and grow up with your children. It is time for you to be a Mother, and not a "Sister," it is time for you, if there Is time left, to take off your partying shoes and come out of the clubs (so to speak) with your daughters, put on your church shoes and dress and take your children to church (in a manner of speaking). It is time for you to be an example to your girls. Now is the time, to become aware of your mistakes and work on change (*if this is not for you, just read over it, my dear sisters, God has something for everyone*).

Being a mother one must show unprecedented support, yet stay in her "motherly" corner, as to not solicit her own personal, hidden agenda amongst her children. Some mothers willingly live out their lives through their daughers, as in the cae of Jone Benet Ramsey, a story that I watched and watched and watched. She was found dead in the basement immediately after she lost a pageant. The Mom and Dad says that someone broke in the house, and killed her, what a bunch of crap (my opinion)! When a mother tries to live her past life out with her daughters or daughters, it will become a disaster! Know this!

Moving right along, In the Bible (I Kings 3:16-28 KJV), King Solomon had to make a decision between two mothers that argued about a baby saying 'He is mine and the other saying he is mine, one said their baby died during The night and the other said one, she stole my baby, yet while I slept, the other's one's baby died." It was a mess, but what the King decided to do was to allow the baby to be "split" down the middle and the 'selfish" mother said, yes, let it happen, while the other decided "No"-let her have him. The king knew from that act of sacrifice, that the true mother was the one willing to give up her rights, (1 Kings 3:16-28, King James Version) to see her child live, and this caused her to be rewarded her child. She was willing to allow life versus death. The point was to show, how as mothers, we must often be "selfless," we must always think on the best interests of our daughters. We must give up our rights for a wrong situation allow the "girls" to mend, grow and continue to live. In saying this, mothers, do not allow one daughter to hold you hostage against the next daughter. In other words, do not allow the guilt of one daughter, to keep you from relating to, or hold back from another daughter. Sometimes in relationships with sibling girls, it can be really easy to slip into "siding with one daughter" over the next, because of the personality of the children. All daughters have different personalities. One may be an outgoing extrovert (finds stimulation from the outside or outer things), while another daughter or several may be introverts (tend to be quiet and dis-tant, not as talkative as the next, moody, etc.). One of your daughters may have a personality that is weird that, you "yourself (mothers)" cannot understand and you become confused or uneasy, because you may feel you could never "really reach" your daughter, don't believe this, a mother can reach their child whether in good or bad, they will respond. Don't let this stop or alienate you from your child, she is your special being, something that you 'pushed' out into the world, if I may say so, she is something you allowed to move and grow into a creation from God, your child, your daughter.

Point. Most daughters want their mother's seal of approval on serious or sensitive issues . I have spoken a lot of the plight of how "mothers should be", with their daughers. Mothers, I want you to take this information and use it to your good. Take this information that seems harsh and cold hearted to a place of reckoning. To a place of reparation. It will hurt and make you feel bad at times, but when you come out, you will "see the light", you will begin to feel brand new, this is all what COVID-19, in the spirit is doing to all of us, digging out dirt and making us all feel like we should repair ourselves! So- Let's do this! Thank you God!

I am sure you are asking, but how do I do this, how can I get along with this one particular daughter, you do not know my child, she is like a "thorn in my flesh." She torments me with her actions, she did it in my womb and she is also doing it outside of my womb and it is causing me pain still until this day. I know this book is about "sisters" and how they are "torn apart," yet I wanted to explore all venues that led to the sometimes, tormented "sister" relationships. Mothers if this is you, work on talking to all your children, work on letting them know that you are the mother of them all, and that you love them all, but that sometimes "some of them" act in a manner that is most distressing to you causing you to act in a manner that is most, inappropriate (you fill in the blanks). You will really be amazed at how things can and will change if you put forth the effort to make all of your daughters feel accepted, wanted, appreciated and most of all forgiven.

One final point on Rachel and Leah. Now let's move on, even further. Let's back track and explore a bit more. Rachel and Leah (From Genesis 29, King James Version) were not bonded. I say this because, sisterhood is supposed to be a serious bond and connection like none other, but in the 21st century, sisterhood has become a place of competition, jealously and torment. Let's look back at Leah. Leah was a blessing within her own rite; she had prominence and power at her fingertips. She did not realize the very thing she carried, delivered, and received was the thing that her sister desired (at least that is what she thought). See Rachel was envious in some ways of her sister too, because she wanted children and, she could not bear in the beginning. Rachel had her hang ups as well, but no one knew it. See the Rachel's in the world are the ones that are most insecure and 'without' but they don't get the time to mourn, complain or talk about it because of the pressures put on them by family, friends, society, etc. to perform and produce. This is normally the "Bronze (is the term I will use, for the purpose of this book)," you see Bronze is a high quality piece of alloy used for many different things. The sister that is considered the "Bronze" Is normally the one that gets all the attention, is revered and desired by most in the community in the home, you name it. I was marveled at what Oprah was told by Beyoncé recently during her interview that she is 'just like any other woman'. I know this may sound repetitive, but for some reason, God has me harping on these issues, some of you may be able to catch it after a while.

We often miss this, and we think, people like Beyoncé and others like her, are 'superwomen' when they are just as human as we are, but as Oprah put it 'with more shoes and square feet' (LOL) Often times one sister thinks one sister thinks she is 'better than' or 'more than (and some of us really believe we are better)' but do not realize the sister that seemingly gets all the attention, but is secretly and deeply dealing with issues of insecurity and other problems, you may not even dream she has. She battles herself, but she often keeps her hurts and pains to herself, as she knows she will get accused further, as being the bad 'guy or girl' somehow. The Rachel's in the world are the physically attractive, physically popular, educated, powerful, and prestigious. Now in some cases it is not all about looks. To the outsider it is, but I am willing to bet some of the most beautiful women in the world feel totally flawed. I am sure that through all the plastic surgeries, with the tucks of this 'and tucks of that', there lies 'underneath' insecurity. I saw a show where a woman increased her "breasts" to a size that was astronomical and in my opinion, that was for the constant washing of her masked pain and insecurities. It was not what was going on the outside of her, it was what was inside her head that was tormenting her, desire to have surgery after surgery. Is that you? Are you sister, being tormented by what is inside your head and not what is really the unadulterated truth?

The Rachel's in the world, appear one way outwardly, yet they are really another way secretly. The Rachel's in the world are overlooked and side swapped, because they are taken by the world, and set up to perform unto the world, their families, their children, the community and-so- they do not have time to tend to their own 'garden's. You see the Rachel 'sisters' are the ones that tend to love hard, work hard and give unconditionally hard! They are image bound! They fight to show an image *(yet deep inside, they are not fully what they claim to be). The Rachel's of the world are constantly trying to make sure everybody else is sat- isfied, and secure while ending up with many burdens, and infirmities that are never talked about out loud. This is because of 'who they are'. See the "Rachel's" issues of bareness were not as highlighted as Leah's issues with not being loved. It seemed that the problems that Leah had were very vivid, while Rachel's were not as, because she was 'one of great beauty' and 'beautiful to look upon'. How many times does the sister with these traits get over looked right in plain sight!,

**Understanding the Pain** Let's look at another group of sisters, but this time another kind of sister group-Sister-In-Laws-Ruth and Orpah **(Ruth Chapter 1, in its entirety, King James Version)**. Ruth and her sister, were both married to-two brothers that both died. Ruth took her blessing, while Orpah did not. Ruth decided to stand in faith and wait on her blessing, Orpah chose to walk away not realizing she was in a blessed place with her Mother in law Naomi. You see some sisters chose to suffer and wait, while others chose to take the easy route. What sisters fail to realize that suffering brings blessings and when one sister suffers to be blessed the others will reap the benefits if they 'faint not'. Know your suffering state and sit in it. Know how you are supposed to suffer within and the time that you have to go through to get to your destiny as well as your identity. A special piece of advice though, for those of you that don't quiet get this principal for yourselves, "allow the sister time"; that it is- to reign and stand, this is because sometimes God choses one sister to profit, yet to benefit another. What do you mean by that, there is almost always one sister that is privileged? That does NOT mean, that the one sister that is not in the 'spotlight' or is not as blessed, it just means that one person is equipped enough, faithful enough, resilient enough, and persistent enough to cope with what it takes to stand evolve and take risks. I think that is the problem with a lot of sister relationships, we, as sisters do not realize that not all sisters will be at the "front of the line (so-to-speak)." Some sisters may not be seen at all (it just, may not be your purpose). You see when this realized, then it will make life a lot better. It will enhance one's relationships with one's sister, because,we- all will realize where we- belong and where God ordained for- us all to be. It makes life a lot easier, when one understands your place in the "scheme of things." Remember, that God's sight is not your sight. God does not see things as mankind does.

Don't continue to fret over something that God designed. Don't think that because you have not always been called on, pointed out, or esteemed openly, that you are not special, because you are. In God's eyesight you are the "one," know this that - not all physical positions are as special as you think. I want those of you that have been striving to be in the front and it has not quite worked out for you to realize that being behind the scenes can be just as important as being in front of the scenes, and you know why? Because God has a rightful place for us all. A lot of sisters waste valuable time trying to prove a secret point to themselves and their sister counter parts that they are "just as good". This should not be! It is really a sad thing to see. I see it on television, I see it in real life, I have seen it in my life and how sisters do things to "out beat" the other because they have insecurities that they do not deal with. This causes burdens, stress, separation and a lot of hurt. Facing, who you are and not 'brushing up against (figure of speech)", what your sister is, so that you can grow up and in with your sisters.

If we all understand how to play our parts, this would be the resolve to most sister problems or relationships. Lots of us, blame the other, when it is really something we need to explore on the inside of us. I truly understand this and once you understand yourself, your life will go well with your sister or sisters.

I got more on-this, let's take a look at the Kardashians (reality show stars, my opinion, please remember this), for instance, it seems that Kim (and she is the middle child of the Kardashian, my opinion and personal view) is the most popular of the family, although each sister has their own thing going on. Kim is the middle child, of the older set of girls. Often we think that the middle child is 'doomed' because of the 'so-called' middle child syndrome. Somehow Kim, got pushed to the front and this happens, if you didn't know them, you would think that Kim is the oldest, I knew that I used to. With sisters this happens a lot, a sister that is not the oldest, sometimes, gets forced into the front and takes over the eldest sister's role. Sometimes that one particular sister, may have what it takes to be upfront. We have to weigh the odds. When one sister comes to the front not by rank, but by some process of life, various simulations will occur.

Sisters may get a positive plus (adding positives) or a negative plus (addng negatives) a push forward, (the extra drive), as they tend to feel left out. I have examined middle children, male and female and it seems that they all have this one thing in common and that is drive. The strive to get further, because they are deemed as not high enough to get over and not low enough to get under (a phrase from Michael Jackson's song). If you are a middle child in your sister group, don't get caught in the trap. The "middle child syndrome" is a psychological concept and barrier that is often set in the minds of humanity to enforce a single belief that one cannot go forward because of the oldest child being the oldest, and one cannot "go backwards" because one is always looking down at the baby or youngest child. In other words the oldest gets all the attention, power and knowledge while the "baby" of the family is always the special one, the last born (baby) is seen as, the apple in everyone's eye. This should not be, but it is. We all should have a certain type of self-worth and dignity, not allowing birth order to be warped within our thinking. Now, I will say that birth order is important in certain things for certain people, so I am not saying it is totally irrelevant, because I would start a psychological war. Therefore, let's look at birth order from a perspective of a sister building, growing and finding her place. Don't allow inner and outer turmoil to take your place. Beat the odds!

SPECIAL NOTE: if you are a middle sister that has inner insecurities, due to you feeling that the baby is better and the oldest is brighter, "ditch "those thoughts. Know that everyone has a gift, a look, a talent, a special catch or anointing that God has blessed you with. Do not focus so much on what your sister is doing or has. Get that barrier or strong hold of a "mindset" out of your life. Don't continue to let the mindset take your life to a place of doom and destruction. I say this because I have heard stories of sisters that fight, bicker, and argue so much until they end up not liking each other, "at all" and they show no remorse or shame for it. Sisters, realization is the key. Know where the door is in your sister group. Realization is the key to growth, determination and success within your sister group! Realize your potential within the context of what you have! If one can realize how their potential can really sprout you all forward in life, in order to excel and prosper. Don't let your sister become the enemy.

With one particular episode of "Iyanla fix my life" series- three sisters were bickering and arguing over family secrets and one sister was said to be 'nasty' 'un-caring', rude and unfair to the other two. They felt that the sister covered for their abuse and supported their mom's wrong doing. This sister left the scene and did not come back after several pleadings from Iyanla. Do you see yourself in any of the sisters described? If so, begin to do soul searching. Begin to ask yourself where do I fit in the sisterhood vibe? Am I the sister that loves, supports, cares for everyone in my family? Or am I the sister or sisters who brings havoc on the family avoids, shuns or runs away when things get tough? Test this sisters and see how you come out? We have to get to the bottom of things before we get to the top. So let's take a look at sabotage. Sabotage is the act of delibereately destroying or tearing something or some one down.

Sabotoge I have seen and experienced from afar, sisters that sabotage one another. This is done, by lying on one sister or the other, by destroying relationships, interference, meaning one sister may intrude upon another sister's relationships and cause problems or "rob" one sister of a close friend or relationship. I have seen some sisters who take their sister's boyfriends, husbands or significant others into their own hands, thinking they have finally won, that they have finally gained security or a stance that makes them feel better than, more secured or poised than one of their sisters. These horrible acts can be done by a sister attempting to 'captivate or embellish' her sister's companion with sensual, yet luring ways.

Why does one sister feel the need to destroy the other? Is it because she is jealous, feels overlooked or is it because she is just plain 'ole' full of hatred and malice and cannot shake it. Or is it that she likes the way she feels towards (the evilness inside) her sister. If anyone of these descriptions fit you, it is time to take on some soul searching. It is time to go! Yes go forward in getting to the root cause of this issue and change it!

Key note for mothers (little bit more), take your daughters by the hand, don't pit one against the other. See their gifts and potential and do your motherly thing to enhance push and motivate when it is feasible. Give your daughters what they are due, and not what they are not (as noted earlier) Tell your girls now how you feel about them, intimately don't keep them hanging on a limb, for decades and or- up until the time comes for death bed confessions. Mothers, lets not wait that long. I have one friend of my Daddy's- Betty (this is for your Betty, Love ya Girl, and I may have mentioned this early on in the book) that told me that her Momma told her before she died that she was so hard on her, and not her siblings because she knew that 'Betty was the strong one'. She said to her according to Betty, on her death bed, that- "Betty you were strong and I knew you could take it the others were weak." Mother's don't wait this long and make your child think that you don't like her or care for her, tell her now, while you have the chance. Thanks Betty for your testimony.Mom sisters need truth, your integrity, your comfort and most of all your love, not the Jezebel grip! The Jezebel grip, is what the Lord revealed to me, even as I am writing this book. Jezebel (I Kings 12, the entire chapter), the wife of Ahab was manipulating and controlling, she used her manipulative questions to promp the King to do horrible things. He was so intimidated by his wife, until he committed evil. Mother's don't use your words to push your daughters to perform evil, push them towards good!

__Now__.I want to take a look at a very distinct group of sisters, I want my readers to take a detour with me. Walk with me, while I take you on a journey of twinship and sisterhood. I wrote these words in the table of my, mind, heart and soul, and now God is allowing me to "spew them" out of my thoughts to the world, for deliverance to all! I am so blessed and excited, my fingers cannot type decades of stuff, that I observed fast enough, I am overjoyed. Continue sisters to walk with me on this journey!

**A different kind of Sister (Twins).** Now let's look at twin sisters. Yes, twins. It can be fraternal twins or Identical twins. I wanted to look at this because I have a sister that is a twin, and cousins that are twins, and I watch how sisters that are twins react and behave with each other. A phenomenal lifetime view. In watching my family members that are twins, I began to watch other sisters that were twins and every time it seems- I came up with- mostly some of the same things Let's take a look at sister twins. Identical twin sisters have a bit of a, different walk, I say this because, my cousins are identical we have called them "Neicy and Nessa" all of "their and our lives". I have always seen them as, "two souls in one body". This is because they both have, in my view operated as such. I have watched my cousins from babies to now, as full grown women march to a different beat as sisters. Not only them, but I watched the Mowry twins on television, do the exact same thing! It was amazing, I could almost know what they were going to do, whether they were acting or in live television interviews, and that is because I watched my cousins do it for most of their lives. So let's begin. I watched my cousins as they were small react with their baby coos and aahs. I realized that they were deeply connected, even when they would utter words. They all seemed to come out the same. They walked alike, they talked alike, they did everything exactly alike! We (family) honestly could not tell them apart, only my Aunt, their mother (my mother's younger sister Janie and their brothers, Bernard & Fred) knew them on the spot. These two sisters were and still are connected at the heart, soul, and sometimes mind! They probably didn't know that I paid them that much attention, but I did. I watched how they seem to know the same things and often times, they'd say the same things, at the same times.

"Twin Sisters"

Later, as I got older and they were too; I saw the same exact reactions as older adult young women- with even more exact reactions. I always asked myself where is the line drawn between identical twin sisters, did they ever want their space or was that how God created them? Where does one twin end, and the other begin or vice versa. I often wondered if being a twin is one of the best experiences or the worst experiences. I have seen twins on television that were vicious towards each other's, but similar in their untold actions and I have seen sisters that were twins, hold on to the other and not wanting to let go. I have seen some twins die for freedom, and then vie to be "untied" from freedom, in other words the experience they wanted, was not exactly what they wanted; although the ventured into it. They became the opposite, they become somewhat enemies, to become friends! Yes, I saw and witnessed twins say that the thing that bought them, would often times, destroy them, or at least that was, what they thought. I know that twin sisters share a lot of the same things, their thoughts, their clothes, the colors that they wear, the cars that they drive, the patterns of speech, the hand writings, the list goes on. I have seen twins galore, on television talk of their day's journey and how they function day in and day out yes-"the same". I have seen one twin get married and then the other twin not long after that. Twins, I ask-how do you feel as a whole and then two individual parts? How did God intend for you to function, is one dragging or drawing from the other 's twin's soul so much so until she cannot breathe her own air freely? Or is it the bond that is so dangerously deep that you cannot bear a day or moment of separation. Think on these things, my dear twins!

Twins are a sight to behold, for, me it is seeing God's elaborate, immense creation of two of the same exact beings (in some cases) share the same place in time, is as awesome as ocean water roaring from a hotel luxurious bedroom window, while reading my book (I just wanted to say that, but it's true), yet it can also be dangerous and detrimental, if you do not find it, the separation and the freedom in "twinning"! Yes, "twinning", that is it! Read on! And I ask (yes, I ask God a lot of questions) how can what God created be dangerous and detrimental, and wondrous at the same time. That is because when two beings connect, they either connect for the good and joy of being two beings as one, or they connect and join for the detriment of themselves and each other. But how can this be, how can we go through life in freedom? If we are so internally and outwardly bound? I am glad you asked. Read on!

Twins are a dynamic duo, dressed up or down, but there is more to twins than meets the eye. For instance, I have seen glamour twins from all over the world, portrayed on various documentaries, telling stories of divine, miraculous connections and findings, while on the self-same- token I have seen some twin sisters share, tails of darkness that have led TWINs to deep, dark- destruction. Some twins have journeyed down the halls of darkness, only to yield the enemy's crop of terror, death and darkness as sisters. I have seen the enemy use the double connection inside out, and turned twin sisters into total enemies! If this is you, beware it wont turn out well! Open your eyes sibling twins, if you are reading this and see the blessing in twinship and not the curse! God has come to save you from yourself, to take you back to yourself, right back to your sister! God has created sister twins for love, connection, and uniqueness. I love seeing the famous twins, the Mowry's connect and I also love seeing them in their own separate places, there is room for both, but know that your twin sister is your fuel, your feed, she is the strength for your weakness, she can lift you, when no one else can. Go there with her, now! Find that God has also given "them" on the earth, yet find your individuality, it will make for better sisters and sisterhood (the act of being a sister).

You see twin sisters, your positions are valuable and useful to God's earth, yet when you do not have your own identify (balance) even as a twin, destruction is, and can be apparent. When you use the vehicle of balance, it can be a awesome feat. As identical twins, although you both share the same molding of God, he calls you to be a team, yet he calls you to as much individuality as you can bear, as twins as well! Amen!, Amen! God would not have created the "twin system" if he didn't mean for you to be unified. I would be bewildered to suggest otherwise. God wants you to understand what you bring to the table as one of a whole part, and one of the two parts. He wants you to sanctify your own soul, so that you and your sibling can then turn back and sanctify each other, there is direct line of security linked to the psychological make-up of twins. There is no denying that God created twins to sustain one another in some way. I will say though that twins have struggles, like anyone else that they need to work out, I recall that Jacob and Esau, struggled in their Mother's womb (Genesis 25:22, King James Version), there will always be a struggle for you- twins to either be together or be apart, God has called you to peace according to his word (partial Scripture, latter part of 1 Corinthians 7:15, King James Version). Twin sister, find your place of peace with your sister. Find out if God wants some space between you, or if you need to run to your sister. I have seen twins that were the very split image of each other, that did everything the same, and acted the same. Yet I saw documentaries on twin sisters that were spaces and worlds apart, as they were separated at birth or they were torn apart by some family decision or dysfunction. One thing that all the stories, that I have ever heard and seen about twins showed that they both (or all of them, if more than two) acted, and moved the same! Note this twins, some twins need that "bringing together" in order to become whole! If this is your story or plight, then do so! On the contrary, if some of you need the space or "tearing apart" to become whole, with your twin, then do that too! Find yourself sister, in your twin place, which do you need now? Some may need freedom and some may need the opposite, which is it for you? Ode to the twins! You are unique within your rights a natural phenemon to behold, you are a blessing and not a curse! Be your self, be your twin! It is God's gift!

"Sister-Twins Xs 2"

Sisters are their some of you out there that although you are not twins, you feel so close to your sister, until you feel that you are twins? Do you have such a deep connection, until you do not know what you would do without her, or is it that you cannot stand to sit five minutes with your sister? Both are good and both are bad. Let's continue on. There is more to come on this issue. Sisters, now it is time to know who you are as a sister. Knowing who you are as a sister is very important. Sisters have power, but how often do we misuse our sister power. I was walking in the building one day to work and began to talk to a woman about sisters and she told me she had six sisters and she said. "Can you imagine having 6 of those jokers"? My response was no. Why do you think it is difficult for sisters even of 'old age' to get along with each other? Women in their 60's are crying out for help with their relationships with their sisters. Let's help one another, lets not be afraid anymore sisters to say what you feel, after all in the age of COVID-19, time is short, you never know what may occur. Lets meet and get it all out, no matter how bad it hurts.

I guess you all can see, by now, how much I love Law and Order (criminal television show), well, there was an episode where two really rich sisters had different relationships with their dad, one was the business one and the other was 'daddy's little girl'. They hated each other, and stated they had no contact with each other, they only communicated through 'daddy' (in so many words). These sisters had a hate/hate relationship and they knew it! How many of us hate one another as sisters and don't care to hide it? How many of us, live and breath through our parents and do not care what each other thinks or feel. This type of behavior is a travesty!

Furthermore girls, Lets not use our parents as shields or weapons, you see these two women used their daddy to filter their hate for each other, it turned up a mess! Be your own boss sisters, speak your own words! Let's get It right, call a meeting, call a intervention, be willing to accept another person's feelings and opinions! Lets not get stark mad at what our sister feels about us or vice versa, learn to be "tough and take it" it will produce good crops in the end for your sister relationships! This book is written to help you, not hurt you, but we first got to deal with the "muck "before we get the blessing. Burdens before blessing, suffering before joy, pain before relief/it must be. See,we forfeit our blessings because we fail to endure the sufferings from the relationships that sisters need and should go through, "If we suffer as sisters we will reign as sisters." When this book is cristined, meaning it has been read and experienced by a mass majority of sisters, I will then write my book on sister bonding! God has released it to my spirit already!

Special Note: Keep in mind that sisters, no matter who we are, we are all important to ourselves! Let's also be important to one another! Lets walk in dignity! Sisterhood is something ordained by God! Let's keep moving in the goodness of it that God has set in the earth for us.

Special Note for Moms on Momma's girls. This is for Mom's. I say this as an experienced daughter, please do not make your girls into made up manikins "of your ideals". Please do not use carven images to create shells of what you think daugthers should be. Let them evolve into the piece of perfection that they were created to be and not your ideal or idea!

Daddy's Daughters. Dad, I did not say much about you because normally a Daddy loves his girls, in that case keep up the good work and continue to love and support them! Continue to use your rational mind to encourage, push and exhort unity amongst sisters. We need you Daddies of the world of girls/children!

Making Points. Now I want to get down to the "nitty gritty" or as my husband says the "grit "of it all. I want to explore something Biblical to make a common point. Hold on, God's amazement and wonders never cease to perform ! All of this is for your good. Let's Continue, this is the deepness, I warned you about.

Let's go back to the "good book" and look at another set of sisters. The book of Ezekiel refers to two sisters: Oholah and Oholibah. Ezekiel, King James version Chapter 23 versus 2-19 and then versus 22, 28, 32, 34, and 35. The scriptures describe first Oholah meaning Samaria- as the older and Oholibah meaning Jerusalem as the younger sister. The scripture refers to these sisters as sinful. Oholah although she was a married woman, she continued to be sinful and sleep with men referred to as Assyrian solders, the bible notes that once she started this evil, she was not able to stop. Often times a sister no matter where you are in the 'birth order' yet- you begin to indulge in a particular sin and it is let aloose, so to speak. It does not matter, it can be lust of envy, back-biting, and lust of hatred towards one's sister. Because of the act of "tasting the particular sin (no matter what it is) in the case of Oholah, she could not stop (as the sin deepened)' . She (the sister) begins to be obsessed with feelings of disgust towards her sister (this can and does happen in life) Moving right along, let's look further at Oholah, before we go onto her sister. Because of Oholah's lust towards sex obsession, she was 'turned over to her lusts' and she and her children were totally destroyed. Now I know I will get persecuted, but it is okay, but sisters, how many times do we 'turn ourselves over' to our lusts of the mind and heart when it pertains to our sister or sisters, and cause our children to inadvertently receive the likenings of our emotions and feelings causing them to pass this rebellion down through generation The seed is from the heart, from the core of our being and can be dangerous and penetrating to the core of who we are and our children. The seed is to the, hurt and demise of the sister bond and group and ultimately of any female group of sisters to come. When we act this way towards each other, our children tend to suffer or 'internally die' with us because of the problems or issues that we have with each other, as sisters. I used this symbolically to prove and show what goes on in the heart of a sister. We need to clear up our stuff, so that our secrets are not made manifest with our children to come.

Lets deal with this now sisters, lets hit it head on, the tension (when we are all in the room), that we,tend to act like we don't see or feel, the whispers in our mind that we don't say, the eye balling that we freeze when they look toward us, lets deal with this stuff, it is time out for the craziness. Let's not allow, the backlash, the jealousy, the lack of trust, the feelings of insecurity, and the feelings of big me, little you, tear us down or break down from generation to generation. There is a harvest that God has planned for sisterhood! Beware of your heart because, the bible talks about our heart being desperately evil. Jeremiah 17:9, King James Version says the heart is deceitful above all things and desperately wicked. Who can stand it? You see with Oholah she had wicked desperations within her heart and it affected her life. How many times does the wickedness of one's sister's heart affect the other sisters? It is time for acknowledgement to take place within the age of Obama, technology,and now the indisputable, Madame Lady Kamala Harris, our first female Vice President of the United States, social media and the like. A major deliverance needs to take place when it comes to 'sisters'. We need to realize how we really feel about each other and stop 'faking it' or 'fronting (as the children say today)' we are causing harm to our children and future generations. We are adding generational curses in a new way, because we are allowing our children to see our 'messed up behaviors, attitudes, actions and lifestyles' towards each other as sisters'.

Behaviors. Now let's look at Oholibah's behaviors. Oholibah saw all the things her sister had done according to Ezekiel 23:11, King James Version and the Bible says she wanted all these things more. She was worse than her sister, how many times do one sister see the bad, evil things that her sister does and she in some way, somehow replicates them. I am sure you ask, how do I know, of course you do, well I have to be transparent here and say, that it is first hand experience. You see, Oholibah had a different taste although she was just as sinful as her sister. You see sometimes one sister that, appears to be good is really not, she is dealing with selfish desires and issues as well as the other, yet-one is just more vivid than the other. It misses none of us! This sister was referred to as 'worse than her sister, the younger one that is', you see both sisters sinned, but this one sinned even more because she did not care, the Bible said, she wanted men and more men, sex and more sex and she let them see her naked body and did not care, at all. See, the point I am making here, is that often times although the 'sister issue' can 'go bad and real deep' meaning they all have issues, ranging from the cut to the core. One sister has her issues, while the other has hers, it skipps none of us and I repeat. Some maybe obscene, ruthless, treacherous and plain evil, while others are even more obscene, ruthless and plain evil, some sisters are evil, but it is not seen with the naked eye those are normally the worse kind. It can sometimes be that one sister is just a bit more brutal in her thinking, acting and responses towards her sisters and others, you can just never tell, until it is actually told (lived out)!

Lets look at this thing with a open eye and no longer closed! Consequently, one sister maybe more prone to gossip, prone to lie, prone to start up dissention amongst the group. A backbiter, deceiver, busy body, meddler in other people's matters Is this you, or the other sister maybe have traits where she is subtle in her actions, but to the same evil? Do you see yourself in either of these sisters 'symbolically speaking'? Do you have issues that you are obsessed with and you just cannot shake? Are the acts immoral and indecent? Furthermore, do you ask yourself, or say to yourself, if she can do it (with evil insecurities, see some of us have evil insecurities, we feel we are not doing as much evil as our sister or sisters, so we chime into the evil side of things as well, without it being as noticeable)? We all have to admit at some point in our lives, whether young or old, we have envied our sister or sisters in some way, all the while wanting to do the good she did, or the bad she did (which cup is yours). This is a true confession of the soul.

It is okay to confess it, if it is good for the soul according to scripture. We have so many problems with our sisters, but we want to 'save face' as we say because we really don't want people to know how we really feel about our sisters. The problem though, is that most of us that are sisters tend to live a lie, because we won't confess and say how we really feel so that we can get along. See adversity will come and will dwell amongst us, but hiding and covering it up, makes it shine a lot brighter than we all think or know. These are big mistakes, my dear sisters! It is a really big mistake. What is the hidden truths sisters? Think about this.

In looking further at Oholah and Oholibah, both sisters had serious issues. One sister loved sex, and the other loved sex too, but in an immoral and indecent, way. The bible states in Ezekiel 23:19, King James Version- stated that Oholibah 'did not stop there, but she became more immoral and acted the way she acted 'back in Egypt'. How many times do we revert back to acting the way we did in our younger years? I know I said earlier that when I was younger we got along a lot easier, but there were times when me and my sisters 'just could not say one or two words before there was confusion, animosity and disagreement'. Oholibah had gotten worse and because of this, she had to suffer for her sins. We as sisters, although we want to deny this, we suffer because of this very thing, as sisters. There is just no way of getting around this, when one sister does a bad thing all the other sisters involved suffer. This is fact and truth!

You, my dear readers, is -that- what happens in the long run, is that if the situation is not addressed, things take a negative 'backward' turn, because Oholibah wanted to go back to her younger days, she wanted to go back to Egypt where she felt men had sexual powers, and more powers, she was infused with his (the person she engaged with that caused her to sin) thoughts, how many of you are infused with bad (joined with your sin). Because she (Oholibah) was so engulfed in sex, and the actual 'lust of sex'. See, this is what happens with us sisters, is that we often develop a 'lust for hatred', ' a lust for jealousy', a lust for envy," "a lust for persecution," and a lust for feeling she (meaning your sister) does not deserve this (secretly, in your heart) and you do (instead, in your heart, secretly)! Fill in the blanks, if there is more.Because of the refusal to take responsibility for what is really happening with us, we have created a mess! Why do we often wait to the most inopportune moments to 'take jabs at the one we say we so-call love' and hold dear? Why do we as sisters try to put one sister down and try to be-little one another inwardly and outwardly, what does it prove, what does it gain? If we say we love our sister, then we need to be a sister? Lets not embarrasses, ridicule or take shots at our sisters in public, let's hold those thoughts until we are in private quarters, I say this because I have talked to and interviewed countless sisters that tell me things pertaining to how a sister embarrasses her (continually) without fail, at family get-togethers and functions! Why is this so? Why does one sister, always have to take the brunt of the 'jokes and sarcasm' and the family say things like "Awl you know she is crazy, we don't pay her no attention"? "Let it go"! Is this good relational skills or is this just a 'brush off' to pounce off more sin? Think on this!

How do we go proceed, in order to improve our sister relationships from this type of inner battle? How do we stop the issues? How do we stop the bruises and the pain? How do we stop the betrayal? How can we make sisters trust each other again? Let's look at the word betrayal. Betrayal has been defined as the breaking of trust or a presumptive contract that produces moral and psychological conflict within a relationship amongst individuals, organizations, communities (common ties, I added this, as it was given to me), etc., as defined by Merriam's Online dictionary. Betrayal is a word that scorns the soul. Betrayal is hurt that hurts for a long time and breaks something "on the inside", of you when it comes to sisters. Sister betrayal is the worst form of hurt that one can experience, as God intended for sisters to be together. God planned for sisters to "take their shots" together, not at each other. It does not matter if you are a twin sister, surrogate sister or any other kind of sister mold, created or developed in life. Because when betrayal hits the soul it ejects you onto fallow ground. Betrayal is like an arrow being thrust into one's heart. It is like something ripping the inner security that connected you and your sister right from beneath your feet. It is one of the most painful forms or rejection in life. Those of you that have survived sister betrayal, let's see a show of hands!

When a sister endures these types of emotions, she is at a lost, she feels alone, she feels empty. The very arms that reach out to embrace you, turns around and breaks you. Yes, this is what some sisters feel, yes it is! We must acknowledge betrayal in our sister groups. We must confess and speak on this topic in our homes, in our churches or religious organizations, you must open up and speak on how it feels to be hurt by your sister, you must yell it loud, that at times you feel that your sister is your enemy. When betrayal hit, there is then broken trust! Let's talk about trust now. I think we are ready for this at this point, hey why not, we are in deep now! Trust is defined as a reliance upon, a confidence in or an ability to rest in. Do we have reliance upon, on or in our sisters? Think on this. Do you have the ability to "fall back, like we used to do back in the days, and a particular person would catch you". Do you feel that secure with your sister or are you peeping out the corner of your eyes suspiciously at your sister? This should not be! A sister should be able to look at her sister confidently in her eyes at all times, she should not have to wonder if shadows are behind her back. We have to decide if we feel one way or the other. Be truthful with yourself and your sister, now is the time. No longer allow yourself to feel like your sister is your enemy. Stop hiding your insecurities and bring them all out, let your sister or sisters know how you have been feeling and what has caused this to be so, it is time to come on out! No more hiding!

If you think on; young sister trust (back in the good ole days) I can remember playing when were were little and outside together. We felt one another, we loved each other without even knowing it, but we did. Do you remember those days of sitting outside, getting your hair braided, while the others were either playing hopscotch or jumping rope, playing simon says, and all other types of fun games, all at the same time while your hair was being pulled, tugged or laid to the side with a straightening comb? We didn't have Facebook, snapchat and text, we had telephones without hold, we had hollars across the field and down the street, with our hands "cupped" so we could hear each other when we talked and we had to take turns on the phone, when we only had one in the kitchen at times on the wall, you remember those days!. We had polaroid cameras (hoping that the sun didn't blind your good side out in the picture), that we either pulled out from the side, or took them to the "drug store" to get developed. I just wanted to add this as a point of reminiscing, how good the days were back then, as sisters and family, and how deep the bond went, we don't see too much of that, it is a rarety and that is why I highlighted my Aunts the Sansbury Sisters, because they are a jewel of a sisterhood bond, even though they may not think it sometimes.

Sister Readers, know this though, your times (who you are in your time and space) may not have been what it was with my sisters, I just wanted to take your mind back to that state of being when you were young, bonded and together as sisters! Don't you just wish it could be that way sometimes again? Another piece of goodness that I am sure we can all relate to is that when we fought as sisters, that would be it! It would be over and the very next day, or even that night we would be back friends, but now it is not that way anymore! Why you ask? It is because, time has caused us to lose our values, in what we hold sacred, and dear, as sisters. Sisterhood was a bond, a connection a force, yes and to be reckoned with. We wasn't out to totally destroy each other, we just wanted a little action, back in those days! Sisterhood was different back then, we did "small time" arguing and never had all the big stuff when we were smaller. If we fought, we would make up quick and fast, we handled our problems promptly and quickly, because we had goals, we had to go to church on Sunday and look pretty, so we handled our issues on the spot. Sisterhood bought excitement, togetherness and love, it was just a fine time!

Do we do that now? Of course not (sadly, but we do not) we now, go for days, years and months without talking to each other? Is it because over the years, we developed low trust towards our sister or even hatred? Do you remember times when you felt you sister was trying to thwart the attention of someone or something you cared about? Do you remember watching your sister, rob you in plain sight, your emotions, your property, your relationships? Do you remember when this occurred, do you remember the time? It happens, a lot more than we want to admit. A lot of us lose our connection, when trust is broken, but it can change, it can be rebuilit,there is hope for the broken sisterhood bond. It is time to acknowledge these feelings so that your life can change.

Being a sister is a bond that is different than any bond in the world. God wants us to stay connected, as much as possible, I know some are saying, but what happens when I am sorely betrayed, there is an answer for that. Let's look at the forms of betrayal to determine the level and type of forgiveness warranted.

Examples of Acts of Betrayal/Offense

1. ***Intruding on an outside relationship*** –This maybe a close friend (BFF), male friend, someone that you are intimate with outside of the sister bond. A sister may reach outside of your relationship and connect to your friend, confidant or significant other, on the side or behind your back, - to do several things, such as "talk behind your back, steal the relationship, or manipulate the situation at hand, all the while secretly trying to move you out of the way".

2. ***Gossiping about you or something personal***, secretive or shameful (about you) that you shared with her-This may include acts of belittling, talking to other family members, friends (so called) or other sisters (about you). Sharing a secret that you confided in her about, that was painful.

3. ***Stealing (***this mean stealing your things, money, position, power)- A sister that when you are in her presence, is always trying to silence you and "move" you out of the way to make you seem little or insignificant. Stealing personal belongings (from childhood to adulthood) and blaming you for it, making parents or other family members believe it's you, when its' her. Removing or "knixing" your place, emotionally, mentally or psychologically (when you are together or amongst family friends, etc., making you feel as if you are not on her level). Purposely leaving you out.

4. ***Identify Theft-*** When your sister totally steals your identity and no one else can see it with the naked eye, except you and her. She is fully aware that she has stolen your identity and she continues to do so, and has done so for all of your lives.

5. ***Victim Preying—***Preys on the families functioning, portraying herself as the victim always and projects her victim preying ways onto a specific targeted sister sibling.

All of these offenses that occur amongst or between sisters are horrible and are considered "high dollar crimes (if I may use this analogy)", also they often produce estrangement and long term alienation. It can be difficult dealing with someone you shared the same womb with, to betray you in this manner, especially when we are supposed to be connected at the soul (so to speak). These offenses are, offenses that, in our carnal opinions requires the utmost sentence! Although it maybe true, God is saying, there is another way, if all parties are willing. This is the key to rebuilding, restoring and rebranding the sister "tie-In".

When a sister offends one or several within the sister group, it can be a difficult task to make it right again, but if all sisters are willing to come together to release and relate to one another deeply; it can be done. I caution you, that the initial meeting will be a difficult one, as truth that has never been told needs to and will come out. The group needs to be prepared to deal with the pain involved in the reconstruction of the mold that carries the sisters. Sisters, I know that you feel really bad and hurt by the acts of what has been projected onto you or the group, for many, many years. God wants you to deal with this! Work, process and deal, work, process and deal. Do this over and over and over, until it is all done and you feel empty! Once you are emptied out, you can all heal. It will MOST definitely feel weird, and that will be your sign that it is working. Know this my dear sisters, that God can mend it all, if you allow him to do so! The Lord says if you are "willing and obedient (Isaiah 1:19)" you can eat the good of the land. The "good (the good, the righteous) land is the place that "sisterhood" breathes and lives. The "land" is the connection that will lift you higher and higher through his ability to push you into increased love and happiness. True sisterhood brings joy, peace, love, and happiness. It brings about sharing, it gives, it hopes and it believes.

Coming together and walking through. When sisters go through, we want to be there for each other, we want to share in our, pain, but we can do it if we really try. Sisters, if disconnection is apparent, it is now time to reconnect. It will be very, very hard for us to share our pain, and it must be done and not in an "Iyanlya fix my life hour (no disrespect)". No longer stand on the outside watching your sister be in pain, come together and make it right! After all she is your sister! God wants us to do better at this, he wants us to be there to guide, redirect and restore our sister's soul, when she is wrong or when she offends, but then wrap your arms around her in complete love! We all have offended, in one way or another, or at some point towards our sisters, so let's get It together, Michael Jackson has a very old song, that says "Get it together or leave it alone"! Lets get it together and "NOT" leave it alone! Let's get the loving back!

Sisters, if you feel nullified or powerless, you are on the right track! This is where the healing will begin! If you are still not feeling it, then you may need to just fall back until you do, but don't give up. Don't' hold a grudge, it makes things way worse. Holding a grudge can sometimes wear out and lose it's effect, so let it go, it is probably something really petty that you are holding on to.Sisters when you feel this feeling it is now time to figure out a plan of action to restore the link,the connection as you know it to be. Sitting in one's stupor no longer feels good, it may have felt good in the past, but it no longer feels now. God is calling us out of those old time trickery and games. The devil has held up the mounds of sisterhood too long. Let's look at this thing for real and fight for our truth, our power and our gain as sisters, our validity! It is time to move up and out of this rut sisters. Read on!

**Releasing.** It is time to release the offenses of one's mind and heart. It is time to explore the issue, by taking a shovel and digging deep, remember those days when we used shovels, to dig up whatever our parents told us to when we were in the yards (for those of us that are southern girls, this would be exclusively for us, no pun intended). Speaking, metaphorically, that shovel represents cleanliness. We began to shovel the dirt, the grime, and the mulk. Let's do this with our sister clutter- and all the feelings or emotions that came with betrayal, hurt and pain. It is time to let go and let God handle it! God says it is so, so, lets prepare and then work! I know it has been weary and taxing on your soul, sleepless nights, things gnawing at your soul, unfinished business, fights about family stuff that cannot seem to be fixed and worked through. It can be done though; rest assured! God knows the end from the beginning and he saw it all when it happened he was right there. Take the following steps, if all are willing, this is the time for reconstruction!

Knowing and being able to face the emotional remake, is vital to the success of the acts of mending the sister bond. First things first, let's take a look at a few things that need to be done to get this process started and to make it a success.

1. _**Confess-Confession**_ is good for the soul. Confessing your offense, meaning- how you were offended, how you felt -when you were offended, your actions and your thoughts towards the offense.

2. ***Transparency*-** Is a must; telling everything, no matter how it sounds and how long it has been, being totally open about what you feel and think is vital (All sister parties involved must speak and share honest feelings of the heart and soul, no matter how painful).
3. ***Brain Storming***, all must add ideas, thoughts feelings towards healing and resolution.
4. ***Resolution*** (problem solve to create healing strategies to fit all sister's involved life styles, personalities, etc.).
5. ***Practice*-** the healing process due to betrayal, will not take an overnight "hit," meaning healing may take a while, a long while, so don't have false expectations.
6. ***Deal with Expectations*** –Take the time to talk about expectations.
7. ***Note keeper/Gate Keeper/ Facilitator*-**Have a responsible, detailed sister in the group, take notes, to keep a tally of conversations, negotiations, strategies and to provide feedback
8. ***Hire a Professional***, Hire a professional, Not Iyanla (LOL, Joking, I love the show, don't get me wrong), but hire a reputable professional to come on board for professional counseling, guiding and coaching (maybe a counselor, pastor, life coach, etc.,)

Rebuilding trust is important, as God has something in store for you as sisters, even if it is nothing but leaving a life example for the next generation of your children or family to see. I am hoping this memoir/book is reaching who it is supposed to. I spent some serious years pouring this information in word documents at times and places, unbeknownst to me (in my car, at work, in the library, on backs of scraps of papers, in the tablet of my heart, in conversations with my husband, long nights, you name it, writing notes as the spirit hits me, no matter where I am at)".

Read on! Have you ever watched a television show and said, boy that is sho'nuff' me and my sisters, we need to make a reality show, or a "show"- period. I bet we can make a whole lot of money … Yep..that is what we do we sit and compare and analyze but we never really face our sisters. Let's get together and face the issues, let's not be like reality show sisters and hold things in for long periods of time until they swell. Depict your truth and let it go, speak, talk and process! Let's not be the descriptors that describe the Braxton's, let's be our own unique, authentic, God ordained self (No Pun intended, Braxton's, I love the show).

**Mental Note**: Do you as a sister, feel that you -have to constantly prove herself, to your other sisters? Consequently if you have a sound sisterhood, one should be safe in the arms and presence of one's sister. One should be knowledgeable, resourceful and ready. Let's get there. There is a place in sisterhood, where chaos bring peace. Stop bringing chaos and not ending in peace, my dear sisters. Allow everyone's chaotic creative side emerge, so that peace can arise.

Do you look for the peace in the chaos, or do you straddle for more chaos? Are you a chaotic fiend or a peaceful friend? Do you feel that sometimes it is not good to maintain peace amongst sisters, and you cause it constantly?. Do you feel that chaos, brings totality? How, what, is your notion toward sisterhood, we all have our notions, which notion is yours? I could name a million notions and ideals that we have towards sister hood, but I would be writing forever, what my purpose is to bring sisters back together and make sisters think individually as well as collectively in order to go to deep levels of bonding and security. Consequently, to make you explore your sisterhood position and the dynamics of how your sister group functions, to dig deep and heal the hurt and pain. Do you feel that you and your sisters need to 'get it all out' in order to heal and be relevant? I do, I think it is deceitful to hold grudges for years, and end up in detrimental states of being, due to suppressed feelings of hurt, mistreatment, ill feelings etc. I think we should end this total bowl of mayhem to make things good and make things right. It's time. To further exploit this issue, in order to move forward. Just to give you all a little taste of how bad sisterhood can get, I had a student that talked about how her sister married her ex-husband. She felt - that it was planned. She had not doubt her sister slow walked her ex-down to get "at her (so-to-speak)". Why do we do these things? Who can handle such betrayal, and why would something of this sort occur in the first place among and between sisters? Think on this, this is just one of few examples that are out there "lingering around" with the sister brood, which is yours? Don't let the devil trick you anymore when it comes to your sister.

__Feeling like a sister__. Do you not feel as a sister, and that some things are sacred and untouchable, no matter how it went for you and your sister or sisters, presently or in the past? Do you feel that acts of violation are daggers of the soul? I would never (as told in the story depicted above), ever in a million years consider talking to, in an intimate way, to anyone that so much as even suggested he liked my sister. But is that the case always? No it is not, how many times have we heard and seen deceit on this level when it comes to sisters? We have some sisters that kill, destroy, torment, accuse, abuse and neglect their sisters, all because of jealousy and hate I continue to ask the question why? Why is this so? How can we build trust again amongst sisters? How can we build the bridge to love, support, and bonding? How can we also be open with our sisters and tell her or them, how we really feel without arguing, fussing and fighting (at times)? What will it take to repair a hurt so deep? Go back and read the pages above if you missed it.

__Now looking back at__ Oholah and Oholibah in the book of Ezekiel, King James Version (Chapter 23, in its entirety), the story just does not end with their sin. The Bible explains their consequences, and how they end up, because of their disobedience. The Bible says that the sisters were condemned and deemed guilty of their sin. The Lord did not let them get by with their devious acts. You see sometimes we as sisters, do not realize that whatever we do to each other, we pay for it no matter what. That is why it is important to treat your sister or sisters with kindness, love, and respect, because one day the reapers will come. Ezekiel 23:36, King James Version says "Ezekiel son of man it is time for you to tell Oholah and Oholibah they are guilty"! God is saying to us, if we don't try to make the crooked ways straight, things will remain, in a bad place for us as sisters, now and forever!

Furthermore, God wants us to be reminded of our wrong doings and errors in ways of thinking acting and behavior, as sisters. God told Ezekiel in Ezekiel 23:36 to remind them of their evil ways. They have been unfaithful, by worshipping idol gods (arguing, backbiting, deceiving, lying, hating, revelings against, strivings, against one another secrecy, so on, and so on,). The scripture shows how they committed murder by sacrificing their own children as offering to idols. They have stopped respecting the Sabbath, this passage of scripture is being used to show how a group of people disrespected God, but in the same token, I will use this passage to show, how we disrespect each other as sisters. How many times do sisters leave the respect far away from the circle? This is something that we all need to look into when it comes to our sister or sisters. How many times do we forget and break the covenant of sisters, by falling prey to our own selfish desires and motives. How many times? Well it is getting time for sisters to modify and change their behaviors towards each other. It is time to get a "new mind" and, "a new heart" towards each other.

For those that are serious and want change, it is time to make a change. Read further. The Lord goes further in his warning of the two sisters in verse 46 of Eziekel Chapter 23, King James Version ... "I will get rid of sinful prostitution in the country, and I will warn other women everywhere to not act as you do." The Lord is now calling for sisters to act and behave differently. In this horrific time and day we live in he is calling for restoration of sisters, a "re-pulling' of his power"! A re-manifestation of his glory among sisters. A redoing, a rebuilding, a restoring, let's get all that God has for us, as sisters, let's cry together, push together and birth together. That is why I love Gayle and Oprah's sisterly bond. Their sisterhood is something that is special and heaven sent (in my opinion), they are always together, and in sync. They are close to the heart and this is how sisters should be, it is a total blessing to see friendship go as deep as Oprah and Gayle's sisterhood goes. I have heard - many times Oprah-rang the bell of "applause" regarding her sister/friend, Gayle, and Gayle has done the same, she has shouted to the highest mountain how good and dedicated of a friend that Gayle is to her and vice versa. To the point, she had her own telephone line, straight to Oprah! Now that's sisterhood. Oprah talked about how proud and supportive Gayle is of her when she achieves. Are you as proud of your sister, when she achieves? Do you openly voice it to her, or do you keep looking and watching waiting to find fault or mishap? Or do you blatantly find a way out of acknowledging and congratulating her feats? It's time for a change!

The Call. He is calling for us to do better, act better and live better. It will first take time, energy, healing, and forgiveness. This book is bringing healing to a long hurting line of sisters from all cultural backgrounds, races, colors and creeds, as well as ethnic groups. Matter of factly, so many sisters have been betrayed by someone that is of their own household (I keep saying this so that we all can get the point). Let's continue to look deep into ourselves for who we are and who we want to become. Read this book cautiously, if you have to put it down for a few days, do so because it is really soul wrenching. A book, that I am sure someone' has been waiting for … the scripture states that "We know that the whole creation has been groaning as in pains of childbirth, right up to the present time. Romans 8, verse 22, King James Version states that the creation waits in eager expectation for the Sons of God to be revealed (for manifestations of new and profound information, deliverances, breakthroughs, new mindsets, new, new and new!)". Romans 8 and verse 20, King James Version: For the Creation was subjected to frustrations, not by its own choice but by the will of the one that subjected it to it, in hope that the creation itself will be liberated from its bondage to decay, and bought into the glorious freedom of the children of God (sisters need to be set free from the turmoil that they face and this book has been birth by God into my spirit, body, soul and mind) to help set sisters free.

Sisters think about how you really feel about your sisters. Think of the years of pain, disgust, lies, mistrust, etc. that has taken place between and amongst you and your sisters. On the next few pages, answer the questions truthfully on a piece paper or within your mind to help with self-introspection, to see what you come up with! The questions are developed for your inner assessment of how you feel, continue to feel now, or in the past regarding your sister, these questions are posed for you to really, do some sincere deep soul searching. Its okay, only you and God know the real answers to these questions, read, relax and release. Your deliverance is ahead. If you answer to at least one these questions, you know there is a problem. Let's begin.

Read below and get set free!

Sister Questions

1. Do you feel that your sister causes lots of problem for you and has wreaked havoc on your life for a long time? If so explain why.
2. Do you feel this has been since your early childhood?
3. Think back to the day you felt insecure because of your sister?

4. Can you remember what started this? What was the cause?
5. Would you change anything about that day?
6. Did your Mom play a role in how you feel about your sister today?
7. What advice would you give your mom about mothering female children?
8. Has your experience with your sister changed the way you view other sisters? Your female children? Why or Why not?
9. Why do you think sisters should be close?
10. Do you think that it is okay to not be around a sister that torments another sister?
11. Do you think that betrayal by a sister is easily forgiven?
12. Do you love your sister?
13. Do you hate your sister?
14. Do you envy your sister's accomplishments?
15. Are you jealous or have been jealous of your sister throughout your life?
16. Do you wish to change how you feel regarding your sister?
17. Did your sister die not knowing how you felt?
18. Do you feel guilty regarding your relationship with your sister?
19. Would you change your relationship with your sister? Can you try forgive her?
20. Do you feel your sister is your enemy?

These are a few questions that were revealed to my by the "Holy Spirit", there may be more that come to you, that you need answers for, if so, take a mental note or jot it down so that you can begin the healing and restoration process.

Information. Read the following quotes on sisters (They will break your heart). Sisters can be loving towards one another or they can be evil towards one another read a few quotes from wwwquotegarden.com/sisters.html

1. Sisters never quite forgive each other for what happened when they were five. ~Pam Brown.
2. If sisters were free to express how they really feel, parents would hear this: "Give me all the attention and all the toys and send Rebecca to live with Grandma."-Linda Sunshine.

3. If you don't understand how a woman could both love her sister dearly and want to wring her neck at the same time, then you were probably an only child. ~Linda Sunshine
4. I know some sisters who only see each other on Mother's Day and some who will never speak again. But most are like my sister and I ... linked by volatile love, best friends who make other best friends ever so slightly less best. ~Patricia Volk
5. Sisters don't need words. They have perfected a language of snarls and smiles and frowns and winks - expressions of shocked surprise and incredulity and disbelief. Sniffs and snorts and gasps and sighs - that can undermine any tale you're telling. ~Pam Brown
6. Of two sisters one is always the watcher, one the dancer. ~Louise Glück
7. Kiss a sister's but have her forever, stop kissing her but you lose her forever-Me (Author of this book-Pamela Applewhite).

Read more on Sisters below:

Being a sister and a daughter can be tough, sometimes especially when you are the one that is held responsile for the others. I have observed Elder Celebrity sisters such as Beyonce and Toni Braxton. I compared their actions and words to those of mine to see if there were any similarities, being as though I too am an Elder Sister, let's explore this particular role. Just because its me! I want to be as transpararent and open in my experiences to help some elder sister along the way.

Special Note I have highlighted a lot of information on Elder Sisters, and that is obviously because I am an Elder Sister, read the highlights in this birth ordered position to divulge who you are as a sister.

What are the responsibilities of the eldest sister? A French oil painting created in 1869 by a French Artist by the name of William-Aldophe Bouguereau shows a girl sitting on a stump seemingly holding her younger sibling, smiling with confidence. Isn't that the imagery of an elder sister ... she holds her younger siblings - not only in the palm of her hand, but her heart, no matter how bad she is being treated. In the picture the young girl is holding her younger brother or sister, and she seems really confident and poised in her position. Elder sisters are often left with the burden of taking care of the younger ones, emotionally, mentally, and physically. It seems almost daunting if she does not. Elder sibling sisters almost always take on the second 'mommy role'.. She is the surrogate mother when Mom is out, or when Mom is working or taking care of other responsibilities. Often times Elder sisters are the advisor, the counselor, the bank (yep we become private loan companies and places of withdrawal,). We as older sisters often; when we give, do not expect it back. We see it as part of our inevitable duty to take care of our younger siblings and family in most cases. So many times the Elder Sister's role is misunderstood. The elder sister by nature is first. She is the one that is birth out of her Mom's womb- first and she tends to have a 'first like mindset'. Read part of the following poem by Sharon Olds, written from her book, *The Dead and the Living: Poems by Sharon Olds*. Alfred A. Knopf, 2001. Olds referring to "The Elder Sister" (Maybe his will help younger sisters, understand the older sister a lot better).

The Elder Sister
by Sharon Olds

When I look at my elder sister now

I think how she had to go first, down through the

birth canal1, to force her way

head-first through the tiny channel,

the pressure of Mother's muscles on her brain,

the tight walls scraping her skin.

Her face is still narrow from it, the long

hollow cheeks of a crusader on a tomb2 … … … … … … … …

"The Elder Sister"

This poem elaborates on an older sister and how she came to be, while giving deep symbolic thrusts of who she is, and what she represents, as well as giving "descriptive twists and turns" on what an older sister does, gives, and envisions, not only for herself, but her sisters around her (so-to-speak). The older sister is often the proud one, the one that sets the tone for the other sisters, although she is "hailed and helled (at the same time, if you know what I mean)," she holds this position proudly, facetiously, undoubtedly, gently, forcibly, humbly and the like. The eldest sister wears many hats and at times, she can be seen as the "savior or the sinner" in the eyes of her younger co-horts. The eldest sister is the proudest, the "sister/mommiest," she is the one that holds the "reins" for the sister group! I could not wait to to get this book out, to give "Eldest Sisters" a REIGN! A title, a mode, a position! They deserve it! Don't you think? Let's give it up for the "ELDEST" (Read the entire poem at your leisure, by Sharon Olds). The picture above shows a sister with a "smirky smile" on her face, showing her holding a younger sibling, this picture can throw off, many different perspectives. One, in particular can be (from my own perspective) that she looks to be sneaky (a lot of "us" elder sisters have been coined as "sneaky, subtle and unpoised). The picture shows me, from my own perspective, an older sister, sitting on a stump holding a younger sibling, seemingly tired, or giving off a message of "It's me" "Here I am, what's next (type of thing)" "This is what I do," and I mean a first born sister really does this, she changes the diapers, she cooks, she protects her younger siblings from getting beatings spankings, or whuppings, (as we call them in our culture), she interferes with arguments, she tries to make peace among other sister chaos that may occur with mother/daughter, sister/friends, sister/significant other relationships and the like, but the saddest part of being the eldest, one can be turned on and off, by her younger sibs, as quick as she is turned on. And this can go on, almost immediately after you have invested so much into the other's sister's lives, their children, their husbands, etc. Their husbands run to you for advice on how to deal with them, but do they care? No! I am hitting it straight! They forget about all the sacrifice that the eldest sister role carries. The eldest sister roles, can go into many, many different areas, and it goes a little something like this (this is my personal written and created by "me" rendition of the Eldest Sister (above)).

The Eldest we are,
Seen as a saint, a sinner and sometimes a star

Sacrificing our clothes, our time, our voice and our mind..
Giving deep, dark discretions only to push you in front and not behind …

Rebuking, scorning, telling you what to do …
Is not a degredation, but a position that's warranted for you …

Taking it wrong from what is being said
The eldest sister, no one can lay in my bed … …

The bed of affliction that, I carry each and everyday
Doing things for sisters, that doesn't come with pay …

Of being the first, the last with a God given, granted role …
My dear younger sisters take it in, it's me you need to behold …

Not because I am all that great (although I am, LOL)
But it is because of the breaths that God has given me to take…

To help you my dear baby sister and what you got going on
Lord, help my little sister see what she does is wrong, wrong, wrong

Because she does not know that my eyes blink with deep found tears
Because of the thing that she does not know- that I fear

For her, her actions and her soul
Things I have seen, and done, something you could never behold…..

They don't understand me, the eldest, not at all..
They don't listen until the dial me and call

My cell and my house phone, looking for a fix…
Big sister, big sister, I am in between and twix…

A rock and a hard place, tired of this big boulder…
Standing on my back and hanging over my shoulder…

What you see is, not what you get…
Because the very thing you want I told you to wait-

Wait, wait wait little girl, your time will meet you, you can't handle my stuff
The Elder Sister Role, not a fallacy, but inevitably rough!

You think I don't know, experiences but oh yes I do…
The deep dark hidden ones, ooops, yes those one's too…

It's nothing to play with or to take with a grain of salt.
My role, my dear sisters is nothing to flaunt!

No not to flaunt or to jock for a position.
It is a role that comes with God's rendition..

A rendition that comes with pain, rejection and deep earthly sorrow
A Elder Sister, wakes up looks to the dawn, anticipating tomorrow…

Wondering about her sisters and their sisterly life
Trying to make something of it and to help make it right

Among and between them all the time.
My dear sisters, it's elderly sister time….

So recognize her and who she is and what she stands for…
The oldest of all, see the dawn of my mantle, my cloak the work of its hand, don't
hate or abhor…

The work of my hands it was all for you
The elder sister, what else can I do..

So step back, my sisterly co-horts, it's not your task to take
Only God has put me here for this its me that's at stake…

If you pay close attention to who I am, and what I stand for….
You will realize what God put me here, to do, I am not just a eye sore…..

I am here my dear younger sisters to watch over you.
To listen to you whine and tell you what to do….

So stop resisiting my eminent power, that God gave me from above…
With might and power, and nothing short of…..

Don't keep thinking that "I am ultimately, dead wrong …
I know you like a "book," even though I sing the same song …

The song of love being portrayed, through my actions, my speech and even when I don't talk
The eldest sister not one of you could take this walk …

Because it is tricky, cold, dark and lonely often times
Being where I am at, can often feel like I am engaged in organized crimes….

I love my sisters even though they don't believe it sometimes, with all my inner heart …
I would give them anything, even though they think at times I would not…

Because I am the eldest, girl a coveted role …
I am the first, and the last because- I have given up my soul..

To this birth order, that was chosen just for me.
The eldest sister, the heavens endowed it to be …

This mindset of the eldest sister- is often misunderstood by the younger siblings. We are often seen, I say **WE-** because I am the elder sister of my set. Yes … (how else would or could I have written this book, hand, heart, and paper) … The elder sister tends to have a superior complex where she takes on a role of power, authority, wisdom, talent, etc. The poem exploits the role, yet it tells you of the job duties of an elder sister. The elder sister is full of stuff, I mean she is like a toy box full of nameless things. Back in the old days we had toy boxes and a whole lot of stuff was in side of it (I will never forget that toy box) and when you went to look in it, you looked for whatever worked, the eldest sister is the "whatever works type of girl," she tells you, if you come to her, what she knows, what she has, and what she can give. The eldest sister can be resourceful. If you trust and believe she can be a box of many things. you name it the elder sister has it, she is and can be the most resourceful of the sister crew. An elder sister is full of things, confident, self-assured, yet weak when she has to be, for the sake of her sisters and that always equals to being the "providing specimen (so-to-speak)". I must say, yet we know that the Elder sister gets seen as the bad guy or the bad person that everybody else in the family looks down upon., the "know it all," the "think she is the badest," the "think she got it all", the "think her children are the smartest," "the one who's always "butting into everybody else's business," "the one that ain't nothing," "the one that you love to hate,"! Yes, I got more, but I will stop there, I think you get the picture."

I want all younger sisters to remember this. An elder sister is not someone who comes to 'bully her way around" but she comes to protect, love, secure, and provide. So many times an elder sister is 'stripped of 'her "elderly sister's garment" by jealousy, deceit, and backbiting of another sister. I will use a male this time to demonstrate what I mean. Joseph in the book of Genesis was a special child. He was born to his Dad in his old age. The scriptures says his dad loved him more and that he had a "coat of many colors." I will deal with that later on parental love and comparisons. The Bible demonstrates a strained relationship between Joseph and his brothers because they knew he was special. Genesis 37:3-4, King James Version states: Now Israel loved Joseph more than any of his other sons, because he had been born to him in his old age and he made an ornate robe for him. When his brothers saw that their father loved him more than any of them he could not speak a kind word to him (immediate sibling hatred and jealousy). See Joseph was truly a special child, and I think he may have known it and that is really not a problem. The obvious problem came in when the brothers saw, how their Dad reacted to his position, to Joseph's favor, given to him by God. You see eldest sister roles are given to that particular sister by God, not by man, not by the pastor, not by the parents, but by God, yep, she is the eldest because God made her to be and not the other way around . We should all be confident in who we are, as long as we do not boast and brag (too much, LOL). Joseph's brothers began to hate him because he was favored, not knowing the entire time, that Joseph would be the one to bless the entire family and bring them out of famine. This is often true of the elder sister (this is repeated a lot throughout the book, know there are exceptions, my dear readers). The elder sister is often times (I am not saying that other siblings cannot be favored, please be assured of this, the elder sister can forfeit her blessings as well) a special feature in the family line. Another sister though, can bump you up to eldest by default (if you are not the eldest by age, you can be in spirit and know that God will reverse it and show you as such), by nature, by personality, by forfeit, or several other reasons, but it can and does happen. Keep this in mind please! How many times do we hear, "My oldest sister raised me," "If it was not for my older sister I am not sure where I would be."

"My oldest sister used to keep us while my momma worked," "My oldest sister took care of us." (This is a crying point ladies) … How many times does all the hard work and dedication get overlooked? How many times does it seem like the oldest sister is trying to 'be it all," "do it all" and "act it all" … yep she really does this, but not to the family's detriment, she does it to bless others. Let's look back at the oil painting this young lady is carefully holding her younger brother or sister. He seems comfortable in her arms and does not seem worried at all. You see God created the older sister to be a 'steady place, a rock, a shield, a fortress" but so many times, as Joseph in the Book of Genesis Chapter 37, King James Version was stripped of his priestly robe, so is the elder sister stripped of her garments because she is misunderstood. What do you think would have happened if Joseph's brothers would have known he would be the one that saved them from starvation, and poverty? Look at it this way, the eldest Sister, maybe the one that can bring you to your destiny! Often times when an elder sister is stripped of her position, she is 'shoved' into a foreign land just as Joseph was all alone, to suffer with strangers in an emotional, physical and psychological foreign dungeon. Let your eldest, be who she is, you will be rewarded by her fruit!

Joseph suffered long and he suffered hard. He was falsely accused of sleeping with Potiphar the ruler's wife and he was put in jail. How many times do Elder sister's get falsely accused of doing and saying things that she had no intentions of doing, meaning, nor even thinking about, ending up confined doubly because we are seen one way, but perceived and acted out in another way. How many times does the oldest sister get accused of "thinking she is the best," "thinking other siblings are the worst", all of these thoughts and statements are misconceptions. Often times the Elder sister just 'speaks her mind' because that is how she was 'woven'. Her inner being is equipped to 'straighten' others out, but only in hopes of helping them ultimately. I will say that elder sisters have different personalities. Some are nicer, some are meaner, some are gentle, some are hard, but behind it all there is a little girl hoping, planning and caring about her younger sisters. I read an article that discussed how Venus and Serena' William's oldest sister took care of them before she died. This is how the elder sister lives. She lives, breathes and makes her being to care for the younger siblings. I noticed at an award show where Beyoncé shouted words of 'love and care' to her sister 'Solange' that is the 'forte' of Elder Sisters -we are always concerned about the welfare of our younger siblings their heart, their will and their emotions. No amount of money, fame, or fortune can replace the feelings that one has for their younger sister or sisters. Sister's it is okay to ride the coattail of your oldest sister in some things. For example, many have said that Solange is 'riding the coattail' of her older sister, news Flash, it is okay to do so, I say this to the sister that is fighting hard not to be "that" you are selling yourself short. Your oldest sister has the goods, believe that and receive that, stop running and hiding from her success, her success is your foundation, your push forward, she does not care if you are endowed with it, you do yourself and injustice when you fight against it!

From what I can see the Eldest Sister wants the best for their siblings, from Beyoncé, to Toni Braxton, to Judge Toler, to now our first Madame President, Kamala Harris. It is really obvious in the citing's that we see with celebrity sisters, although they some are open and some are private, some things you cannot hide, regardless, it is always seen and interpreted by those that have experienced it. And that is the bond of sisterhood. Sisterhood is legendary, it is monumental and it is something that is not inconspicuous. Being sisters is an adventure, know this and explore it. Now back to elder sisters, I just love this part (LOL)! You see the elder sister's goal is to provide, and take care of her sibling sisters. The act of becoming rich and famous without being able to share it with your sisters is really a useless feat. Material possessions is the least of it all in the mind of the eldest sister. One of the main goals for a sister with siblings is, being able to share with others, but especially with one's sisters.

Being able to set the pace for your predecessors is one of the most fulfilling things for a true Elder sisters to do, in life. Believe me! Look at Oprah Winfrey, and Gayle, as surrogate sisters. We all know though, that Oprah found out later, that she had another biological sister and look at what happened, she took her sister in and respected, her, loved her, and was resourceful for her. It is what sisters are supposed to do. Oprah's sister that she came to know, Patricia, on the other hand, dedicated her life to respecting Oprah and not betraying her. She held a place of honor for Oprah, even before they met! How powerful is that!

This is something that I want all the sisters, reading this memoir to get, if you get nothing else. Your elder sister is not out to get you, she wants to care for and love you. She wants to provide for you and help you to become who you are intended to and supposed to be. She is not trying to 'exalt' herself over you, she is trying to be that person that can bless you. Sisters if you can get this about your elder sister, you will really be blessed. I know some of you are thinking, it is too late, my sister hates me. She will never forgive me. I cannot give you all the answers, in this situation, but if she is a true Elder Sister, and if I know myself, she will let you back in but with caution, just giving "fair warning". I promise you this though, she will at least listen to you, eventually! It never fails, one way or the other, the Elder Sister will be just that the elder sister. You must respect her and give her her props! Wow took me years to get this all out, but here it is! Elder Sisters take this into your heart, younger sisters, you do this same, it is just what was explained and expounded upon! Let's keep this thing moving and move forward! Sisterly love can be the bomb! Or it can be a bomb! Know this. Read on! We are almost there!

Birth Order Lets now take a look at other birth positions in the sister order. Many times you have the second oldest, the yelling baby and then the baby when it comes to larger sister families. In some cases they are smaller sister sects that include 2, or 3 sisters. All in all no matter how small or large sisters- encounter issues.

Sisters that are second or even third tend to follow the lead of the first sister, they are the clear sighted and the stable minded one's mostly. They have issues with feeling left out, but they tend to cherish their oldest sister, they are her mirror, her side kick and sometimes her employee (smile, lol). The second sister, depending on how many sisters are in the group is dedicated to making sure the eldest is confident, secure and she follows her closely and would not harm her, generally speaking. She is the image of the oldest and the oldest over the second and third sisters, she tries to keep sisters after her and the oldest "in line." The second's sister's personality puts her in the role as "go-to," secondary leader, she is detailed, nice, and submissive (just to name a few).

Third and Fourth Sisters, and so on- follow a general rule, they are normally followers and group oriented, they will go along with the program, the fourth sister, is normally the news carrier, the one that adds drama to the sister group, the personalities vary, but they normally flow together. If there are more than 3 sisters in the group, with the exception of the baby in the group, they are all "grouped together" and they think alike. They won't betray each other too bad, but they tend to "clique up with other sister siblings throughout time" to mix and match with other sister personalities and form alliances when there are issues as they come.

The baby sister, we all know who she is and her character, she is always the spoiled one, wants her way, tries to take "her little stances" against the sister brood, has her own agenda, "so she thinks," makes subtle, dumb mistakes, takes our money, our time and other stuff, that she knows she can- yup, I said it, got to be true, but when she makes them, she runs to her Eldest in secret, with her tail tucked in, once she gets her momentum back or re-newed, then she is back to playing the baby role, with all the other sisters, with her little small seen in-dependence (we elder siblings, subtly laugh at it, sometimes, for real, yawl know it is the truth). She wines to the sister, that she knows she can and will listen, when everyone else in in opposition of her actions, thoughts or beliefs and if she cannot get the sister group to move on it, she puts on her "baby suit (not bathing suit)" and she cries and whines to the mother or person that carries the mother role, the one that will easily pick up her "little baby up" no matter what, even after she has violated, and that is the BABY SISTER!!! No pun intended. But we all know this is true!

More on Sister Groups There more and "more" types of sister groups that I would like to refer to such as twin sister groups, celebrity sister group, and others. First,

I want to start out with talking about twins sisters. With twin sisters, I recently saw a movie about two twins on a particular network, the twins were doing everything together, even working together and living together. This is normally the dynamic of twins, On this particular show, it appeared they shared dark secrets with each other, that only they knew about.

I have noticed that with twins, they can be inseparable and that they love each other deeply and soulfully. Twins are a special, yet unique group of people Twins are made and created by God. Twins are almost always connected differently than the average sister, they are what I refer to as "One soul in two bodies." I have watched my twin cousins act in a manner that reflected this very theory and thought process.With twins, they share a bond of "talk," a bond of "think (meaning they think the same things, at the same times and as mentioned above, they often times say the same things, at the same times). The bond can be unbelievable at times. I have seen on television and in real life, twins do certain things, even when they are in separate environments at the same time. I have seen some twins not be able to live without each other and I have seen some twins not be able to live with each other, even though they are still connected. What do I mean by this? I mean this to say that, twins are a created phenomenon by God that cannot be disguised or deluisionized. They are one, yet two. Let's look at this bond to see how sisterhood can be. It is a marvel, a wonder, a mystery. Twins are a being that resides in the same world at the same time. I have viewed and seen documentaries on sister twins, that cite one or the other -being spooked by their sister's presence, due to feelings seemingly like they are overtaken and smothered. I have yet on the other hand, seen and explored twins sisters that have experienced tragedy. I watched a show, although the show was an act of art (fictional), the one twin wanted freedom so bad, while the other one wanted control. God wants us to bond, but not to the detriment to the other. This story, didn't turn out so well, as it actually ended up in tragedy, because the one sister wanted total domination of her sister's soul. Sister/twins, if this is you, let up some, don't control your twin sister's soul, its not healthy, by no means. Things like this tends to happen in real life, I have seen it! Let's not be so weak, until we have to stand on someone else's soul to be somebody! I am here to tell you twin girls, that

God doesn't want that for your lives, "Yes" being a twin can be fun, devilish and witchy at times, because of the secret switches you can make to your own credit and idealism, but God is saying there is another way, "Twin Sisters," it is time out- for one twin to take up the slack for another, "to the bad". Sister/twin it is time to find your true sense of self, even if you do feel totally connected, and lack the ability to separate, at times, there is nothing wrong with being, identical, but there are times, when God wants you to know who you are as individuals, in order to create your own unique duality (I am sure this makes sense, to you twins). I have lived around and experienced twinship all of my life, with my cousings, and siblings. My family has one set of identical twins and 2 sets of fraternal twins and would have been three sets of fraternal twins had my grandbaby's sister lived, little Memphis! So I can speak truthfully and with experience on the life and mindset of twins.

Let me restate that, God made TWINS and no matter how horrified it may have been for some, let me say that, it may not have been this for all, God is saying that to find yourself, is to know yourself. Twin/sister-set your own guidelines, as individuals and, as sisters, as a person, as a mother, as a student, as a daughter, as a wife and then as a group. Don't wait on your twin to fill in the blanks. This is what I heard the Mowry twins say in so many words, that at one point and time in their lives they had to find their own paths, in order to be together. I also, read some articles on a set of twins that are well-know in the world of psychiatry, June and Jennifer Gibbons. These twins, were born and grew up in Wales. The identical twins were known as the silent twins, for years and years, they didn't speak to anyone but "only" to themselves, but in a weird way. They were seen by psychiatrists and lived at one time in a mental hospital for 11 years. They spoke Creole, but talked so fast, that no one could understand them. These sibling sister/twins, were so caught into each other's souls, until they could not unleash the tie that bound them and although brilliant, they began to commit crimes, as they though they could outwit the world, because of their duality. This did not last long! Know this twins the evil, deceptive gig is up! Lets fly right! God is calling you to do so! The Gibbons twins endured countless counselors and mental health workers, and doctors, trying to unravel the web that weaved their souls, even to their brief demise. The medical professionals ended up, separating the two and put them into two different places, but only to cause them to go into a deeper darker hole. The Gibbons twins are an example of what God does not want for his creative mold that carries twins.

"My Sister makes me happy set of Sisters"

God also want twins to explore and become individuals in their "twinship." God created this blessing, and wants it to be so, but not to one or the other twin sister's demise. Twins, find yourself, find your soul and then find each other, being a twin is an awesome, miraculous experience, learn of it, act of it, yet--be it not to the imprisonment of the other (don't let the twin sister be the "enemy"of the other). This maybe a difficult task, but do it to the degree that you are able. I am not encouraging you to leave your twin, by no means, because as I have learned that twins feed off of each other, the very essence of their lives is centered around their opposite twin. For the most part! Yet there is another part and that is you! God wants twin sisters, to know themselves and be themselves, yet stay bonded and connected as "two in one." I am sure that you that are twins, understand this. It will be difficult making the transition, but it can be done, but as a process. One would have to possibly get guidance or help, from a professional to engage in this tremendous feat. But it can be done, if you are a twin, and want to love and share the space that God has created for you, but not as a slave, but as an equal, a close friend, and a mate. Let me be clear- twins are definitely mates. They are supposed to be the undergird of each other, that is what makes being a twin special. I would be remissed to say this is not so! So in saying that know that God wants you all to become greater and better as "two'! Read on!

God, though, wants the ugly removed, from this bond entirely, and to bring it into the righteousness that he declared for twins to have. The holy place of endowment, for the being of TWINS! Yes, there is glory in being a twin, don't get me wrong, but not that one twin or the other, lacks the ability to function or deal with the outside (so-to-speak). Don't allow your twin sister, be the one that you love to hate at the same time, but the one that you love to love, don't let the enemy steal your joy, your bond, your pure connection by saturating it with ungodly ties and unduly submission. Don't allow yourself to fall in the trap of the " ugly twin syndrome," this is the trap of confinement, mental, physical and emotional imprisonment of your twin sister. Don't allow it to be so anymore, God wants you to be one, yet with freedom.

I know that being a twin is like being married, it is like two becoming and being one, I can speak from my observation of TWINs, as I have three (3) sets in my family, one identical and two fraternal. God wants you to know who you are, and be good at what you are. Don't allow your "Sister to be your Enemy," as a twin, I have seen it happen so many times, with so many instances. I have seen television documentaries, shows, and real life instances where- one twin can be jealous of the other, one twin, tries to destroy or steal from the other, one twin, steals the other's identity, yet while one twin steal the other's relationships (meaning husbands, boyfriends, friends in general or anything of value to their alter twin). It has been horrible, but God has something else for you TWIN sisters, he has freedom, in your joint connection. He has a liberty, that you never knew existed. Yes,- it exists, in you and your twin! Knowing and understanding your sameness, as well as your differences, will bring about a "brand newness" that you never imagined. It is real and it is true, God wants this for you!

"Sister -Twins walking in newness"

Celebrity Sister Groups Celebrity Sisters are the ones that we look to, the ones that we think has it all together. The ones that we think would die for (meaning die to meet or be their best friend, LOL). The sister group that we always think has it together. I will use the sisters that I looked up to for a long time, were the singing group, "Sister Sledge" and the "Jackson Sisters (Rebbie, Latoya and Janet)"! When I was younger, I always thought these sisters were the best, were beautiful and that they got along well. Well over the years, media reported a lot on the sisters, I will say the Jacksons mostly. I heard a lot about them and their issues and how the sister bond was betrayed by lies, secrets, and other unwarranted issues. My fantasy about sisters was broken as I got older and saw that they seemed to have gone through as much as the next sister group did. I saw the fabulosity and the beauty of the sisters that were "STARS" in my eyes, and not what happened behind the scenes. I never saw the deterioration and waning away of what sisters really meant happen upfront. It was not until later, I realized the truth and what was really going on with sisters. Furthermore, I saw celebrity sister's smiling, going on long trips, and with lots of star power, money and fame, yet little did I know there was another story. What I saw or thought was love and connection, was not –to- say the least. I have seen other celebrity groups bicker and fight, as we saw with the Braxton's (Toni,Towanda, Tamar, Trina and Traci) on Iyanla and I have seen the Kardashians (Kim, Courtney, Kendal and Kylee), do the same and act the same. Furthermore, I have seen sisters close their eyes, and turn a blind ear to this or that, hoping things would get better.

What I did was carried, the misnomer that people that have money have perfect lives. Little did I know, that I was wrong!

<u>Notion:</u> Sitting up here- finishing my book during COVID-19, listening to Marvin Gaye's, "Got to give it up", has caused me to realize in life, that God does not want us to destroy each other, just because we are famous, have millions of dollars, fame or forture. As sisters, God wants us to desire and long for continued closeness, like the Wright Sisters (my former neighbors) tend to vie for. I saw on the reality show the "*House Wives of Beverly Hills*", two celebrity sisters, Kyle and Kim (that are on the show), air their dirty sister laundry in ways that you would think they wouldn't.

It seems that money means nothing, for sisters, if there is no love, no connection or assurrance with your sister bond! God does not want us to continue to think sisters- that have money- that- this is all that there is, because it is not. This is not God's plan for us, it is not his plan for us, at all. Sisterhood is sacred and we need to start seeing it as such. No dollar, no name, or claim to fame should draw you to feel that your connection with your sister is not important! We have to take a look at the place that is held sacredly for sisters, and hold this place higher on the list of relationships (for those of us that are sisters)! Know that, no dollar amount or tangible thing, should separate sisters from the love, bond and connectedness that God wanted you to so desperately! Celebrity sister, I say this to you, find your place in God, find the place where you and God can dwell outside of the fame (in order to connect first with yourself and then your sister), the fortune, the star power, look to him, from which cometh your help (Psalm 122: 1 & 2 King James Version). Work on reconnection! Look at who he is to you and how he created you and then know, your place as a sister. I know you thought it was your star power, that would do it, but I know you see now that it has not!

On and On sisters, there is a place of goodness for sisters, believe me, there is a place for sisters to dwell (I thank God for the "Wright Sisters (Cymp, Shoan, Debbie, Lynn and Angie, my childhood neighbors)". There is a pure place that sisters can yield to, to be refreshed, to be revived, and to be restored. You ought to try it. I love to see, every year, my childhood neighbors (that are sisters), Cymp, Debbie, Lynn, Angie and Shoan, take their new found sister trips, they do something different every year and they just love on each other, they bond, they mate and they have fun. They leave their everyday regular lives, husbands, children and those they love, back at home, while they experience the world with each other as sisters. They stop time- to be what sisters should be! They take time to learn of each other and drink from the cup of sisterhood,. They talk, they laugh they cry, they joke, but they dedicate one time per year to their heavenly creation and that is sisterhood, that is God's divine institution for us all girls (that are sisters in one way or the other), to produce, and to fill! Sister's I recommend you all try it! I think you will like it, Ode to the Wright Sisters! I love you guys!

Good Places, In talking about sisters, there is a good place. Let's begin to reach out for this place. Let's stop doing the bad and get to the good. The good place does not allow exploitation, backbiting, cheap gossip and lies. The good place is a resource, a web of safety and warmth. The good places of sister -hood allows for sister to do things such as- babysit for her sister without question, help her with her school or college work and back her up in controversy. A good sister knows how to be and when to be. Let's begin to mature in sisterhood and find the good places. A good sister place, is when a sister is in 'need' and, before she is asks, the sister is there. A good sister place is when a sister will give even when she doesn't want to sometimes, yet she will allow her closeness and desire of her sister's security take prescense. We have all done that. The goodness of sister hood will keep secrets that don't need to be kept in order to protect and guard, sister darkness, that we all often experience! Sure we all have experienced sister darkness, situations that causes one sister or the other to be in darkness, by her own actions or the actions of others in her life, yet it does occur and it can cause us to be left ashamed, cold and oblivious to the outside world!

Yet sometimes a secret is told to the betterment of her sister's life and ability to function properly (we have all done that). It is all done in love though, even though we don't understand it, it is all in the name of love. Yes, we have all got together with one or the other of our sisters to squabble, talk about, laugh about, say, 'GIRL, she knows that is a shame, or she knows she should do better with her kids, husband, job, or whatever it is we want to talk about one or the other sister about." We talk down about our sister's mistakes, when her husband is not what we think he should be (we say to ourselves, that sorry, son of -----), yep, we say it in our heads, in our thoughts, in our dream, out of our mouths, but we dare not let our sister that we are referring to hear it! Yup, we have all done it one way or the other, out loud or in secret. This is unavoidable, yet we got to use these type of scenarios to make our sister relationship better, not worse. A good sister does a lot of things, good and bad, yet let's learn how to keep one another's secrets, and if we cannot, then lets just be honest upfront and say, "Girl, I don't know if I can keep that kind of secret, so its best you don't tell me, yes, lets be real about it, versus pay for it latter with "sister wrath (we have all experienced that too)"! So, let's decipher through what is beneficial and what is not. Read another poem, written by me about sisters.

Read this poem, take it in your heart.

Good sisters are this;

A good sister is one that is close and near
A good sister is one that is dear

A good sister knows her sister's heart
She will never let anything tear them apart

A good sister will tell you the truth
A good sister will risk it all, even if it is uncouth;

A good sister knows when to 'step back'
A good sister knows when one or the other sister lacks

This is because a good sister never parts
She is there to end it and there again to start

The issues that need to be discussed and those that do not
A good sister, let her be at times … she will never stop

Loving you no matter what you experience
A good sister-takes the sister bond serious

Never betraying and letting go
The good sister, I know … … (fill in the blank for your self-reader)

The poem depicts how good sisters should act and behave towards one another in times of bliss and in times of sorrow. Sisters have issues that they have, or that we need to let each other go through. For instance, when a sister gets married, we think we know what is best for her in a mate. Often times we want to rescue our sister from her choice of a husband, and sometimes we cannot because she has to learn life for herself, if this is the case, sometimes it is, and sometimes it isn't, but ether way it is your sister's choice to make. We want to help her through her relationship issues, but sometimes she does not want help, just a listening ear or a shoulder to cry on. Sadly, sometimes we have to let go and let the end show the beginning. Some sisters are secretive and like keeping their personal stuff to themselves. Some sisters love you all the same, but feels at times she can and needs to handle her own problems. When one sister sees a sister in danger, yes, warn her, even try to get her out of it, if you can. Provide all the help, and security that you possibly cam, but know, as sad as it is, that your sister has to make her own decisions and sometimes to her pain and her children's it is sad, but it is so, so true, tragedy can occur because of one's ill-advised or low researched choices and decisions. Sisters, those of you that have been or are currently seeing and witnessing your sister, go through pain in her marriage, accept and go through pain for her, share some of it spiritually, get on your kneews and, pray for her, do what is humanly possible to help her, but if she refuses, all you can do, is pray!

Sister Types Now sisters, I have talked about a whole lot regarding sisters and there is more. But now, I want to take the time to talk about now, is the type of sister we are, and can be. A sister type is like a personality, of the sort, "if you will," it is the description of the type of sister you are or the type that your sister is! There are various kinds! Take the time to read the following descriptions and excerpts on sisters. Find the kind that you are! I will- start out with the topics such as 'the guilty sister', 'the pleasing sister', the trouble making sister', the comedian sister, 'the peace making sister', 'the religious sister' the 'materialistic sister', 'play-play sister' 'the loner/alone sister' '"the I don't want no babies sister', 'the nasty sister' and "the I got to tell you the truth sister." If I have not named who you are as a sister, I am sure you will fall into some sub-category as you read on. Keep reading it gets better!

The guilty sister. The guilty sister is the one that always feels she owes the other sisters something. This particular type of sister holds guilt in her heart, meaning she thinks she has violated her sisterhood pledge in some way or morally wronged her sister siblings whether in word, thought or deed and she spends lots of time trying to compensate in some way for that particular emotion she carries.

I heard Rose (Betty White's character) on an episode of the 'Golden Girls' say that when her sister came to visit that 'she always felt guilty because they did not get along', but what she finally came to realize was that her sister was selfish and cared only for herself. There will always be times when one sister or several in a 'bunch' of sisters will only be concerned with 'how they feel'and not concerned with the others, and in turn causes lots of internal conflict among the sisters. Most of the time when a selfish sister is in the bunch, she will almost always 'place blame' on the innocent sister or sisters, transferring guilt to the heart of the innocent ones. This should not be so. Why does one sister make the other feel guilty? Is it because she is 'strong, fearless, assertive in her thoughts, actions, and ideas'? Is it because the one that lacks those qualities really want to be that way, and because of this, she in turn manifests a feeling she has inside and 'turns it on the innocent one' by accusing her of ills, wrongs, mishaps and the like? Sisters, have you ever experienced this? If so, it is time to stop being the 'guilty sister'. Even if you made a relational mistake with your sister it is time for you to identify the real source of your guilt and attack it, not the sister (LOL), but the guilt. Meaning explore your inner being and trace your steps. Find out how and why, you began to feel this way. What caused you to become guilty and why? Begin to face the guilt inside. Whether you were wrong or right, once you face it, admit, confess, forgive or whatever it takes to rid yourself of the antagonizing wiles of guilt you will begin to feel a lot better.

Guilt is an emotion that can drag on for a lifetime if not dealt with. Before you know it you will be an old aged geyser (smile) and on your death bed, saying tell my sister, I love her when this could have done, long before the end. I say this sisters, because this can happen if not dealt with. If you love your sister and want to make amends deal with your guilt, as soon as you possibly can. I don't want to force or rush you into this, yet I say this in urgency. I say this because I have read lots of self-help, family mending, do it again books that tell you to take certain precautions immediately. I would encourage sincere prayer, meditation, conversation, etc. …., before making any moves. I say this because you may, make a move that the other sister is not ready for and make things worse. Sometimes 'timing' is the best guide. You will know when the time is right, just don't take 'too long' is the key.

The pleasing sister. The pleasing sister is the one who tries to please all the other sisters because of some insecurity she has or mainly because she wants acceptance. Often times there is one sister that gets lost in the 'shuffle of sister cards' and she does everything she can to gain acceptance. Sisters dealing with this, hear me and hear me well- you will never be able to please your sisters enough to gain acceptance or feel validated. Validate yourself, do yourself, be yourself, find your confidence in what suits your style, your personality, your creative self. You do not have to be who your sister or sisters want you to be. Do not continue to create the mess that everyone else perceives for your life. Make and set your own sister path, you are you, so be that! Never try to make your sisters accept you. Be who you are. You were 'fearfully and wonderfully made' according to Psalm 139:14. Never try to please others, no matter who they are and how they are related to you. They (meaning sisters) will get accustomed to this type behavior, and they will never let you out of the prison you helped them create for you. Pleasing family members is sometimes worse than pleasing a stranger. I say this because often times you can eventually break away from a stranger. Family you will always have with you. That bond of family makes it harder to break away from certain curses, we generate personally or inherit. Being a sister pleaser is one we often create ourselves. It is okay to help our sisters and be there in a time of need, but pleasing them is a 'no-no'.

Never accept one sister's entrapment. It may be some long kept secret such as something you were 'vowed' not to do because of family customs or family rules and one sister caught you doing so anyway, don't stay in this place. Never please another because of something she secretly knows about you or witnessed you do. Face up to your faults or doings and let her know you will never be 'swindled' into fear or emotional blackmail. I know some of you are not 'believing' your eyes when you read this. I know, I know. I cannot believe I am writing this. I give all Praise and Honor to God for this Writing/Memoir" his precious "Holy Spirit" is pouring this out to me in his name-to give to sisters to set them free or bless them even more. He said I will 'restore all things'. This is only to make us all better sisters, keep reading!

Now sisters, no matter what race, religion, culture, background, neighborhood, income bracket, job, rich or poor, is better than the next. I want you to, at this very moment 'free yourself' from your sister's web or the perception in your mind that you think, that your sister or sisters have of you, it can go either way. You determine which way it is. Don't' let yourself go to the misery of misconception or rejection. Loose your mind from the bondage (and be free), loose your heart and your soul from whatever is entrapping you right now! Tell yourself you are set free and you are 'free indeed'. Never accept this agony again. If you are not physically near your sister, then repeat this to yourself. I am free from all childhood fears that I had as a sister or growing up. I free myself froms the warped thoughts that I had back then that -my sister will, expose me, tell on me, or take from me. No matter what it is- whether it be a wealth, inheritance, or an incident I participated in! These ill-fated thoughts, are to torment me (I see it and I know it and I am tired of being held captive), they come to scour me and tear me apart, so now I "REBUKE and REJECT" them, in Jesus Name! No matter what I did, I now want this agony to be re-moved from my psychological make up and being. I want them to be removed from me, and I denounce her hold, and I go forward in power and strength. Do it now! You will be glad you did! Be mindful that she will notice you are free and the enemy will try to 'gain that hold again', but go ahead, it is your time, it is your season to be set free!

The trouble making/negative sister, There is always one in the bunch. The one that carries news and bring news. They always say "The one that brings it will carry it." True saying, True meaning. I am sure I don't have to give you too much of a description. Because we all have a sister that will cause trouble openly or secretly. The Negative Nancy, the Nuisance, the one that buzzes around the sister group, like an aggravating gnat, that you just cannot stop! It is the one that tells something that you know you only told to her and she totally denies that she said anything and will tell you things like 'girl you are crazy' … I did not tell anybody, you must have told someone else because. I am not like that … when all the while the person she told explicitly tells you,, child guess what your sister told me about you … .This is the sister that befriends you just to get your personal and private information, only to spread it amongst the other sisters or family members. This is the sister that talks about everybody, to anybody and has no scruples. This is the sister that thinks she 'knows it all' and does not and sometimes because of her nosiness, she knows a few things, but I digress! She knows a lot because she is the 'town crier'. She gossips about the preacher, the teacher, the bus driver, his wife, the dog, the dog's friend, everyone, everything, and everyplace. This is the trouble making sister. She is very convincing and conniving. She convinces the mother of the brood that she is the victim and everybody else are her accusers and she paints everybody except herself as the culprit. Yep, and in spite of it all we love her still. These are just descriptions, okay (what do you think)!!!! Read on!

This particular sister is to be handled with caution. For those of us that knows her, need not fall prey to her. She is the type of sister that you love and be kind to, but with that long handle spoon and make sure that you do not divulge anything that you do not want told, exploited, kept a secret, or held as sacred out of the bag, because believe me, when she gets a hold of it, it is for sure coming out. She is not the person you confide in. This is the sister that you love, pacify (a little, only to keep her off you back, somewhat of a peace offering (LOL), because if you don't you will be her next target). When she gets bored, she thinks of stuff to talk about and she is not comfortable unless turmoil is in the midst of the sisters. You will know her by her fruit … (her actions, words, and deeds). This is to help you not hurt or separate you any further, this is the armor you have to carry until your sister changes, is delivered or sees the light. This is your shield of protection. Take it and run with it, you will live in peace until the bridge is built between you and her.

The Comedian Sister Now there is a sister that all of us have or most of us that is the "laugh" of the party. She keeps you laughing when you should be crying, and she makes you cry, when you are to be laughing (that is how much fun she is)! She turns every family brawl into a stand-up comedy show. She is the sister that no matter what awful instance you describe or explain she will come up with a laugh! This is the loving sister, the sister that hides behind her comedy. She does not want you to get too close and neither does she desire to be too close to. She is most comfortable in the mode of comedian, it keeps her safe. This is the zone that she knows. This is her place of refuge. She will not ever be caught without a handy joke. She is the one that you have to hang up from getting stitches in the stomach. She is the one that never take sides and never ever talks about one sister over the other. She will only give hints 'between the lines of her jokes'. She is well aware and she will never ever stray away from her lines. This is the sister, that deep inside wants to provide answers to the ever so troubling sister romps. But she fears the outside, she fears the outside of her jokes and what will happen if she does not have one. This is the sister you love a lot, but despise because she hides behind her language of comedy. This is the sister, the comedian. Do you have one, whether blood or bought that you want to come out of that shell or stay there, this is the person with the "third eye", she sees all things as and from comedy and humor, do you know her in your sister group?

Intermission Talk to your sister, encourage her to seek counseling. Let her know that you truly enjoy her comedian side, but that there is a time for everything. A time to laugh, a time to cry as the Bible says, a time to refrain from, a, a time to refrain from laughing (Ecclesiastes 3:4). Let her know of your love, but that at some point she needs to be taken serious, or audition for a show for comedians (this was just to make you laugh). But seriousnly, your sister that jokes at times when it is not even funny really needs to develop, evolve and grow up in a way of difference. Let her know that suppressing issues through laughter can be a plus, but it can be a burden as well. Push your comedic sister to 'be for real, for a change'. (I know this is getting to you right?)

Every one of our sisters has a sigh, whether it is an inner sigh or an open sigh, or finally a word spoken sigh. This is her motto, her life mission, her values, her integrity. But is it always appropriate or right? Judge for yourself, read the poem below and mediate on this for yourself or your sister.

My Sister Sighs

My sister sighs, my sister cries
Sometimes my sister tells lies

My sister sighs my sister cries
Sister, why is this so- why, why, why?

Sister, why are you this very incredulous way
You wake up, and never budge in your soul, to this very day.

Your sighs are good and sometimes bad
Sister, my sister, you make me so mad …

My sister cries and she sighs
The blues that are deep in her hurting soul "way" down inside?

My sister sighs and she cries, just to make a point..
My sister sighs and she cries, make me want to "bust this joint.".

My sister cries, my sister sighs
Will she ever receive or respond with ear inviting righteous replies …?

My Sister sighs, My Sister Sighs, won't let go of the devil's spark …
My Sister Sighs, my Sister cries, evil, you must depart …

My sister sighs, my sister cries break up the fallow ground—
My sister sighs, my sister cries, come on back, around

Let's continue reading this book, it is nearing the end, but it's now getting really good, my dear sisters, keep reading!

The peace making sister. The "peace making sister" is the one that tries to keep and make peace amongst 'all the sisters'. The peacemaker will always try to bring about reconciliation.

She is always there saying "This is not right" or "It should not be this way" or "Yawl please don't do this." She is similar to the "comedian sister" where she does not want any grudges, animosity, hostility and she will do anything to maintain the peace in the family. The peace making sister never fails to call everyone up after an intense argument amongst the sisters and she is always on the phone with the "Momma" trying to get to the bottom of what is going on to make everybody understand the other person's side. She is the one that 'tends to everybody else's garden and leaves her's unattended'. She is the one that is so busy trying to keep the peace until peace is no longer apart of her inner self or for that fact; her very own. She has forfeited her place of peace, her place of reckoning, so that everyone else can be fulfilled, but to the cost of her very own! Are you this sister? Think on this? What is the goal of the peace making sister? Is it too, self-fulfilling? Her goal is to make sure everybody loves each other. She has seen what disruption and mayhem causes and she despises it. Maybe she is such an advocate for peace because she witnessed parental divorce or someone she loves dearly relationship fall apart because of the lack of peace and harmony. Maybe it is because the feelings and flashbacks of no peace 'haunt her' and she despises this aspect of relationships. The peacemaker loses sleep at night to make sure that peace is there for others often times forgetting about the peace she needs in her own life. She will go countless hours without sleep trying to solve others problems and often get into terrible fusses and fights with her husband or significant other because she is so focused on bringing peace to the unduly sisters. You my sister, if this is you, set your boundaries too! Don't keep forfeiting yours for others, it is not worth it! Find yourself and then you find yor peace!

**The religious sister.** Now this sister is all into her "Word." Every day and night she is talking about the word or her religion. She believes in every word she reads, and she does not stray from it. She will quote scriptures, passages, whether it be from the Koran, the Bible or her Religious book, and she is the one that when the conversations go awry, she suggests getting on your knees and praying. She is the one that rebukes the devil at every turn and 'denounces' spirits in your face. She is the sister that is spiritually insurmountable and she is the one 'you love, but hate to call'. Yes because she is that gentle, yet loving sister, but when you call you really just want to talk to your sister … but because she is religious bound., it is hard for you to get a 'glimpse' at her because she, too hides behind her religion. This sister is the one you can depend on and honestly, she can get 'a prayer; through'. She is the light of the house and her presence does truly make everything feel alright. Yet, making you nervous at the same time, around your not so saved, acquaintances. You feel safe with her though, as somehow her spiritual connection, makes itself known. She is strong hearted and she does not stop, for nothing, she prays through the night, and she will get a break through. She knows the pulse of God and she can talk to him, in a way that is unbelievable, yes she is that sister! She will pray in tongues on the phone with you. She will stop you were ever you are, on the street, in Walmart, in front of the grocery store, at the club, yep she will sense you, and will come if she needs to, and walk right inside the club and get you or straight up tell you, "it's time to go". She has no fear, she only fears God, she is the one! She will pray in the club with out shame if she has to. Although she is fearless in that sense, she still will respect your wishes and walk you outside to the car, to pray and get a response from God! She is the one that you feel safe with. She is the one that just to hear her voice makes you feel like somehow it will be alright! Yes, and although you know that you were trying to get your twerks in, you somehow feel good and guilty, at the same time, as you go back in the club. She is that sister, yes the sister that keeps the spirit "high" and uplifted. She is the religious sister.

She is the one that makes you cringe at her coming but at the same time, she is the one, the light bearer, the one that gets the job done and seems like the spirits listen to her and respond to her immediate requests. This is the sister, although religious, you can trust, rely upon and depend on to be firm, consistent and on point! You trust her, you feel her, even when you are out there sinning, she is the sister that is weird, but good at the same time! This sister is resilient and passionate about truth and change. She is the sister that you love to be around, but just don't want her to talk 'too much'. She is the one that is not afraid and is the 'silent power' of the bunch. You know that with this sister although she is bible toting or koran fearless. She exuberates a strength that none of the other sisters have. She is the one that even your "momma" leans on, although she would never admit to it (your moma that is) Her children are neat, well-poised,clean hearted, and looking". We all "Rise up and call her blessed (Proverbs 31:28-even when we don't want to some time) There is a sense of purity upon her, but yet at times. You feel overwhelmed with who she is. She tends to smother the atmosphere with her presence.

The religious sister is the one that stays in church or the temple all day and night and her entire life is centered around her beliefs. She is the one that begs you and begs you to come to her church or place of worship. She is the one that one day when you finally try and go with her, she scares the 'wits' out of you with the rituals endured or performed. She is the sister that knows you are afraid and comes and 'rub' your back and tells you to 'not resist'. She is the sister that although you stayed in church for eight hours, you somehow trust in her more than you do the other sisters. She is the one that you can confess anything to, because she has a serine spirit, a just spirit, she is calm and non-judgemental at all times, only when she has to be, she is that sister! The religious one, yes, that's her! This sister although a diehard religious girl … at times knows when to 'pull the cover back' and not mention religion. She is a smart, wise, firm, sister, yet she does not let all people know who she is. She maintains a good demeanor, she is always positive and she will go out of her way to help you … This is the religious sister. Although she is a fanatic at times, she pushes you through to the otherside as she always has your spiritual best at hand. She is the one that you can present your deepest fears, sins, and mistakes too. She never tells, anyone nor does she ridicule you about your faults or weaknesses. She finds a way of wisdom to let you know how you strayed, and how to move into the light again. This is the religious one. Are you this sister?

<u>**Special Note**</u>: Now we have read quite a few descriptors on sisters, and their style, personality, and flair. There's a few more. I wanted to break at this moment to ask are you "feeling and seeing yourself or someone you know"? If so, does this help you with understanding and seeing your sister or yourself in a different light? Continue to read this book with a renewed sense of understanding and figure out which direction you need to take with your sister. How you can work on your relationship? Understanding her is the key to growth, connection and the "turn-up of sisterhood (a millennial saying)", I just had to say that"! LOL! Let's continue on with the descriptors. Let's engage ourselves, so that we can figure out who and which one we are! Let's know our characteristics! Moving right along!

<u>**Materialistic/Educated/Chanel/Gucci, Style Sister.**</u> Now we have the material-istic sister. She is the one that loves material possessions and is defined by them. She is the sister that you really do 'hate' but only because you are 'blood' relatives do you deal with her. She is the sister that is always talking about the next $5,000 bag or Red bottoms she is going to purchase. She is always talking about 'stage shows' and 'popular plays' she frequents. She is the one that secretly rubs in your nose the fact that she has, it and 'you do not'. She is the one that your "momma and the preacher" praise because she makes them, embrace her "bigness", style and flair. She forces you to embody her with the lashes, high botoxed check bones and plastic, waxed everything else! She brags, she brags and she brags, she is that sister that is on all levels, phases and stages, she can be living in the projects, driving her gifted Mercedes Benze, but always clocking something new or telling of her new project furniture and where she and her "boo" is going next. She is

Always bragging about what she ordered from Tiffany's Macys or some other cite with Ghetto to Glamour Clothing! She makes you want to throw up, or get ghost (another millennial term)!

This is the sister that is 40 years old that acts like she is 20. She is the one that said she was going to medical school and did go, and you- can never live it down. While you going to school online (nothing wrong with that) and, work-ing at Starbucks, all at the same time. She is the sister that is always talking about Oprah and how she wants to be like her one day, with the same billion dollar stash. She is the sister that knows all the college and university names and the Presidents of each. She is the sister that walks in the door and demands attention either of her title or her style, because she is over the top with every accessory, every car, every outfit. She is the one that everybody secretly and openly, tend to hate. She is the sister that talks of Jimmy Choo, Ralph Lauren, Tom Ford, Vera Wang, and all the names you never heard of only on the red carpet. She is the sister that has her Tablet, Laptop and I Phone all, in her midst at all times. She is the sister that is talking about the "Dow" and you thought it was "Soap." She is the sister that knows the "ups and downs' of the market and she is always talking about people she knows personally who were promoted to CEO at IBM. She is the sister that talks about her dreams of leaving the country to travel to places like Cancoon, Maroco or Dubai! She is the one that says she met "President Obama and the First Lady" at a benefit Dinner she attended where the plates started at $7,000 each. She is the one that knows people in the six figure club and working on the 7 digit club. She is the sister that everywhere you go, she is filing reports, talking about figures, speaking in a business language you never heard. This is my materialistic, educated, 'aristocratic sister'. Do you know her?

The evil hearted sister. This one I call the evil hearted sister, plain and simple. Those of you that are reading this book right now, know exactly the sister that I am referring to. This is the sister that was born a 'bad seed'. She is the one that everyone knows she is just that. She is the one that sabotages major events with her contradictions, fake episodes and attention seeking behaviors. She is the one that makes all the excuses in the world, yet wants nothing, for nobody, not even herself. She is the one that makes you think she is loving and kind, but in the back of heart she is nothing but evil. She at times make you wonder; where on earth did her fertilization take root from. She is the one that taunts openly and secretly. She knows that you can see her evil ways and she snickers at you when you see her evil behaviors COME OUT. No she does not snicker with her lips, which would be too easy, she snickers with her eyes, with her body language. She knows who will pay attention to it and who will not and she so gently, but hostilly serves you up a plate of no good!. She desires to see, you (her sisters); suck up the taste of failure and she feeds off of it! This is the one, that you wonder to yourself, is she going where the son does not shine or if that is actually where she came from! This is the one that really needs to be in a psyche ward, but nobody knows it. She is different and evil smarted at the same time, yes this is her, she is that evil hearted sister is this you?God wants even this type and kind of sister to be healed. Pray for your sister and ask God to relieve her from the evil that has beset her for most and all of her life!

Special Note: Sisters, this memoir, is to give you a little taste of sisterhood, and what sisters have been for many years, said or unsaid. God wants us to get the understanding so we can address one another through our real and true understanding of one another.

More on sister traits! There is a sister that comes into your life that is not your blood. She grows onto, and into the family, she can be good or devastatingly bad, she is the play, play sister. She is the sister that we all love to have in our lives. She is with us all the time in our family gatherings, so on and so forth. She resembles the surrogate sister mentioned earlier, yes that is her, yet there is a darker side to a play play sister that we all need to be aware of. Let's get the true understanding of what we are dealing with.

Darker Side of a Play, Play Sister Type. On the darker side, there is a sister that secretly competes with you. She comes along, just to keep you in her sight, she is not a open, outright trouble maker, she does her stuff in between the seams. She goes from one sister to the other, siding with each one. She hides what she is, and coasts along in the family, until she is called out and exposed for who and what she really is. She is the one that secretly holds a grudge with you although she tells everybody else that you are her best friend, her sister, her BFF (we did not say BFF back in the days, we only said or referred to each other as "play-play") She is the one that hates you in her heart, but cannot stand to **_not_** know what you are doing, just so you won't get too far ahead of her. She is the sister we all need and don't need, at the same time. She is the next door neighbor, the kindergarten associate, the down the street girlfriend, the country kin, or whatever you call her or refer to her, as, but she is and will always be the "play-play" sister. She is special, because she plays her cards well, As, she was and is there for all of your real sisters events in life, to include- weddings, pregnancies, business openings, you name it, and she was there!She is the one that has spent the night with you and your birth sisters, gone on trips with you and your blood sisters, sat up late at night and gossiped with you and your biological sisters and then acts like she does not know you, when she is with another set of play sisters. She is the busiest of bodies. She is two-faced and she is known as "Aunt So and So (**You fill in the blank**)" by your kids. She is the one that is an only child, so she switches her sister bond from family to family. She is the one that calls you early in the morning and say "let's do breakfast' or 'let's do church' or 'let's do the club'. She is the one that everybody in the family loves and does not know of her several personalities. She is the lying Libra, the twinned out, two-faced Gemini" or the undercut- Pisces"...the one that is a socialite, the phoney, the liar, the one that secretly tries to seduce your childhood sweetheart and any other man you take serious. She is the one that so many times you want to sever the tie, but do not because somehow although you hate her, you love her, she is my sister, my enemy, BUT she is- the 'play-play one'. Are you this sister?

Read this poem below … (For the Play-Play Sister)

My Sister, My enemy.
She is the one I love to hate
My sister my enemy
Things she did to me- I remember ever since I was eight

My sister my enemy
She drove me to shame

My sister my enemy
Even though we don't have the same last name

My sister my enemy
Told lies on me with no remorse

My sister my enemy
She left me at times with no hope

My sister, my enemy come to me and face me with the truth
My sister my enemy. Can't you see, works me till I am blue …

I love you and I hate you, almost everyday
My Sister, My enemy, no more time to play

Why do you want to keep this up?
Lies, jealousy and distrust?

Clean up your heart and your ways
My sister, My enemy lets change this and go to the next phase

Of our lives before it is time to go
Unto death beyond life's crossing Up Above or Down Below …

And then we cannot say how sorry we are or were... to one another
Let's not be enemies, for the sake of our loving mothers …

My sister my enemy-can't you see
Woven deep inside my soul, let's end this side of us ultimately

Do you know this person written about in the poem above, read on!

Let's Continue …

<u>Situational Ethics with Sisters</u>. Sometimes your sisters can become your enemy when you get married. When you are married, part of you 'transfers in spirit and mind' to your husband's way of doing things. It is hard to realize, but it does- and with this comes change. Often times one sister or the other does not realize that this change must take place, 'in the beginning' but can 'level off as time passes'. It can be difficult for a sister to understand your level of submission to your husband and your marriage vows. Some sisters think that 'sisters come first," NO MATTER WHAT, they feel a marriage, should not separate, but it does. That can often be a misconception. The spouse has to be placed and once he is placed, then things can fall in line, some sisters, call it control, some call it brainwashing, some call it deception, but no matter what you call it, or how you see, it -he is her husband and until she changes it, you have to set back and let it be, not all sisters have to go through this, but a lot do, so let's get the understanding and wait, time cannot crush the sister bond. Be wise and let your sister "mare (mesh with)" with her mate, she will come back, yes she will!Sisters are to come in 'second place' as is any family member, including Mom and Dad, once you are married … you are to 'leave and cleave'. Leave your parent's home and cleave to your husband. Sisters are a bit more sensitive or less willing to believe those particular set of rules, digest and lets move on! We are almost there!

Sisters when dealing with your sister's husband and you are offended by his very presence, make yourself aware of what is really going on. Most of the times sisters are dependent upon one another and a husband at first seems to get in the way, this is because, you feel you 'cannot talk to your sister the same', 'you cannot react with each other the same', you cannot hang out with each other the same. And it just keeps on going. I would say, sisters to just give it a little time. Normally that is how it goes initially and sometimes it does not change, from that, but the main way to not make your sister an enemy in this area is to learn how to not make her have to choose. Now on the other side of things, give your newly married sister time to adjust and modify her lifestyle to what she vowed before God and witnesses. I know she's feeling just as awkward as you are, but because of the purpose of life that includes marriage. Waiting on the adjustment period is always key. Be prepared to not like the changes that marriage, made for your sister, because it will definitely happen, for the newly married sisters, for some of us time has past, but I am sure we all that are seasoned married sisters, know this is so! So take note, newly married sisters, I am sure you 'hated' her for getting married in the first place, because you knew your access to her was going to limited. You saw it coming the day she started dating this guy. Yeah, I know you did. But it's okay, just know that your sister loves you and so try your hardest to wait on the change.

Mistakes. I know for some of you, though, you feel that- your sister's husband simply turned her against you . Some of you may not even be buying that a husband comes first and that nothing should come in front of a sister bond. I know that some of you are seeing this as a joke. I got something for you all too. Sometimes a sister will and does make a mistake and marry a 'jerk'-really and truthfully, there is nothing you can do about it, but pray for her, encourage, love and support your sister until she sees the light. No one sister can make a decision for the other! A sister has to be bought to a place that she makes the decision to change her situation. I know some of you sisters are angry and want to rescue your sister, but truthfully the decision is left up to her, if she is in a situation where the husband is not treating her fairly in any capacity, you will have to remain on her side until the 'blinders drop off'. I know some of you may even 'blame' yourselves for your sister being with this guy, don't torture yourself. Lots of times we as sisters blame ourselves for the way our sister's lives end up. We try to fix, turn, change, help, help, help and it never turns out the way we hope and pray it to happen. We try to provide answers and intrude into our sisters lives, to be honest, most of the times, our sisters do not take advice as serious as we should from one another. We listen physically, but deep down inside we say to ourselves, "I am not listening to her not one bit", she always thinks she knows everything, she was that way all her life and now that I am an adult, I do not have to listen to her and I won't and most of the time one sister will not listen to the other sister, even if she is right, even if she went to medical school, even if she is a preacher, lawyer, astronaut, electrical engineer, relationship counselor, college president, chef, cook, garbage collector, actress, singer, etc. The sister boundaries stop where the blood stops … I am sure many of you know what that means. It is sad, but it is true, some of us don't trust our sisters no more than we can text, email, or Instagram them, it varies (I am trying to bring understanding and touch all basis). Another sad truth. Let's try to get to the bottom of this, so that we can live and come into peace.

I encourage you sisters to not worry about how her husband is treating her, although I know it makes you sad, and it is not easy to do. She (your sister) has to choose to make that change for herself. As sad as it may end up! You cannot do anything about it. I have seen sisters in my life have wonderful husbands, relationships etc., and then I have seen some, 'wallow' in horrible relationships with abusive men that you pray, call, encourage, push, etc. but to no avail. The victory only comes when the sister gains her self –esteem back, her 'self-upwardness, herself consciousness'. You see if you are the sister that is watching your sister be abused, you can call the police, you can do any preventative measure or action, that you feel that you need to do so, but when your sister has no 'sense of self', there is nothing that you can do to save her, she has to see it for herself. She has to realize the dangers in being with this man. To be perfectly honest, sisters, the only thing that I have seen help in this situation is backing off, yet being supportive and praying, When a man abuses a woman (not turning this into a book on abuse) she is lost 'in him'. The power that he has exalted over her mind, has taken over and she 'lives and breathes it'. Sadly some women, never release themselves and end up prey to a man's weakness and abusive ways.

Pray, support and love the sister that has been changed into your enemy by her husband

Lord help

Lord help my dear sister
I can't seem to do it

Lord help my dear sister
I just 'knew it

That this guy she said was 'of her dreams'
Was nothing at all, It was just as it seemed …

Very mean to her and dis-respect-full
Lord help my dear sister, please be mer-ci-ful..

Lord I am depending on you to do this for me
Lord help my dear sister-come out by decree

Decree of your word and your inevitable power
Lord help my dear sister, don't let her stay in this another hour!.

Lord help my dear sister.

The loner/alone sister. The "Loner/Alone Sister. "Is the one that wants to be left alone? She is the one that is 'in the family, but not 'of the family'. She is the one that stays on the outskirts and comes to most of the gatherings, but when she does she seems to not want to be bothered, she does not answer her phone, come to the door, receive a text or anything. She is the one that 'twitter's between 'saved and I am not so sure if I am saved (she is true to herself)'. She is the one that is very moody and distant, but you knows that she likes being around the family during extra-large gatherings- sometimes … The Loner sister can go for days and months and years, if there was not parental intervening -without seeing the family. She takes strangest trips all by herself. She does not talk a whole lot during family gatherings. Sometime she 'laughs really hard' at the jokes of your favorite uncle, but she is strange, but in a 'good kind of way'. The sister that is alone lets you know that 'two and three is a crowd'. She tries to hurry into gatherings and hurry out, but sometimes out of guilt she stays because she doesn't want to hear the parents 'jibber' about why she left so early, why is she so quiet, why is she distant, why is she not engaging. She can sit on the sofa and be still and quiet for hours. If nobody says anything to her, she won't say anything to them. One thing though, she loves the kids and will laugh, talk and play with them, as long as no adult is around. She is strange and weird in a good way. She is the sister that "keeps herself" to herself. She is the sister that you are not going to get to "talk but so much." She Is introverted (inside of herself) and that is where she is safest. She is the sister that is brilliant, but nonchalant at the same time. She is gentle and kind, but will "push' you out and away, if you get too close. She is the sister that will talk to you at times, but if you bug her too much, she will penalize you with her "lack of presence" for as long as she possible can, she is the beautifulist thing you want to see, but she down plays her beauty. She will never let you in to her relationships, because those are "brick stone' solid/ out of the question and quiet entities within her life. She may never marry, she is in love with her aloneness. She loves her significant other, but mostly not to the point of sacrificing her private side. She is the one that is alone and likes it that way!

(More on) Isolation and alienation. Many, many times one sister leaves the others behind because she cannot take the pressure anymore. Many many times one sister is left to herself willfully or forcefully because one or several sisters refuses to compromise. Sisters have fought day in and day out, year in and year out because they refuse to let go to the other sister's feelings, ideas, thoughts intelligences, ideas, projects, or what have you. This causes one sister or the other, to alienate herself and move herself out of the sisterhood brood. Sisters we need to wake up and see- what we are doing to each other. We need to realize that sisterhood is a powerful force, and that inorder to be a force, we have to improvise and compromise in order to get along, grow and develop. We need realize how important it is to be someone's sister. God created sisters to be there for one another, while taking your sister's spirit in your hand, caring for it, being gentle with it and comforting it- when she is in need.

Sister/Self type. There is one type of sister out there that is alone. She is the sister that you always see, but never hear (*another version of an isolated version of a sister type*). She is not like the loner/sister, but she is the sister that feels inferior and insecure. She is the sister that has lots of gifts, but has never been able to 'come forward' as the prize possession that she really is. She does not know herself without her sisters, she is the one that is 'lost 'in the shuffle and does not speak often, only behind closed doors and in the annals of her heart. She is the one that wishes she could have done more, but got caught in life's shuffle of sisterhood and 'just being there'. She was the one that had a lot to say, but did not say nothing. She was the one that believed in her sister's plight and lost out because of it. She is the one that had lots of views that were totally different, lots of deep level thinking towards sensitive family topics and not just family topics, but other topics, but she allowed her sisters' view to dwindle, her insight, her plight, her advocacy, her ability to press into a thing, a thought, a word, a deed.. a lifestyle, an endeavor, a duty, a deed! She gave away her rights to things that were valued and hallowed. She went too far with taking on the- the sister pledge, and lost her dreams. Had this particular type of sister done something, in her prime, she would have been in a different place.

She is the one that has a secret 'love/hate' relationship with her sisters, that she hides and keeps 'pressed deep down inside' She is the one that wants to be set free, but time has now passed and she feels it is 'too late' or she is 'too much of this or too much of that' to make any waves, she is the sister that loves/yet hates her sister 'brood', she is the one that will remain silent until possibly the day she dies about how she really feels in honor of the 'sister code' .. "Thou shall not betray, talk against, state your views, disagree with, go against, leave, do not listen, keep your mouth shut, tell them they are wrong, tell them they are morally out of line, tell them they are making 'foolish mistakes'. She is the one that knows it all, but "goes" to say nothing. She is the sister that feels-that- being quiet when she should speak up, is a sin against the sisterhood pack. She is the sister that at times, hates it all, but she stays because she always heard the words 'echo' from "her momma's lips." "Don't betray your sisters" "Stick with them" never walk away from your sisters. This is the sister that has chosen to suffer, instead of speak, She is the sister that no one pays much attention to, but is the smartest one of all she is the sister that is despised by one sister in whom she would least expect, but she is the one she has done the most for the and "treaded out the corn for (as the Bible says in I Timothy 5:18, speaking metaphorically). Is this you? Are you the sister that has tortured yourself for most of your life, taking the backseat to sisterhood flaws? If this is you, 'stand up'.

I call this sister, 'Sister/Self" because she is deep into herself, her thoughts, her notions, etc. The Sister/Self is the one that remains inside of herself only to not reveal who she is to the rest of her sisters. Her sisters walk by her day in and day out, to not know who she really is and have made her weak for all of her life. She is the sister that felt overlooked and has accepted this as her 'm/o'. She has told herself deep in her-'self' that this is the way it should be, only but wishing in her heart of hearts that it would be different. Sister, dear Sister, you have time … you are still here and you have time to make yourself shine and be somebody. You can continue to grow and sprout if you take that first step..the first step to what you always wanted to do and be. Sister take care of yourself, do not allow everybody else's gardens to be 'attended to' and not your own. Take the time to cultivate who God created you to be and stop making excuses for your sisters. Take off their 'mantra' and put on your own individualized 'self- created mantra, that God himself gave to you!' It is time. You have time to further- create your own individuality and still love them, at the same time. You will not abandon them. It is alright to say this time. "I don't agree with you all." I think that you were wrong the entire time..etc., etc. Take a stand when you need to and free yourself from years of error and mistakes.

Special Note: **Take charge and change your name girl, it is your gift, it is your season, it is your blessing, not there's … Go forward!**

Another thing about the loner sister is that she will get 'one-on-one' at times with one sister or the other, only at one time,while distancing the time she speaks to each one. She is a good sister, but at times, you don't know if she is good or bad (because of her introspection of herself, being on constant watch, of herself and within herself, sounds weird, but I know you, yes, you the one reading this knows this is you, for whom it applies). She is generous, but she won't let you take advantage of her. If you do try to 'pull the wool over her eyes', you can believe it will be a long time before she talks to you, that is how she punishes you. She thinks nobody knows or understands her ways. Yet there is a straight "ace in the hole" perception of who she is by at least one or more of the sibling sisters within the group. This type of sister does not tell you her business at all and she is very offended and defensive when you ask. Do you know this sister? Is it you?

The I don't want no baby's sister type." Yes there is one in the bunch that does not want children. She freaks out at the sound of "Are you pregnant.?" She is always caring condoms around, always counting her birth control pills and always panicking when the topic of pregnancy comes up. She is the one that is married and her husband is begging her to have a child, adopt a child, anything a child. She is the one that is married and does not desire to be, as she doesn't want to be married, although she wants sex, and because she was raised to be married if you want to be intimate. This is the outgoing sister, that has no scruples, but has them all. She is the mix between "I wannna be right, but I also wanna be wrong" and has the split -in personalities that pop up out of nowwhere. This is the one that 'sickens you out' with her tantrums on NOT wanting or having a child. She is the one that sees children as brats, won't babysit or come to birthday parties, because she believes she will get the 'pregnant bug'. She is the one that makes you want to 'grab her by the neck' she is the sister that says "I don't want no babies." She is the one that believes that children are a burden and not a blessing. She is the one that believes a child will 'mess up her figure' She is the one that calls you crazy for having your house full. She is the 'one' that hates to read the Story book of "The old woman that lived in a shoe." Do you know her? Is it you or is it your sister?

**The nasty sister.** The nasty sister is the one that you know not to mess with too much, 'because she is enjoyes being nasty". She has the nasty look, the nasty attitude, and the nasty disposition, she is the "Nasty Girl"! She is the one that we all avoid. She is the one that eats trouble for dinner. She is so nasty, that there is nothing much too say except- she is the one that makes everyone love to hate and avoid her. She looks mean at every turn and smells of it. When people see her in the store, they know to go down the other isle, because they know if you so much as even smirk at her wrong, she will be ready to stir trouble and be glad about it! Yes, because she enjoys and intentionally loves being nasty. She enjoys making everybody miserable, because she is miserable. She is the kind of sister that has no limits and sets no boundaries, she indulges affairs not of her own, she will take what she can to be just that a "NASTY GIRl!"

The I got to tell you the truth sister. This is the sister that speaks the truth, even when she does not need to. This is the sister that does not realize that some truths gets you in trouble. This is the sister that is so truthful, she incriminates herself when it is time to apply for her food stamps. She is the one that really does not understand that truth sometimes mean..."Keep your mouth shut." She is the sister that thinks telling the truth means telling you what another sister said, not to tell because she did not want to hurt the sensitive sister's feelings. Is this you? I don't think I need to say more about this particular sister. What she fails to realize is that sometimes the 'truth' hurts and some people cannot handle the truth all at once. She is the sister that is too smart to be dumb! Need I say more?

Descriptors. All in all, the descriptive monologues given on sisters are hear to make you aware, make you laugh, make you cry, and make you say "AMEN" to at least one or a few, so that you can see yourself or your sister and come to terms with who you are, in order that you can all be healed. I am sure you can see yourself in at least one of these sisters or maybe several. Being a sister is a highly esteemed role and can be a ventricle to use to maintain blessedness, yet at times, it can often times be seen as or full of turmoil, strife, suffering and pain. Let's move on!

What about the sister that is really your half-sister, but is of a different race. Let's read up on that, how do you handle this situation? What is your perception of her, what is the bi-racial sister's perception of you? Let's see how she is described.,

**The Biracial/half sister** is a sister. that is of a different race. A sister that your Mom or Dad bred, from different means. A sister that was created in a different womb or was from a different seed. A sister that may have been born of a different culture or life style than your own. A system of difference that entered into your life that was of contrast, yet oneness. Someone that was different than what you know, different in terms of what you know as a sister born of the same blood. A sister that flowed through similar means that you did, but something is obviously different, yet the same. You do by no means look the same, but she is yes, your sister. She sits at the table to eat with you and the other sisters, but somehow you wonder, who is she? Where did she come from? Why is she sitting here with us? Why is her color, her tone, her make-up different than mine! Read on!

"The half sister (when we were kids)"

This sister is the one that you want to be proud of, but you can't because, you cannot quite figure her out, as- she always holds her head in a direction, that you are unfamiliar with, she is the one that pays attention to things that you do not, she is the one that understands culture in a different way that you do not, she is expansive, she is abstract, she is "so not you," yet she is you. How can this be? She is the one that does not act a certain way in public, when you do. She is the one that you feel ashamed of, yet proud of at the same time. She is the one that you want the world to know is your sister, yet, you somehow don't, you just- though-, for the life of you, cannot get close to her, and neither can she to you (inside or out). She is the one that you watch out the corner of you eye and while she looks 'right back at you'. She is the one that you all talk superficially and smile, at each other 'curtly' even though you both know deep in your souls that you don't quite get this 'sisterhood' thing, between the two of you, even though your mother or father, has the same name and so does she. It feels, tastes and sound like a sister, but is it really a sister? You both somehow know that 'you are enemies from within'. Yet you both ask yourselves, "why are we so connected, yet disconnected"?

Read into the minds of the two different looking/colored sisters above.

Sister 1.*I know my sister hates me and I think I hate her. She came into the world with skin oh so much fairer than ours. She came in as if she was a princess to the world, and I was furious with Momma,. I really was, how could she do this to us? How could she change the family portrait, how could she add a color that that is not properly coordinated?" How could she invite stairs, sneers and snarls? People calling our Mom the "Nanny" or asking them is she a foster child? How could she be so careless. "I think I blame her the most." I remember playing hopscotch and a car stopping and saying 'Hey little girl are you okay'? I recall immediately trying to protect my sister, as I am the oldest and the person in the car said, "I am talking to the little cute one," sorry. My sister was too young to answer, I took her in the house and I told Momma what happened and all she did was look at us and say 'I hope you are okay'. Momma never explained this was the beginning of the rejection and the separation of my sister and me ". She never once explained this to me, that I would grow up resenting her, to the point of not being able to be in the same room with her, talk to her, cohabitate with her. My sister of a different race and I have not talked in 10 years. I never knew bringing a different race into the family would cause me such pain. I never knew that I would hate my sister as I do my enemy, only because of her color and the difference that she brings in. "My sister my enemy."*

Sister 2.I was born of a different race and I am not ashamed of it. I was born with skin that stands out differently than the rest of my sisters. I love my sisters every one of them, but this one sister of mine. I cannot embrace. She is the one that watches me all the time and when I think she is not looking she is still there. She is the one that does not talk to me even though I reach out to her, she is the one that makes me feel as if I don't belong or as if I am an outcast. I love my family, although at times, I don't know why Momma did this, because it can be challenging. I have wondered to myself, why I am the only one with hair like this, skin like this, features like this. But I let go to my heritage, my family, I know within myself, God allowed this for a reason. I accept who I am, but my one particular sister has not, she cannot and will not open up. When we were kids she would protect me in the beginning, because that is what all older sisters do, but as we got older, no matter what I tried to do, to let her know it was "us and not us against each other" it made it worse. She would walk in front of me, walk past me, sit behind me on the bus, stand a distance away from me when we waited for the bus. I did not know what to make of it, talking about reverse 'racism'. I had a good life, but my sister the one, that I hate to call my enemy—but she is, made my life a living hell at times … Momma did not make it any better because she always tried to 'pacify' the both of us. I refused to stoop to my sisters level, so after many years of trying to make her happy. I gave into what she wanted. I became her enemy. I never purposely did anything to harm my sister, but I did a lot of ignoring and blocking, 'whew that took a lot of energy'. I would not go anywhere she was when we were hanging out and if I knew she was there or got there and by mistake was not informed, I immediately left. My friends would always wonder, what was going on between me and my sister, but I felt that was the family secret, I guess that was my Daddy's side of me, to stay true to your family bond, no matter how you felt. Do not turn your back on your family or insult them with 'outsiders'. That is just what I believed. But my sister..she fought me hand and foot, even though I never argued with her, humiliated her or even contradicted one word that came from her mouth.

My sister fought long and hard to 'seal and sanctify herself' as my enemy. She fought really hard to put the wedge that she felt "all along" into existence. She made it come alive! She fought so hard until I think it took Momma to her death. You see my momma was what they refer to as old school (I don't use such terms)," but I heard them say it a lot. She did not believe in 'causing harm' where it was not. She believed in just letting things be. So because that was how Momma was, I never said anything. I let my sister 'rant and rave' all the time. Talk down about people of my skin color, make snide remarks about my hair being fuzzy or stupid looking, always talking, always saying, always snooping, always in and out of my affairs, but I never let her know it got to me and that is what I think killed her the most.

I would talk to her only when she wanted to talk to me. I always had a book in my hand, so when she started, I would politely leave with my book in my arm and open my window and lock my door. I knew that one day, I would leave and pursue my dreams and never have to deal with this. I wonder about my sister up until this day. I have not seen or heard from her for many many years. I love her, but I finally came to refuse to allow the emotional blackmail to control me. I finally realized that I was not the curse, created for the family. I finally decided to move on. I finally decided to let her have the 'enemy piece' she so much desired. Is this you, the- "cup" of biracial sisters? Is this you? Are reading this and getting the revelation at the same time. Yes, let's prepare to take this issue up with God and the one you both have been avoiding all this time,, yes, your biracial sister! It is time, yes it is, to confront, release, deliver and be set free, God and your Momma is watching and waiting for you to bury the hatchet, yes is is time!

Analogy of the two sisters When you have sisters born into one family that have been bred of a different race, it is almost always a hard feat to overcome. In observation of sisters born of different races and values. Most of the time the sisters have a hard time accepting each other due to physical appearance, mental states of being, values, customs and beliefs. It is almost like being in a two-part-distant-relationship, only difference you both lived in the same house-hold. I will use an analogy of the movie "*Imitation of Life*" where the daughter appeared 'white (physically, she obviously had a white daddy)' and the mother was 'black (physically)." The mother tried to do everything she could to make her daughter feel accepted and loved. But she, the daughter refused to accept that she was "black" so she would play with the "white children" and act as if she was from a white family, but it would always lead to shame and pain for her and each time she would end up feeling dismayed, rejected and loathed of who she was. The story ended up with the white looking- daughter leaving her black roots and disowning that side of her, but when her mother died, she couldn't live it down, the guilt nearly tore her apart, all though, this is a fictional portrayal of a mixed race (interracial) relationship, this represents so many of you out there! ARE you sisters of two different breeds walking in an actual movie that really, honestly and truthfully "imitates your life," are you all playing the parts of the two characters. God made us all, we are all his creation. He wants us to know that skin color is not a barrier to relationships. I realize that certain countries ban different races from cohabitating together and it has caused throughout the years, unsurmountable pain and grief. Sisters, that have lived this "to the bone," God is calling you out of this "rut"! He is calling you to face who you are, face your fears, face your sister, stop ignoring each other. Don't be ashamed, leave SHAME to itself, let shame be buried, and let your relationship come alive, it can only come alive, though- with the two of you coming together, confessing your faults to ye one another so that you can be healed. James (KJV) 5:16-"Confess your faults to one another and pray for one another, that you can be healed."

"The half sister part 2 (we grew up)"

See what we need to get past as sisters and in this world, is that we are all created equal and love has no boundaries, therefore when it comes to race we should not judge. We can make it easier, if we love one another, as sisters. If you want your bi-racial sister to be a part of your life, 'bless her and not curse her'. Accept who she is for what is inside of her, and not what you think is on the outside, not what you view as an issue, that is really false and blinding. Don't believe the lies that the devil is contantly telling you to paint a picture of a person whom- 'thinks she is so much more affluent, rich, better looking, educated than the you." Please "switch" the mindset! Quickly! While editing this book, God gave me a theory (that is what psychologist do, they create theories)! God gave me one on July 6, 2020,called the "Makeshift theory (really he did).The theory explains, first what the word "makeshift means". The word "Makeshift means a- expendient and quick substitute! The example came, when I delived this message in a prayer call message, on how when we were kids we created little or maybe even big forts. The forts were your momma's covers draped over chairs and we used those as "substitute houses", we made them quick, fast and in a hurry, before our 'momma" would make us stop, those were our substitutes, we made it work and we enjoyed them, we also made "makeshift food in mudpies". So in God revealing this theory to me (I need to add this theory to the field of psychological science, maybe I will, just thought I would throw that out there, LOL)! But moving right along, God is telling us to "make the shift", "make the change in our thoughts", "our beliefs, our stances, our moods, our outlooks, our minds, make the shift", as you "make the shift" out of old types of feeling this way and old types of feelng that way, with, old worn out emotions and thought processes, you will begin to see life differently. You will begin to feel a deep inner, psychological, mental and emotional "shift of change" all over, but you must do it expendiently and quickly! Give it a try! The Makeshift theory! Do it an watch the change come forth in your sisterly relationships,. Do it my sisters, "make the shift"!

So lets keep going, there are other sisters out there with deep rooted issues and problems that are biased and racist! Lets accept people and not colors of skin. All and all we are the same inside and out, only with different mindsets. Let's continue to come to a realization of what is and what is not. Let's continue to explore them (the theories), in this time of civil unrest (even though I wrote this book many years ago, as I edit, God keeps adding more revelation, as the times change right before my eyes, his ways are surely not our ways, Bless my God)!

My sister (s) that are a racist, out there- As we move through life, we may be aware of this mindset and maybe some us are not as much aware as others, but there are a group of sisters out there, that sisters are racist and one, just one in the group is not. The belief is that any race that is 'less' than or 'incapable of' living up to the norms and standards set by their particular 'born in' race, Is not appropriate to live and dwell in a normal society. This set of sisters fight with each other, because of the one that believes malisciously, while the other does not. This sister group is in constant battle because of this. One sister believes in the thought that 'all are created equal" and the others believes the opposite. Many sisters are at odds, due to this predictament, and cannot come to terms on either side. I have seen some sisters become enemies because they hate the fact that their sister loves or enjoys 'being around' this particular 'non-race' or irrelevant group of people. Read on! Hold on to your seats, this memoir has something for everybody!

Sister racist The Sister racist believes in the discriminatory view that anyone that is incapable of having the specified traits of 'her race' they are to be isolated into one particular area of society and that they do not belong with the 'our group of people'. This sister believes that the opposite race is illegitimate and illiterate to certain knowledge's and they do not deserve to function in- normal society. The sister racist feels there is no exception to the rule and has no empathy for the 'degenerate race'. She feels that the rules have been set, although 'ancient' and that to change one's beliefs would be a total disregard for what the ancient leaders of our society has set. My sister, my racist enemy, sister believes that nobody is better, she believes that if you cross the line with 'racial blending' you have cross the line with the system and you should be 'ousted'. This is the type of sister that you have to relate to on her terms or you will not relate to her at all, to attempt to make her see your side of things when it comes to racial lines, would be of utmost disrespect. This I will warn you is an awful state to be in, as I truly believe that we are all created equal, accepting or not accepting your sister is a serious choice one has to make. Sister/ enemies of this sort carries years of pain and heart ache, simply because one sister is not racist and the other one is. If you are the sister that is on the side of not being racist, the only thing that you can do, that is possibly the safest thing to do is constantly pray for you sister. It will require you taking the risk of forfeiting your relationship with your sister at times, and on different levels and spaces in time, if you believe the opposite and have believed this way since you were a child. It would take 'stepping away' to set your boundaries, and limits, yet still love your sister. I am sure you the sister that is not racist has stood in "hard places', places, where your heart was broken to pieces at conversations and citing's of things done that were not kind or human like. I am sure you have prayed, cried, talked and done things to keep you family out of trouble and various other issues, you dare not discuss out loud. You have been mocked, scorned and abused because due to you joining, against your will, being what the other sister or sisters stand for. Because you know what is right and knew - that being a racist is not what God has for sisters. Racism that is rooted within your sister, and not you, was planted in her 'deepest heart' when she was a child, yet you kept clear. Your sister, she was trained to believe that this is- what is just right and fair in the "stream" of racial status and position. You on the other hand knew what was wrong, unjustified and incorrect!

As you- felt the inappropriateness of this, as a child or growing up, you would inquire from you teachers and adults, you felt you could trust- regarding race and how God saw us as different colored species. You asked yourself, how can I be so different than my sister or sisters in regard to thinking the way I do, versus how they think. You, this particular sister (on the good side of things) believe that you are not like your sister or sisters to the core and you do not desire to be. You saw a glimmer of this in your Mom, but she decided to cover up her goodness to walk in darkness. Over the years, you have realized the truth, you are not them and they are not you.

You are now, sickly seeing, that-the one that you- grew up with, allowed to fix your hair, and tuck you in as disgusting, disregarding and evil in the sense of race and relations. *First Person,* I now-watch my sister from the corner of my eye with contempt and disgust because of what she believes to be for another living, breathing, human being. I love my sister, but I hate my sister, yes, I hate that part of her and I don't know what to do. I hate the fact that she or them- hates others based on the color of their skin and not who they are. Because of this 'evil' that rests within my sister or sister's heart, I am making a decision and I am making it now. This issue has to be dealt with! I cannot be torn between the two any longer, I cannot be "luke warm", as my grandma used to quote from the Bible!

First person continued -I believe that we all have access to the same of everything and that the 'general scope of people are the same" no matter what race, creed or color (as was quoted to me by the Holy Spirit one day, during my first day of psychology). I will quote from the King James version of the Bible where it says …"Nothing is unclean of itself." I interpret that scripture as saying that when we are born into the earth we are not born "as" unclean. We tend to 'make ourselves unclean with behaviors, thoughts, attitudes, systems of beliefs, value systems, or anything that contributes to our psyche as a whole, what we read, hear and apply in our daily lives all contribute to "uncleanliness of heart, soul and mind". All these things contribute to 'us as a people in making ourselves unclean'. I say that in essence to state that the sister that hates people because of what culture or colors they come from does not realize that we are all people, alike and the same.. We are 'cut from the same cloth'. Romans 1:13, 14 says "Let us not judge one another anymore, but judge this rather that no man put a stumbling block or an occasion to fall in his brother's way." Verse 14 says I know and am persuaded by the Lord Jesus that there is nothing unclean of itself." Amen!

Sister Saint (She loves them all- racism) from the mind of the racist- sister that sees the sister that loves diversity. This sister does not understand how; her sister in whom have, both- been born of the same blood and womb, accepts 'other people's' blood in her life, she cannot see how this can continue without there being some separation. Listen to her heart. *I cannot understand my sister, I love her, but I hate her. I do this because, she was not 'raised this way'. She was not told to 'like them'. She was taught a system of beliefs that we are 'all different'. Why can't my sister see this, why can't she see the damage she is causing, we will never make it mixing that way. I want to be her friend, sister and confidant, but when I see her 'drooling' for the 'mixed relationships', my mind says no. I don't understand it. I get confused sometimes. Because I work with a little boy that is of the other race and I feel sorry for him, but I tell myself he deserves it. I tell myself it is what was 'handed down to him', but he is so little and so fragile, how can I be a nurse and care for people that are different, maybe my sister is right, maybe … I had that* *thought just once, but I later realized after talking to a family member, I would be betraying myself and my family values, if I changed my thought process., if I became a Democrat. Republican is what my Granddaddy was. And what I shall forever be. But back to my sister, I think she is making a terrible mistake. I think she is really going to suffer from walking away from what we believe, or is she? How can she love such people? I love my baby sister, though ... how can I give her up? I don't know how I can make it without her in my life, but we have two different set of beliefs. How can I chose, my heart is hurting. What do I do??? Maybe I am not as racist, as I have led myself to believe that I am. Why do I feel this way? Why do I support racism? I see this little boy and I want to touch him, but I can't. I long to hold and comfort him and I think he knows it, every time I come around there he is looking ... but I can't I got to stay strong to what I believe that is "------ Power (fill in the blank)" ... I feel so bad ... I am a racist but why am I racist? Why am I this way? I searched my soul, but I don't know why I am a racist ... I hate my sister, but I admire her, she chose to stand up and believe in what was right and I chose to follow my 'Great Granddaddy's plight' ... I don't know why I am this way. But I know that my sister she is brave, the one that I love at times, then I hate. I love the way she does things that I am afraid to do, but then when she does them I feel as if I could 'choke her' because I wish I had the guts to do so. Am I such a coward as I call other people of other races? Am I just as guilty, as the plight I preach secretly every day, Am I a hypocrite of all hypocrites? Is my sister the one that is right and we are all wrong? How can this be? How can I abandon all I know and cherish? This is our family's heritage to feel superior, but is it still worth it? I am confused. I guess my sister the enemy is more astute than us all ...*

Think on this, my dear readers, this is to help, heal, and not hurt!

Sister "Surprise" You My Enemy "Sister" "There are some sister relationships where the sister totally catches you by surprise with her malice, or hatred. I was watching Whitney Houston's character, *Rachel Marron – in the movie- "The Body Guard"*. In one of the scenes, there is a part where the sister, whose name was *Nikki*, hated her sister (Rachel Marron) 'all' along and paid a "hit man" to kill her sister. This was and is a trajesty, but hatred of this sort happens a lot in today's world! It made me realize how much "flesh and blood" can hate each other. This woman hated and envied her sister because she eventually spoke that "It was her and not me", she said near the end of the story that she wanted to be who her sister was. How many times do we secretly want to be who our sister is, or have what our sister has? God does not want us to be jealous of our sister, like Nikki was in the movie, "*The Body Guard*", and if this is you, it is time to let it go! It is time to get your mind away from the evils that the devil has invoked, so much, until you want to see your sister out of this world! No! Not SO! I want to elaborate further to allow whomever is out there, with these tendencies to realize this, and get help for these traumatic urges. The sister, *Nikki,* in "*The Body Guard*" movie, was not as popular as her sister *Rachel Marron)* and felt sorely betrayed, empty, insecure and being in her sister's shadows. For that, she plotted her own sister's assasination. She paid someone as the story goes to 'kill' her sister. The sister planned her sister's demise, and did not show or have any remorse until her nephew was at risk (a fictional story with true undertones). This sister had worked closely up under her sister and "right beneath her nose was jealous of her". She even told the assassin, to not finish until the job was done! This movie was art, imitating life. Art of any form,, always has some truth or "life" in it! It is always from the life and heart of its creator in some shape or form "real life"! Or at minimal what they imagined or someone close to them, it was in some way, whether an experience, real or imagined.

Is your life imitating this piece of art? Do you have this level of hatred, envy or jealousy towards your sister, or do you know someone that does? Sometimes the truth can be cold, painful and heartless, but it is just that, the truth! I heard, someone say, that "the truth does not need any support"! If this is your truth, then there is a definite call for you to go get some immedient and expedient help. The sister having these feelings needs to get to a point where you are no longer jealous. Jealousy eats up at one's soul, let's not do this any longer. Sister's lets all open our eyes and see what we need to see, so we can get healed. It is apparent that jealousy has become your pathology, your pattern to life on-how you feel and sometimes act! It is time to get down to the core of this issue and get deep down into the pit of one's soul to be healed.

On the other side of the story, Whitney Houston's character, *Rachel Marron,* was depicted as blindsided, as she did not know such evil existed within her sister's heart, she trusted her with everything she had. Sisters on the other side of this let's not be ignorant of the devils devices, lets be aware (2 Corinthians 2:11! Although Whitney Houston's character never displayed any knowledge of her sister's hatred for her, I wonder if there are ever signs with some of us that have experienced, the blind side, that is often so obvious, that we ignore? How many times do we place what we see and feel in the denial box? We often keep such family secrets hidden up under the rug. We often endure ways of the culprit from our family members that are never addressed due to the "shame it may bring on the family's name". The sister that is the culprit is never addressed and often times, wounds are festered and tragic things occur because of the lack of addressing the one that is the root of the problem. Is this something going on in your family? If so in order for healing and resolution to take place the agony needs to be addressed. The issue that is really obvious is what needs to be looked at, observed, processed and talked about. Not only will this help you (the one that is experiencing it) but the others involved, the sister that has certain underlying issues, needs to be talked to. I know that for those of you that know what is going on you need to sit down, talk to your family to find out the best way to approach the situation. You always want to handle the insecure, enraged sister with care. This is because the bible says, "Words from the mouth of the wise are gracious, but fools are consumed by their own lips (Ecclesiastes 10:12)". In other words, (the words of a person such as this is their way of life. They are consumed by 'what they think, by what they feel and what they know). Wisdom requires stillness, maturity and well thought, out level headed processing, not impulsive overacting. Wisdom is justified by her daughters (Matthew 11:19).

Explore, note and digest the pain that we cause Often times as sisters, we cause each other lots of pain. Some of us, atleast, cannot be honest with our sisters. But now is the time for us to do so. Some of us deliberately do things to emotionally scar our sister, some of us lie on our sisters, some of us imitate and mock our sisters (to the point of agony), some of us lure our sisters, some of us set our sisters up, I have said all of this throughout, so that it can stick, but now as I am a few pages to the end of this book, it is really time for a change. It is time for a change from us all! We are are guilty of some and maybe not of others instances in this book. The extremes maybe the latter, but at some point, in some way, we all can relate to this God inspired memoir!

Sisters, I want those of you out there to digest every word in order to get healing! If you have ill feelings towards your sister, It is time for a change. The feelings of insecurity, mixed feelings inappropriate, indecent feelings. These are not the feelings that grandma told you to have.. These are the feelings she warned you about 'jealousy, malice' envy, and spite'. These are the feelings that when Grandma recognized during play … she said "Honey it is not nice to be jealous of your sister"! These are the feelings that she tried to give you a story or a old fable to, make you aware of the dangers it would cause as you grew up. These are the feelings that she tried to 'mask' you from. These are the feelings she knew that if you acquired would be destructive and devastating- for you and your sisters. I want everyone that is reading this book that has a sister and this particular scenario applies to you, try to think on the day you began to have awkward feelings towards your sister that you felt you could not control. I want you to begin to "seize" it, with all your heart, mind and spirit, as to get rid of it! What the devil plotted in your brain, was a trick. It all was inner deception. This is not the way you were created to be. It was inner evil, inside that 'crept' up in your mind that led you to believe that 'your sister was and is your enemy'. It is time to prove him wrong. It was and is the devil's job to make you feel that you are not a part, of anything, that you don't matter and that you are useless. These are all entrapments of the mind that the enemy has used on us all, as sisters. He (the devil) has tried and made his ambitions happen successfully, to keep you and your sister apart. Needless injections of pain, you have encountered because of the projections in your mind being played over and over again! Now is the time to deal, it is time to war, and fight my dear sisters.Let's get rid of this evil that has tormented the sister group for so long, let's destroy the enemy's camp. He wanted you to miss out on a lifetime of love and blessings as a sister group, whether 2, 3 or 4 siblings, no matter what the number of your group, he wanted you apart, separated and not together! Can you see it now! Get rid of the mirages, and complexes in the mind! Let's do the work sisters. I am being for real. I guess we don't always tell you that after reading the book, you have to take steps. I mean do some work to make the book be as helpful as it needs to and can be. This is what the writer hopes it will be. I have read so many books by Bishop Jakes, Joyce Meyers, Rebecca Brown, I mean you name it, but I failed to 'put the work' in although they were life changing writings.

Furthermore, I saw to you sister, do not 'get off' on your sister's pain, no matter what 'race, ethnicity, nationality, tribe, culture, etc., you come from. No longer look, snicker, and laugh at her on the side or beneath your breath, regarding any issues that arise with or about your sister and her pain. Don't advertise her pain anymore for clearance, like when you are in a store and there is a clearance rack, meaning we will take anything to get it out of our doors and shelf. WE want it gone, don't do that to your sister, don't advertise something valuable at a cheap price just to get it out of your way, don't play with your sister's internals that way, stop or at some point it will become dangerous. Don't make the same mistakes that I did, make all attempts, you and your sisters can and have -to use this book as a guide to put the work in, if you have to highlight areas as you go along, when you gather together to get some of this stuff out and on the table!

Confess.We all have to face our fears of confession. Confession is a scary thing, as for one, we don't know how our confessions, will be looked at and two, we don't know if our confessions will be accepted as a good excuse or not. It is always a gamble, and left up to the individual at hand to decide. For instance, you know how it goes in the court room, when the judge makes a decision on how much of the confession he will accept as an excuse and how much of it he will not, it is all in the judge's hands. This is how confessions are in real life! I had to realize as a sister that accepting your fault is room for self and inner deliverance. Sometimes you are not fully able to say this because your 'pearls will and maybe trampled'. Matthew 7:6 says "Do not give what is holy to dogs and do not throw pearls before swine, less they trample them under their feet and turn and tear them to pieces". This definition is obvious in, explicitly, saying to not "persist", in giving what is of value to someone that is not appreciative of it, because your undying efforts could be rebuked and scorned or even directly attacked. Be careful and prepared when you move forward with deep dark confessions According to a website www. bible.ca/ef/expository-Matthew 7:6 that the words 'dog and swine' were used in allegory form to show symbolism of animals such as pigs and dogs as standing for worldly, unappreciative, and uncaring. I by no means am calling anybody's sister a dog, or a pig, but I want us to take a look at the true hidden meaning in reference to this topic.

Ask yourself- is this you, is this your sister? If so, then things need to be processed, looked at and resolved. I say this because when you, as one sister continues to go to the other sister in an apologetic, helping mode and the other sister that is not so welcoming is constantly rejecting you, then some things need to be reassessed. There is a time for everything, and if you have tried everything, then maybe you need to look to other alternatives. I emphasize, that if the following behaviors describe you, then you need to find other means. Don't keep going back and forth, back and forth and nothing is getting accomplished. Don't allow yourself to be put down, let down, scored or ridiculed. No do not stand for it, stay calm, yet persistent, that you will not continue to take harassment and that if all are going to come to the table, we all come in a manner of respect, integrity and fairness, allowing all of sisters to have fair, honest input without yelling or screaming at the point of explanation, now I am sure the yelling may occur at some point, but not at this point, this is the time of "letting it all out". Sister, let's be fair! Set your ground rules, have a monitor and run the group type of therapy in an organized way, it can be done, I know you all have one creative sister in the bunch. Keep reading!

If you have been looking for your answers, but afraid to do anything about it, here they are. Do not continue in this way, time is out for that! Lets mature and move forward. . I know, some of you may be tired because your were made to do it all of your life, well it is time to "make the shift, remember- "the Makeshift Theory". Lets apply it now. Don't worry about how this is going to make family members feel. You are going to have to go for it at this moment, or you will lose this open door!

God wants you, all sisters that have a broken relationship to come together to "make the shift" he wants you all to come together in cooperation to work towards mending what has been torn. God is saying to sisters out there that have been broken for years, but you still feel just a little "flutter of hope" or "flutter of something" deep down within, to come together for the sake of love to make it right, in the times of the Pandemic, although I had plans to finish this book, a long time ago, I kept getting delayed and God knew why! God wants to restore all of us, in all areas that we need with sisterhood being "top" on the list! No matter what it takes, it needs to be done! God is telling us, that lets not hold back any longer. In order for us to fix the group, we have to make decisions in order to come into our own sense of self and being. Sometimes the raw has to come out first, sisters get your heart prepared after the phase of organization and discussion, in order to get the raw out. This will require us having to be ruthlessly-honest, vigilant, and instant,. We are told that, we are supposed to be truthful at all costs. But how many times do we "hold back' out of fear of hurting our sister's feelings. How many times do we not say and speak humbly, yet lovingly, our true and entire heart? How do we not allow our very blood to know that we are in disagreement, even it it means, separating for a while to let things settle.

Another story………………………………………………

We are almost there! Keep reading, my dear readers!

Cinderella.The Cinderella story depicts three sisters, but where, the two of them hate the other. I have seen some Cinderella stories where there are sisters against one another and at times one seems cornered. I will say that no matter how this story is depicted in fairy "tailing" or real life, the results always end up the same. We have to stop allowing the Cinderella syndrome to hit our homes and sister groups. I didn't elaborate much on this story because so many of us, already know this story and how it ends up. Lets stop isolating one over the other due to indescretions, it is time for us all to grow up. Sisters stop fighting against one another and grow up! Cinderella always wins! I have seen jealousy at is peak over the silliest of things over kindness, over weaknesses, over closeness, over lonliness, over children, over parents (relationships) over money, over perceived power, over fame, it doesn't matter jealousy always tries to rear its ugly head! You see we are not jealous of our sisters mostly because of material possessions, although this can be. We are mainly jealous because of their confidence, self-esteem, their ability to make friends, their ability to make a bad situation good, and sometimes the sister has nothing and she still gets the bad end of the stick (so to speak) There are some sisters who are jealous of their sisters that do not 'have a dime'! It is just sometimes, Some sisters are jealous- "just because"! Horrible isn't it! But we know this is so.

Be assured that God created everyone with a gift and talent. You may 'not' be popular, 'always liked' or 'noticed' because that is not your particular call God has delivered to each and every one of us, sisters, just what he wanted us to have! It was his choices to make us African American, Caucasian, Indian, Jamacian, Italian, Russian, or what ever nationality or race that he saw fit and not the other way around, once we realize that God does the chosing, we can get a long better, at least I hope so! Realize who you are, my dear sister, a lot of times sisters do not realize how uniquely special they are and they spend lots of time "out of them- selves" trying to destroy. It can be one sister against the other or it can be two or more sisters against one (or however it goes). I mean the pairs are ongoing, yet the main point is that it is time for sisters to see themselves for who they are. It is time for sisters to understand the differences, and know their strengths. It is time to "remove' the spirit of jealousy, and envy and replace it with 'peace and joy'. It is time for you to acknowledge that you are a beautiful sister no matter where you came from. No matter where you are located within the birth line. It is time for you to stop making excuses for who your "sister is and who you are not". Stop focusing on somebody's else's' business and focus on yours. You say, my sister is my business … well not in some cases.. If your sister and you are two grown living adults. What your sister does is technically "not your business" unless she invites your there. Our sisters are "**not our property**." She is not something you own. You were just birth from the same "**cana**l." You were 'in most cases' just living in the same house, the same bedroom, using the same bathroom, but that does not make her "yours, your personal piece of property."

Sisters need to learn as they grow-up to set boundaries amongst or between themselves, because early on-throughout time, your life changes. Your thoughts change. How you feel changes and the things you felt and saw as a child is not the same as you are, as a grown up. Your sister may not like your 'jokes' any- more or maybe she does, or maybe it is something else she feels different about.

It is okay to differ and change when you are a sister. That is a lot of "sister problems,". We often do not agree to let our "sister" change, we want her to be the same person that we knew from the age of 5 to the present. How many times do we hear these words..."my sister changed when" … ' She changed when she got married, she changed when she had a baby, she changed when she got that job, she changed when she met this guy, she changed when she got new friends, she changed when she got that house, she changed when she got that car, she changed when she became a preacher, she changed when she moved to the United States, she changed when she refused to obey our cultural values, she changed when she got 'her white coat', she changed when she won the nobel peace prize, she changed when she got six figures, she changed when she adopted those kids, she changed when she stopped smoking, she changed after she got off drugs, she changed when Momma died, she changed when she lost weight, she changed when she came from that sabbatical, she changed after the loss of her child, she changed when she got her visa, she changed when she wrote that book, "**SHE JUST CHANGED."**

How many of you saw yourself in those statements. If so, it's "good". I wanted everyone, reading this book, to see what they have been doing to themselves and their sister. Take note of the -one comment that applies to you. Meditate on those words. I mean just think about, what is behind those statements. Think how limiting those statements are. Think on how the sister that you are referring maybe feeling about those heart wrenching jabs, that have been projected onto her for ages (so-to-speak). Making her feel guilty all because of your secret, hidden insecurities, its "confession time", oh yes it is! Keep reading!

Did you realize that these types of statements can, cause a person to feel guilty about herself and her accomplishments? Do you realize that this statements 'ring 'in your sister's mind constantly. Do you realize that every step she takes towards her destiny, these words are there? Did you not think your words did not affect your sister? Do you know that another 'sister's words can be damning (I hate to use this term, but it's true)'? Damaging?, Hurtful? debilitating? Sisters let's stop being petty, let's stop getting mad with our sisters, over something that can be handed in a manner of seconds.. Let's stop being mad because our sister has moved out of that place, that you once knew. What place you ask? The place that we held dear and near, to each other, as children. Accept that your sister is no longer the person you knew,at times, when it is apparent. Know that she has developed and evolved into something she desired for her own life. It does not mean she does not care for you, love you, or admire you, it just means she does not have all the time she used to, when you all were playing out in the field and yard- yet she still loves you. Sisters do not, and I mean do not dwell constantly on the past when it comes to you and your sister's relationship. Yes, it is okay to love them, call them, check on them, text them, or 'tweet them'. Just know that if she does not respond right away, today, tomorrow or, next week, understand that she maybe be busy, (with the exception, if you sense something is truly wrong). Give her some time, allow her space to be herself. Allow her 'a minute (as they say)'...just stop jumping to conclusions about your sister. Stop believing what has been told to you in your mind about your sister. It is not true. It is a spiritual lie … Adjust and move on.

Sisters and Sisters, lets all mature and grow up. Let's start-- as sisters being frank, open and honest with each other. Let's talk like we are our age and not our "SHOE SIZE" as our Mothers and Grandmothers told us in the past. Let's speak the truth if it is bad, speak it if it is good. Let one another know if you like something or if you do not like something. Let that sister know if she is being honest, faithful or supportive to the cause. It is okay to disagree with your sister, tell her, hey I don't like this, hey you can do better on this, or this is totally not acceptable. Let her know when she is being dishonest, let her know when she is not telling the truth. Let her know when she is being the "bad word" that we all tend to or want to say, but we just tend keep it hanging up there in that little "CARTOON BUBBLE" in our minds. Tell her and be free, it is alright to be mad, but not too long. Don't be too mad too long, because you will become accustomed to not having your sister in that space and fighting to win it back, is just too hard to fight to keep it, once you have hit a certain age, take it from me, moving towards reconciliation maybe hard at a certain age! But stll yet, Let's get it right sisters, on the "come up (as the millennials say)," let's leave a legacy for our new comers. Our sisters that we see have the potential to be powerful! Let's stop all this madness! Life is short.

Let's see your adult sister as your adult sister, let her know what it is you want her to know. Don't hold back anymore. On the other side of obedience is a blessing. On the other side of the readers receiving the writings of my heart that are coming from God and his precious "Holy Spirit" is something you never ever dreamed of in regard to your renewed and restored relationship. It is time for those of us that have been suppressing and hiding things because we don't want to hurt each other's feelings to speak it 'OUT." Stop holding this inside. It is too much to bear. If you want to improve yourself and your relationship with your sister, it is time to 'get busy'. It is time to make a change like never before.

__*A few more important descriptors.*__ I had to a few more descriptors in here- it was ringing in my soul! I am sure this happens all the time, when the child you birth seems closer to your sister, than to you. Read it and weap (just a figure of speech, LOL)! We are almost to the end!

__*The sister that befriends my child and makes me jealous.*__ This type of sister is the type that is very loving to your child. Very helpful and giving. She does anything she can for your child, but 'you don't like it'. What makes it so bad is that your child really likes her. "she is his favorite aunt', 'his buddy' 'his friend' someone he can go to for anything. This is something that, is seen amongst sisters all the time, when one sister has a child that she does not know how to parent and you somehow end up parenting her child in a 'aunt's way' and you develop a bond with that child, in a way that the mother does not. This can be a root causes of jealousy amongst sisters too. One sister gets mad because she cannot reach her child the way her sister can and she somehow works on 'turning the tide'. Meaning she does everything within her power to sabotage her child' relationship with her sister. She backstabs, backbites, and makes her child feel guilty, thus sabotaging the aunt/child relationship. And the first words you hear, is "that is my child anyway (making the child ultimately choose)", "Who do you think you are." "What are you doing"? Some sisters will even ban their child from seeing their aunt, because she cannot stand to see how they relate to one another or she will make excuses with the child, as to why it is ;not convenient' for her to see the child at the time, leaving the child feeling hopeless and sad. This happens a lot. Has it happened to you? If it has, **you sister, yes you!** Re-evaluate your motives, reevaluate your child's relationship with your sister to see why they are bonded. Check it out and see if it is really God ordained because they both may need something from each other that you cannot provide. Maybe it is special, because your sister has the personality traits that are tolerable of your child's personality. Maybe it is just a special relationship made to build and tear down and rebuild (so to speak). This meaning to build up a child's character and destroy any issues that are unwanted, some aunts just have that special touch. One of my sisters, Jenny has a close bonded relationship with my oldest son Tyrus, it is like she birth him herself. I totally undertand that, and I value that to the highest, but some sisters are not like that, they beg, borrow and steal to keep you away from their child all because of their insecurities (I am by no means talking of any relationships that are evil, criminal and disrespectful). Is this you? If so- Take a chance and allow your child to love and care for and be with his favorite Auntie! Move out of the way, my dear!.

Furthermore on Sisters and Nieces and Nephews. We as sisters, are made to take care of one' another's children, as you are her replacement, often times- but, at the same time, letting her child know, that this is your momma,- but not allowing that child to 'see your sister as momma, trying to rob her of her place is a whole different story. Sisters that are helpful to their sister's children, tend to be somewhat of a sister surrogate. You see, if we, as sisters, were to connect in that way, what in the world could we achieve with our children, our husbands, our jobs, etc. I mean we could build things, spiritually, naturally and forever. I hear Oprah and Gayle all the time, speak to their connection their "building and support" of their friendship/sisterhood. The long life establishment. Yes, sisterhood is an establishment, a fort, a movement. It can be and will be, if we let it. If we can understand how to work it, it can make us and we can make it, we just got to "Get it together."! We got to know how to move through the annals of time in sisterdom! We got this thang! Let's do it, Read on, My sisters! Furthermore on Gayle and Oprah-I can see Gayle as the sister that Oprah needed and desired. I know she found her birth sister, but I am sure that nothing could replace Gayle's support, strong opinions, or need to tell Oprah when she sees something that needs correction, yet in love, endearing, 'holding', prompting, or pushing. I'll bet Nothing (all of these are my opinions) takes the place of that. Oprah and Gayle are, in my view are intertwined, as this is my opinion strictly! Okay Oprah, don't yall get mad, Please, but It appears that Oprah's connection to Gayle has opened so many doors for Gayle (although she too had her own doors opened), again this is my personal observation, Gayle did not beg, exploit, take advantage of her friends power and fame, but she only supported and was there for Oprah. I have heard Oprah say that Gayle encouraged her in things that she really wanted to do (for shorter words) And for that it seems like anything major Oprah is involved in or anything whatsoever, Gayle seemingly reaps from as well, and there is nothing wrong with that. This is how sisters should be. Gayle, in my opinion, understands her role and she does not overstep her boundaries, seemingly and she is just as famous and popular within her own rite as Oprah is (this is my opinion and I think I am right about it). I really admire that … Why is it that we as real birth sisters cannot do the same, or use Oprah and Gayle's relationship as a template for those of us "birth through the same womb"? Sisterhood requires sacrifice. In order to be a true sister! how much are you willing to sacrifice? Think on this!

After all of this sisters, some will say, after reading my book---I don't care what you say Dr. Applewhite-I doubt if this will work and I doubt if me and my sister or sisters will ever be close!-Girls, read on, (but after all this pouring out, struggling, pushing, birthing and weariness, of writing, you are telling me that you still hate or have issues with your sister),? let's see if there is some justification in your still hating, disapproving of, non –trusting, not believeing, non-acting, towards your sister, let's just see. Let's read on (I am almost finished) … I know some have read the words above, and to this point and have said, well I am not too sure about this or I still got some real serious issues with my sisters. I know some of you are saying … there is nothing that I think in this world can repair our relationship. I know you think that maybe your sister betrayed you in a traditional, notorious, cultural or ritualistic- way that is unforgivable. I know there are our foreign sisters (from cultures outside of the United States) that have different plights than we do here in America. I wanted to address your issues too as well sisters. So let's look at how there are foreign sisters- out there that want to break away from certain customs in your culture that seem unfair and you were 'exposed' 'ratted upon, snitched (as we say in America) or openly betrayed. You thought you could trust your sister but she took something very dear and near to you or away from you. She stripped your confidence, by this betrayal. She forced you to do things unthinkable that is not allowed in your cultural norms. She was deceitful and spiteful and she put you in a place of vulnerability. Cultural norms vary and somethings that are allowed in America, are totally disrespectful and at times punishable crimes, in other cultures. Your sister did something that you think is punishable, you think she deserves the worst extent of all, even death! Don't think this! Don't believe this! I know cultural norms may even support it. God is calling for something different, he is calling for a shift in your thinking, right now, 'the makeshift way". Don't hold on to old time values, and beliefs, if it is damaging your sister relationship.

A person reading this memoir knows who they are. I know what has been written from the heart of my spirit (divinely inspired) flowing through me; is your life, issue. But I tell you what you are feeling towards your sister is like a blockage that seems unclearable. I know what you feel in your heart, she deserves the ultimate punishment as stated by cultural laws, rules, and regulations. Maybe she does, but not by you. Her punishment, payback or repercussions will come from a 'higher power'. Do not take her detriment to your gain. Do not allow what she has done to turn you into what she is? I am speaking to you! Let it go. Forgive her and then allow the time it takes to process full forgiveness take it's course, know that forgiveness takes time. I will first ask you to 'put it down' 'walk away from the pain' and "Set It," Yes, Set it, as if you are picking something up in your hands (imagine putting something on the table, in the trash, in the garbage disposal) Take the time to do it step by step, in the imagination. Then next plan for the actions! Nothing negative, but all positive to cleanse and renew your spirit, soul and mind. Take it and let 'the animosity' down' the 'intense feeling of hatred 'you have. Time has a way of honoring requests. Time is a tool for cure. Time is the boss. Now begin your journey! I speak to you my African Sister, my Asian Sister, my Jamaican Sister, my Italian Sister, my Caucasian Sister, my Indian Sister, you fill in the blank, if you are a sister, this is for you, and you know who you are!

Think on these things my dear sister and 'release'. It is time to forget what she began to do to you as a child that your Mother never noticed and you kept it inside, because you wondered to yourself, "Is this how sisters are supposed to be" and you somehow figured it would get better, but it didn't. It is time to seek salvation for what you created in your inner being towards her that nobody knew and that she started and placed the blame on you. It is time to see yourself separated so that "Time can Lead" "Time can execute." Nobody can take the place of what time can do to a situation. Place time between you and the person you deem as your enemy (your sister). Reshape, renew and restore yourself for now. Maybe you need professional support, maybe you need to confide into someone you saw that you 'wished' was your sister and she wanted to be that for you, but customs forbade it. Take a chance, and find this person that you know is trustworthy. Seek you heart, seek what you have always felt inside, but did not want to hurt the person you shared the same 'womb' with. The one that you took care of supported, provided for. Do what will help you feel best, for once. Don't wear another person's heart inside of you. Wear your own. You will feel a surge of activation, release and freedom, if you walk away from something that has been bothering you all your life. You see sisters, we all, no matter what custom. (I had to stop and write this by unction that came by God and his Holy Spirit) have secrets that need to be released and surged from inside. Someone was looking for answers and picked up this book by divine inspiration to find their answer. I hope it is you!

False offenses and made up lies Let the false offenses go, whatever they are, and where ever they come from, my sisters' let it go in your heart, where ever the accused is standing let it go and let it go forever. Whatever the devil has posed that is false, let it go, let the made up lies of the heart and mind be cast as far as the east from the west! Let it go. Years of false accusations have surrounded the sister brood, we all have different ones of them, but whatever it is, it is time to let go. It is time to let it go into the pits of hell!

Special Thought: "On a positive note": I wanted to share with my readers, a story about sisters that are real, sisters that are connected. As you know there is always a good and a bad, a ying and a yang, up and down, high and low. I wanted to add to this writing a very good example of how sisters should be. Let's Continue

**Sisters, for real, God bless her Soul, she has since then gone on to rest, Betty Moore, one of my aunts best friends** ... I saw this lady I had been knowing from a little girl. She and I were talking and she said to me something about her and her sisters. She said that she and her sisters were 'prized'. Meaning they could not make it without each other. She said that they talk every single night, and cannot get rest until they do so. God rest her soul, Mrs. Betty Moore (I may have mentioned her earlier), she is now deceased (See my Last Chapter on "The Death/Loss of a Sister)" I looked at her and said., 'wish it were that way for me'. Sadly it is not. What is so different with the sibling relationships back then as to now. And if they, meaning the lady above had problems, how did they overcome. What is it that they understood about sisterhood that we do not understand in the 21st century? What is the secret to their sisterhood success? How do we obtain it now? What do we do?

First let's look at loyalty and what it means to be loyal? Loyal is defined generally as faithful to one's oath, commitments, or obligations, vows or loyal conduct. Is it that sisters in the 21st century lack faithfulness to their commitments as sisters? Is it that during life growing up as sisters, one sister failed to show commitment to the other? Was it because of this, the sister, lost faith or confidence in the other? Or was it that one sister was not loyal in her conduct, actions or ways? What do I mean by making these types of statements? For instance did one sister, leave the sister "trough" by saying, acting or doing something outside of the realm of what was appropriate or aligned? Did one of your sisters "in time" embarrasses you or say something that she knew you were totally sensitive about? Did she disagree with your lifestyle in some way that damaged your bond with her? Did she go to your 'mom' behind your back with a trusted secret or violate you in any way that seems almost unbearable? What was the 'root' cause of the issues that caused you to not believe in, trust in, or even like your own sister? What has caused the relationship to be strained, only you know? Ask yourself this question until you come up with the answers, trace it back as far as it needs to go, to begin the healing or removal process.

Do you want to know? Then search your soul, it is there. I say this because sisters it is time to mend what you thought was not at the point to be mended. If you desire to have the relationship of a life time in regards to being a sister it is time to work on these situations and find the cure, as Ms. Moore (the sister group I mentioned before) and her sisters had, in which- was connectedness and love. Do we all share this at all times, even in the bad times? Take the risk my dear sister and go for love, take it all for love and work on mending what needs to be mended and corrected!I am sure you are re-living at this point, the things that your sister did to you. I am sure your mind is thinking at the moment …"No she does not deserve it, after all she cursed my name, she cursed my life, she even told me I was not worth the body God created me in." I know she said things that would make one weep tears bigger than a crocodile!!! I know, but if you desire to 'conquer' this 'giant' then you are going to have to 'press through' this situation. You are going to have to struggle through the fears of the results. You see. that is what keeps most of us from talking to our sisters, because we don't want to ex- perience the rejection or put ourselves in a position to be hurt again. I know that your sister before -you all 'broke up' did something that haunts you day in and day out. But think of it like this, what you are now- doing is evidently 'haunting you' equally as much, because it is on your mind constantly. If this is something you need to do 'not only for her' but for yourself as well, then it is worth the risk, even if she is not receptive or responsible enough. You see you are trying to 'clear your heart, mind, and soul'. It is really not your responsibility to clear hers, that is entirely left up to her if she wants to receive what you are saying or not. It is up to your sister if she wants to 'break the bread' of forgiveness and call up the realm of redemption. Work on your, own conscience.

I haved always noticed during the investigation periods on criminal shows that I watched, that the investigators would- make all attempts to 'work on the conscience' of the suspect or witnesses. They seemed to be trained on 'how to get to the conscious' or the 'core essence of the soul of the persons involved. They would pull out what they needed with cues.They tend to 'bank on the fact' that something deep down inside that is imbedded as- goodly will rise to the top to evade the darkness, and pull out the truth. It is a method. They seem to believe that a value of some sort, whether good or bad will creep up to get the meaning or to the bottom- of the story to the light. Go to your core, go to your values and make sure that they are all reached and attracted in order to get to the bottom of the issue do your in "internal investigation"! I hope you ladies are getting this!

Using the principals of investigations will help you to heal, go to your set of 'core values' and allow them to take up residence- for healing, and for being set free..

Being Still. Have you ever experienced a time, when your sister was shaken, because you were 'still", just simply still not saying anything, not reacting to anything-, meaning, just non-moving, non-speaking, the old world definition of still,,just still in your soul' or still 'in the peace that God gives when we tap into it'? Do you recall her asking you constantly things like "What's wrong with you"? "I know something is wrong"? even when nothing was wrong. Some cannot handle silence, but know that silence brings deliverance and often enstills God's peace that surpasses all understanding! It was revealed to me- by God's Holy Spirit the Principal of "house staging," he showed me that when a realtor stages a house, they do it to set the pace or feeling for what they want you to get. We can all use this method with our emotions to the good or to the bad! You decide, if you want to set your feelings for positive outcomes or "be set up" for negative outcomes.

Don't keep going through and over the same things over and over in the place of sisterhood. If you have 'already lived' through this, do not repeat the same things ... I quote this from a preacher, that I love to listen to sometimes' Once you lived through something it makes it easier for you to face or deal with that situation, when it comes around again'. You see what we fail to realize is that, once you go through something the next time it should be easier to 'process through' the next time. It should be a lot easier to deal with the blows of frustration, stress, or whatever comes with the situation. That is the key. Tell yourself 'I have been here before'. Repeat it to yourself over and over again ... I have been here before and I will move past it in order to get to the "good." Once you do this my 'dear sister'. You could take the steps to doing what it is in your conscious, spirit, and soul is telling you - to do. You will feel the burden lifted once this 'feat is accomplished'.

Sisters revamped Sisters we go through so much. We have lots of trials and tribulations. The preceding sisters that were described throughout this memoir is real. One or- several of the sisters described, could be me or it could be you. Ask yourself, does sisterhood- need to be 'revamped and re-defined/ Or even "re-glorified"? Does having a sister mean having a close and cherished friend. Does sisterhood stem from 'blood relationships only'. Do we have to honor 'sisterhood' when it goes against what we believe? Do we trust our sister that we have been born from the same womb? Do I know who my sister really is? Do I … sometimes - just don't know? What it means to be a sister? Do I define it by what my "Mother" tells me it should be or do I define it by what I know to be true in the depth of my heart. What I feel is 'real, just, and right'? Do I have to stay back and allow my sister to do the heart crushing things to me and 'laugh within herself, secretly and hideously' at my 'fumbles, slips, trips, and falls'. Is that what having a sister is all about? I wonder about these things. Do you?

Sisters we have to take a few more steps and now; here we have - in which is walking in the "Darkness of sisterhood"………………………………………………………………….

Special Note: As I near the end of this book, I want to open a few issues that we rarely talk about is when we lose a sister to death. I want to open up the physical manifestation of losing a sister to death, right before you eyes, as well as spiritually before your eyes, both are tragedites and hurt you deep to the core! I hope this blesses and delivers you all at the same time!

Important Note on Death of a Sister. In this book, I have talked about sisters and a lot of unfortunate occurrences, that take place in being a sister. I would like to stress one important area, that I may have not addressed that, is really serious yet, freightening. I am sure there are some sisters out there that need these words, desire these words and want to be set free in a way that is not able to be described with words, and that is "losing a sister to death". The loss of a sister to death, is horrible! This experience is one that makes the heart feel as if it is "not even able to drop". It appears in my experiences of seeing close family members and friends lose a sister that when one sister's voice is taken and there is nothing you can do about it, it tares, into the soul like a rocket unannounced . Losing a sister is not like any experience one can fathom. The emotions that rip through your mind and tear into your head, like a headache that the human body cannot cure. The moment that she dies, is not like a moment that one can put in natural words, but let me try......when a sister dies (meaning literal death) and then when a sister dies (internally and spiritually amongst sisters). Walk with me!

God inspired this to me, it was a special inferred writing inspired by the Holy Spirit- on when a sister transitions, there are some sisters out there that have lost a piece of their heart and soul to a sister that is deceased that need resuscitation. Read on my sisters:

The Death of My sister (Naturally)) Losing a sister, is, I am sure, - one of the scariest things that can happen, to a sister relationship. I would imagine. I have never lost one of my sisters, but I have witnessed countless family members, friends and relatives, lose their sister or sisters. Losing a sister, by observation and research is a horror. It is a horror because when she takes her last breath, a part of your breath goes with hers, especially if you are the oldest or one that took care of her, looked after her or managed her life (Listen to her thoughts).

(First Person).Losing a sister is a tragedy, that is not described with natural words, but with inner whoa and dispair. Petty, restlessness, hopelessness and doom, thoughts going back and forwards in the mind, of "what if, what if, and what if." Racing towards the clock to find answers, when there is none. Waiting on time to say to my sister come on! Toiling, Toiling into the abyss of the after life, not being able to escort her is devasting. I look and I search, saying to myself, this just cannot be. I could not understand where this comes from, it is too early, not now, no, no, no! I saw you as a fighter, I saw you as a winner, but now the time has come, I know it, I can feel it, I am your sister! Please don't do this to me, don't do this to us, I am helpless, in away I have never been before! I hate to sound selfish, my dear sister, my dear love, but this is wrong. You are not standing, girl, "come on"- this is not the way it is supposed to be We fought and we argued, but now this is not how it is suppsed to go! You are supposed to do something and I react, now there is nothing! I don't like this!. We are supposed to grow old together and laugh on, porches of our kids running and playing, this is too sudden, too fast and too wrong! Please don't leave me, I thought you told me you would stay! I am overwhelmed with grief, I am not sure I can take it! Pause!

*(Second Person)*Once a sister takes her last breath, it mobilizes you, your feelings and your entire psyche. It takes you into a spiral of emotions and mind thoughts that are not enough to put on a paper..

*(First Person)*The day I lost my sister was the day that my heart revealed an attack, that I never thought was known to man." The day, she uttered her last breath, I seemingly thought I lost mine. It was unclear as to where this-- was going and some days, I still don't know. I saw her laying there and wanted so much to say, let's go, get up, listen to me, answer me, laugh with me, cry with me, but there was no more atmospheric matter- that could conceptualize any human inference from me to her. I was baffled, my heart was not broken, but subdued! Subdued, by outer forces that I cannot explain, subdued by inner forces that were not explainable. I am still at a loss of losing her, yet I contend. My Sister and I, had this type of thing going on, where we loved, we hated, we sighed, we cried, we fought, we did a lot of things, that all are coming to my mind and I cannot stop the thoughts. I want to grab time and say, "Stop, bring her back," "Bring her back," but I know I cannot! I know and feel that she slipped, yes slipped, right out of my hands, my heart, my soul and my mind. I was hurt by the travesty that carried her into another hemisphere, another realm! I was not happy or pleased with- the initial transition. I was appalled, shaken, hurt, and unsure of what had taken- place. I was indignant, I was not in myself. I was not out of myself . I don't know where I was . My sister, My sister, where are you? I asked? I could not look at my parents. I could not give them an answer, nor my loved ones, as I was as lost as they were! This could not be real! I contend!I want to forget this day, yet I want tro remember this day, as it was the last day that we were connected. The thread of our connection just stood still and I didn't know where to put it! It was just there!

It was not until now at this very moment that I realized that we were bonded in the deepest place of life, in the crux of intimacy, that I never even knew existed! I am hurt, angry and confused, all at the same time. I need one more minute with her, one more second, but I know the Master has unctioned her forth, as she stepped out of mortality to immorality. I know this is so. I just was not ready to let you go. I miss you, I call you sometimes, just to hear your voice on your cell. I hold you near, my dear sister. I miss you, my arms miss you, my mind misses you, but I will move, so that you can be free I will never forget you. I want to see you again, one day, just to love you, to hold you, so that I can talk to you on the mountain of sisterly love. I want to play with you again, the way we played as little girls, I want to tell you I really love and appreciated you in my life, I want to play in your hair. I miss you so much! I really do! I will say to you and to God, I needed more, I finally understood what she needed, what I needed and, how to make it all fit. When she softly slipped away, I felt it, I encountered it, I refrained, as the "pull" was so strong, I thought when I opened my eyes, I had slipped with her! It was not anything, I had ever experienced ever in my life. I felt like nothing, I felt that I had lost and failed. I am here to say that the death of my sister was something that I will always encounter, good and bad, she was me and I was her. Yet I know she is in a place. A place, I long for and desire. A place of peace. A place of wholeness a place that gave her a renewed body, not like the one we have, a glorious body. A lift, a flight, a joy that I could not keep her from. I saw you laying there and I knew you were happy, although we were not. I knew you made it! My dear sister.We are no more or no less, we are "there"! We are in and we are out. I love you my sister, you died, and I shall always encounter your goodness, your love, your faith, your drive, your strive, you are me and I am her, you are my sister, I love you through time, and love out of infinite- time, I love you always and forever- through the seams of God's infinite powers and unseen connectors that keep the stream of his love from one channel to the next. I will never forget you, my love, my sister! I miss you forever!

The Death of a Sister (Spiritually) Losing a sister naturally is one thing, but losing her spiritually is another. Losing a sister to chaos, mayhem, rejection and betrayal is a travesty in another whole direction. Losing a sister, because one cannot come to the realization that one is blind and disillusioned by one's acts of non-aligned inner court relations is as much a tragedy, as is a natural death. Losing a sister, because one cannot see as one, or think as one, is like losing your sister to the grave.

Losing a sister because one eats the bites- of jealousy and sips the drinks of discord is a frightening experience. One's own flesh and blood, one's own soul keeper and intertwined "wind" that connects sisters is forever tarnished, by some 'man-made" concept that is formally a lie and piece of indwelled poison. Losing a sister to the annuls of misunderstanding and fight- is as tragic as seeing your sister lay in the bed and take her last breath. Dying to the tie that binds is hurtful and painful and a place that darkens your mind when it happens. Go into your soul to see if this is the place that you are in. Did you close the door? Did you stop breathing breath into each other or did you allow the snakes in the GRASS to sneak up on you? Do you remember those days, when the grass was not cut, as a child and you would look down and see a small green snake or hear a rattle, you didn't waste no time moving did you,, because you knew what it was, so now and why is it different with the snake of a person or the snake within you, to allow it to happen now? Why? If we can explore the truths from within ourselves and acknowledge our mistakes we can destroy the 'yoke' that the devil created to keep us apart. I want sisters that are not talking to each other anymore to delve into what started this and ask yourself, are you apart because of some responsibility not your own? Where you standing up for someone else's plight and ended up not speaking to your sister? The one that you were once close to? Is it a unbearable pain that you can barely stand because of the stance you took for someone else that caused this to come upon you and your sister? Think on this. If this is you, you need to go to your sister and get it right, something needs to be done and done soon. Don't let nothing separate you from that loving sister bond, if you are at each other's throat, because of your children or grandchildren's stuff, let it go. Is there some truth to what was said, if so acknowledge it. There is no reason to be mad at the truth. Should these truth's been said sooner and you just let them go? I mean the "truth is the truth"! What truths did you hide for so long that caused things to get out of hand, no matter who, what or where it is about. This needs to be sorted through and handled. Don't let the devil hold your souls any longer! Don't live the lie that he wants you to live anymore.

In the End This memoir is set to help, deliver, break chains, strongholds, unruly tradition and unfair and unequal values that may been having a negative bearing on the bonds of sisterhood. I bought every piece of knowledge, resource or information to this memoir, I have done this, through years and years of watching, listening (to God), praying and researching sister relationships. Because I want sisters around the world to acknowledge the truth of what they have experienced, come to awareness, be set free and return to closeness. Some of you may have been waiting for this, while some of you will be angry at the 'frankness', 'yet true' 'cut to the soul and bone' deliverances. Deliverance does not come easy. Sisters don't do this anymore- conceal pain and truth. I want you all sisters, in the future to see the whole deal with hurt and pain upfront. Don't let years of pain linger. Talk about it, it already hurts anyway! We

"My grand and god-daughter, (what do I see)"

Caption: A special note on this image, we took my oldest granddaughter Tytiana and my god daughter Cayla to Atlanta to Lego Land several years ago, I couldn't help, but notice- the bond that they shared at the time, it seemed to be a inner connection not put together by hands. It was something that reminded me of a time when me- and Cayla's mother, Lena grew as sisters. I would always watch Tytiana and Cayla and wish that me and Lena's sisterhood would have stayed as such. Yet- a moment in time, pricked my heart as the girls spent time together, opened up what sisterhood really is and aided me in my redemption of the bitterness, the distance and separation that occurred between me and Lena (Cayla's mom). They are all grown up now (Tytiana and Cayla), this was several years ago, but I would be remised to not speak on how time repeats itself. Me and Lena grew up as sisters, but something tore us apart as time progressed. It is funny how time repeats itself, this picture of Tytiana and Cayla's time together made me laugh, it made me cry and it made me grow"! It made me realize that sisterhood is a devine connection that never stops, it stays no matter how far apart or close that you are. God ordains sisterhood!

As I have gotten older the scripture says "I was young and now I am old" Psalm 37:35. I said that,to say this … There are some of us that are sent here to hold the door open for our sisters so that they can be pushed or even shoved into their destinys. There are specific sisters in the sister set that are called to do this or maybe several others, it all depends. You will know who this sister is, by her fruit! You will now be able to identify her by her fruit according to Matthew 7:16. What this means is that your sister will have traits that show her as the leader, as the pusher, as the one that will stand in the midst of persecution and not run away. This sister is the one that is the one that takes risks that no one else does, this sister is not afraid of her authentic- self. Sisters in your groups of sisters, determine who that is and follow her, you may be missing out, because you won't trust the process, you want trust your sister's guidance, in which is her love for you, her time to groom and prepare your soul.You may have been avoiding her rights to minister, coach and give you what God has in her hands to give.

Don't miss out on your blessing, whether it is a birth sister, or someone that you have Called your sister don't hold yourself back anymore, don't let the enemy make you see backwards, don't let him reverse what GOD IS doing through your SPECIAL, chosen sister. You are missing the push, the stamp, the label, don't do it any longer, those of you that know you need to follow her, then you follow, those of you that KNOW you need to LEAD your sisters, then you lead, if you are going to be a little scary cat (no pun intended), then know that this job is not for wimps. If your sisters are not willing to submit or go with it, then just let it be. We all have decisions to make and it only takes a moment. I heard a SERMON preached by Bishop TD, Jakes, that revolutionized my life preached on September 29, 2019 during his Sunday morning services, "If I would have known it was ME," let me tell you ladies or whomever is reading this book. I have found me in a greater way, even though I had already begun my path, he pushed me right on in to it "even more so". The basis for the sermon was him finding out that it- was "HE that God" had in mind, if throughout his LIFE had he had known it was him, even though he doubted himself for a very long time, things could have gone a lot-differently, a whole lot sooner. He went on to say-even when the stadiums were full, even when they fought to buy his books, so on and so on, things would have or could have gone differently in a lot of instances. Is this is you, Do you know it is YOU? Are you ready for the "YOU"- that God has prepared and ready now? I am, I am not waiting! I am HER, I AM SHE, I AM, the ME that I was looking for and I am going to take full responsibility for her, as not only a sister, but as a child of GOD, as a wife, as a mother, and whatever else there is for ME to be, before I leave this earth! Are you with me sisters, who are you, find that JEWEL inside of you. Use your sister's talent the one that is the "POINT GUARD" of the group, who is the one that makes you sick, but you know she be RIGHT about it (country talk), who is the ONE that can turn WATER INTO WINE (speaking metaphorically), who is "the" she that sees the future and challenges it no matter what? If you are wondering if I am describing me (meaning you), then YES, I am! I want to be a blessing by sharing this side of me, so that those sisters that KNOW this, can feel these words RESONATING deep down in their souls and PULL their sisters out and UP, Toni BRAXTON DID it, BEYONCE did it, one of the STAPLE SISTERS did it, MARY, MARY did it, just to name a few. Where are you sisters? Where are you? Calling that one SISTER or sisters-- to STEP up, do it, you are able, SEIZE the MOMENT! It is your time, stop WEIGHING in the balance it!! Just do it!! You GOT it girl, stop suppressing it!

When you hold back truth, that is decades old, you are not only SCARRING yourself, but your sisters as well, no matter who you are or who they are. You are doing more hurting that helping. When you rescue your sisters from pain that you have experienced in order to set them free and forward them to their destiny, you WIN. Don't do them an injustice anymore. Don't stick to tradition, a lot of times we think the older, wiser, innovative sister is always it, but not always. I needed to say this as to not isolate sisters that 'wear' the 'older sister BADGE, in other forms and not just by age... I have seen 'baby sisters' operate in the 'older mode' I have seen some 'middle sisters operate in that mode' –yes the mode of being the oldest, but not actually the oldest. It all varies, and REMEMBER, you will know them by their fruit.

Always operate in distinct truth and honesty. You will be honored in the long run by your 'co-sibs". They will eventually- tell you how valuable your truth and protection was over the years. They will see you as a solid resource for life, they will see you as the 'iron pillar' and the 'brazen wall '. When you speak the truth in an unyielding way, you will ignite an eternal fierce- spark within your sisters' lives that will never go out. Those of us that 'remain in the background' create many, many problems for our sisters in the long run and for the relationship between us. Truth creates growth only! Lies, cover-up and bring about denial and enablement. And this is inadmissible in the SISTER COURT! Not doing (speaking up) -creates and causes disruptive –torn-covenants between sisters.

Sisters if you are concealing pain on behalf of your younger sister, you have to let it go. If you are reading this book and shedding tears, it is because you know what you are reading is true. If you know that you have covered for your sister for too long, it is time to let it go. When I say 'cover for', this is what I mean. You have been the emotional scapegoat for your younger sibling sister or sisters (no age rank). You have allowed what she felt, acted and looked like as a child 'carry over' into adulthood. Now is the time to change!

You have used your ability to protect and save your sister hood as a crutch. You think, how can I leave her, how can I let her go? Change! This should have been done in the very beginning. Now it is a lot harder, because there are so many years between when your baby sister fell and busted her nose, verses, her now, losing out on the very intricacies of life. It has now come to be something more serious than a nose bleed. You have stood and watched your sister commit unruly acts and say unruly things that has caused insurmountable damage to the connection that God has created! A sister not willing to follow God's plan-and let her go until she sees the light, causes more problems that you can ever imagine bargaining for.

You see Leah and Rachel (Genesis 29-35) didn't see a sister bond, at all when they wanted that Man! Get it! Rachel had one focus (to bear child). Leah had another and that was to be LOVED, no one was thinking about how to connect! At times sisters we have to both stand on our own two feet, we have to leave our sisters to their selves even in turmoil to let them go, when we rescue them from their suffering- it causes more stuff! Enabling a sister causes a lot more trouble than what it is worth. Toni Braxton said that she wished that she could have gone on her own, in a prior interview, and that she would have soared higher- but she was scared because she was dedicated to the cause of taking her sisters along. Sometimes sisters cannot always go where the one that bears, the most fruit goes, she has to go, bears and come back later. I am just going to make it as plain as that, and when she returns, you are supposed to be growing and learning form what she left behind, gleaning, wanting and waiting-yes change! You sister BEARER of the FRUIT (hear me well), you have a plight to carry, you have to know when to let go and let God. Sometimes bearing fruit unto the sister brood is letting your sisters grow, so that what you have put into them can maturate. Enabling your sisters for two long can also be damaging. God says an unjust balance is an abomination to him, Proverbs 11:1. And I say again, enabling is just as wrong as denial from all parties ! Don't fear letting go, BIG SIS or whomever the designee is categorized in this role. Stop worrying, if a grain of wheat falls to the ground and dies, it will bear much fruit, but if it remains it will not bear (paraphrased from John 12:24, KJV).When you come to this point, there will never be an end, unless you decide to make it one. Wean yourself and wean your siblings, whichever the case maybe. Stop falling for the games, go back and rework this thing and reset it, 'straightforward'! Be truthful about how you feel regarding your sister's ability to use you mentally, emotionally and physically. Let her grow up and out- from allowing herself to to use you and you, my dear sister-grow up from allowing her to continually use you-let this go (I know this all makes sense)! Know this, that the feelings will come with a lot of discomfort and you may even have to get counseling, as this is a major psychological change that will take place. Enablers have to seek help too- you know, as they are psychologically prone to doing and being what a person wants them to be to keep confusion down and to satisfy some pathology inside of them as well! So., my dear sisters- when the release comes, there is an emptiness, that cannot be fathomed, so it works both ways, both will feel an emptiness, because those sick horrid places will no longer be there. It will take some time to adjust to not being a user and to no longer being used (key thought to keep in mind).

Let's change, let's go back to how it should be. It has taken me several years to write this book I started in 2012 or earlier, at the "spur of a moment", while WATCHING LAW AND ORDER--and the wind of God bowed and blowed (over the years) and then it stopped, so I had to stop! So one day this October of 2014, all the way up to 2020 after fasting and praying the wind of his strength came back and I completed and finished this entire book in a total of 8 hours on one given day (minus the updates). So people, take this book and absorb it. Read it all, word for word and twice if you need, take notes, take it on your sister trips, read, it take it to the Threshing floor of your heart, refine it, get mad at it (but pick it back up, now, LOL).Always remember. To try to fix what you can fix, and what you can't leave it, don't try to overrule someone else's decisions. I had to learn this the hard way! I have some 'sister/friends' that I have been with for years and we have a perfect bond of a relationship. WE fuss, we argue, we avoid each other, we don't' talk for days and years at the time, but they are my sisters and they are not who you think they are! Sometimes the sisters you thought you had, are really not that at all. Sometimes you think your birth sisters are the only sisters you have. God sends us BLOOD sisters, through his son. WE are bonded through his blood and it is perfectly alright. You can be bonded through a lot of others ways, but feel the deep connection, as if it were a blood sister. That is okay, it happens. I will say though, that sisters- if there is any hope left. That I would encourage you to try to salvage what you have. I met a lady on the elevator at work and she was talking to me about her 5 or 6 sisters. She said to me..it is nothing but a 'big ole mess'. She said. I have one sister that is the 'trouble maker'. She stated. That her sister 'gets on the phone' and calls around snooping and looking for anything negative, scandalous, or gossipy about one or the other sister. I said to her, . I would rather not be bothered and she said the same. But I got to thinking to myself. Sisters should not be that way. One should be able to rely on their sister for honesty...integrity...support and the like... Sisters should be able to problem solve and find solutions though, when there is a problem.

Thought Stopper: "Do you feel close enough to your sister that you would fight for her? Why or Why not?

I saw something on FaceBook and it said would you "SLAP your sister for 90 million dollars?" HMM—I think we would have to discuss this and then we BREAK each other off a peace later. I think we can mend ourselves off of 90 million dollars, don't you? I just added that to break the monotony, to make light of this serious book! SO LAUGH!! LOL!!

_**Another story before I close.**_I had an encounter with a person for several years that was the eldest of three sisters ... she seemed to be 'bossy' 'rude' and "overbearing' at times to her younger sibling sisters. For some reason they were intimidated by her ... but I never said anything because of my friendship with her. I declared myself an innocent bystander ... I noticed though- that elder sister relationships can break or make a sibling connections. I say this because I am one ... not that I am perfect or anything ... but I have tried to be the perfect sister. Where this particular one has not... (in comparison)...she bullied and pushed her sisters around...never gave them a time to speak or should I say for 'not so long periods of time'...their opinions were of no use to her...she would 'overpower their thoughts and sometimes their actions by her manipulative 'big-sister' power ... I am guilty to some degree for exalting my big sister role. But I would only do so in terms of helping. This particular person... (in my personal observation) used this to her sibling's demise ... I said that to say this, let's not bully one another as sisters! Lets not hold things over one another's head. I know I have said a lot and repeated a lot, but I did it at the unctioning of the Holy Spirit, it lets me know that repetition is a teacher! Sooner or later it will get in your head! We are almost to the end, keep reading!

**Ladies.** this memoir is to work on the 'enemy' connection that we have with our sisters and bring out the BEST in our relationships and to expose the ENEMY within. In order to get some type of healing or deliverance from the hatred, resentment, or animosity that sisters carry or have carried for one another over the years, almost to the grave, or even so 'to the grave'.

Being realistic in the end Let's be real about how we feel, let's- let go of the "secrets of our soul" regarding our sister relationships, so that we can be totally free. I know the pain is bad, and really bad, but there is nothing that God cannot heal! Let's take this pain and set it aside! It is time, my dear sisters!

Being a Good Sister-We have visited what it feels like, sounds like and tastes like to be a "enemy" to one's sister, now let's revisit what it takes to be a "good" or "real" sister. I notice that the Braxton's argue a lot, but somehow they are still bonded and I will applaud them on that (my opinion). I would like to take the instance of bonding from the Braxton's, to share with the world, what it means to bond. Bonding is defined in most cases as to "join or be joined" to someone or something else typically by means of adhesive pressure. What does that mean to some of us? That means, in taking that definition and applying it, is that sisters are supposed to be closer than glue, and even "tighter "so to speak when problems arise, instead of doing the opposite and splitting problems up the middle and everywhere else, problems should ultimately bring sisters together. Remember what I mentioned early about a friend of my Aunt's, (now deceased, Betty Moore) told me, "Pam, I do not know what I would do without my sister, we talk every single day (God Bless her Soul)." She said to me, "Yawl young girls are like that though, my niece told me that she and her sister don't speak for months and even years" (She said that is the most craziest thing she ever heard, in so many words).

Some sisters see their sister as their sole enemy, or even their nemesis. But I see others that are totally different. I read a Facebook comment, a while back, by one of my first cousin's Jennifer Williams saying to her sister Janae Williams McDowell after she had gotten married, "This is my sister, my friend, sometimes my enemy, but (paraphrasing) all in all she is my best friend (is what I gathered from the post my cousin said to her baby sister). Remember the days when Moms would dress two sisters alike, even if they were not twins, that was

Jennifer and Janae! I Remember it would be from 'head to toe, the same, even the color of their ribbons', those were the good ole days of sister hood bonding, when you did not even know that your sister was your enemy, because your momma made you close by dressing you alike until people probably "thought you were twins (LOL)." So in saying this, I want to encourage all sisters that are at "war" with your sister to work on your relationship. I know you say this is hard and it will never be because-, you don't know what my sister has done to me, and this may very well be the case, I cannot judge that. I can say though, that you can be in a good relationship with your sister, then try to do so, try to take the opportunity to be a "Good sister" and not a "Bad" sister. Work on developing a sense of "closeness " "with your sister, by taking her out to eat, sending her a card, doing something really "weird, that you know she will love and cherish. (something totally out of character to bring things back together)," even reminding her of something from the past that you all loved and bonded on to bring back that sense of closeness, those are just a few examples. You may have your own unique thing you want to do to bring your relationship back, but make a move and try to do so. If you feel bad about all the things that have happened between you and your sister and you know that you, yourself were the culprit in most situations then you be the 'bigger woman' and begin to call the shots, in other words, try to work on getting back in a relationship with your sister.

Sensing.I sense in my spirit that there is a sister out there, that has held a grudge with your sister for years and you now have an opportunity to get it right, you know that your sister may not have much more time, it has been weighing on you to talk to her before it is too late, it seems to you that in real life, when a sister betrays another sister in the manner that you have been betrayed (yes you reading this book), there is no way to even consider this, but I tell you as you read this book right now in the name Jesus Christ of Nazareth, you can do it! Don't let another moment pass you by, as you wait and wait to no avail. You will feel so relieved. Letting the burden of holding the betrayal be your salvation! Do it now!I have learned that holding a grudge is a very hard burden to bear. I know that there are some people that regret not speaking to your sister that is now deceased, I know some of you wished you would have made that connection with her before she left the earth, but it is never too late, ask yourself for forgiveness and then release it to God, being a sister is really not an easy task and some of us, may not ever be able to "verbally" make amends because just as well as there are sisters out there that want to do the "right" thing, there are some out there that want to do the "wrong thing." And maybe it is just not feasible at the time! I get that too! Keep reading, we are near the end!

I hate to even mention this again, but for the sake of sanity of some that are reading this book and to eliminate any double talk, I want to assure those that know that their sister hates them and there is 'no making up' due to their declarations, that you are banished, you, need to make peace with yourself and this can be done. You can first forgive yourself for whatever it is you have done to offend your sister and then you can pray and ask for forgiveness. Our Lord and Savior is always there to listen and care for your heart! Sister, I would like to encourage you, that if you feel you have done all you can do and to do anything else, it would probably be detrimental to the both, or each of you, then I would say to pursue peace, in other words, just leave it alone and allow it to "come back around." My Grandmother, in whom was a nurse would always say that if you continue to pick at your wounds, they will never get well! Sometimes you have to allow the natural process of healing "take its course." I have learned this the hard way. Sometimes we can want resolution too quickly, and it can do a lot more damage than- if you would just leave it alone. I guess so many people are wondering, how do you know this, I experienced it so many times, in more ways than one. I know that some relationships cannot be mended right away, while some others can, you honestly have to judge if your sister relationship is mendable at this present time. Working on yourself in the event that your sister relationship is presently not mendable is the most important thing, making sure you go into daily mediations through prayer and reading and fasting, can make you a lot stronger to deal with your family member (your sister) when that time comes.

Sisters, this is the time for change, this is the time to take a look at your relationships with your sister or sisters to see where you stand, check your conscious to see if it is clear, check it and recheck it to see if you are where you feel you need to be. Some of us, have held a grudge for over 30 something years, as Sophia, in "The Golden Girls" noted in a scene when her and her sister had a misunderstanding that caused them to hate each other over their men subjects (LOL)! Yes we do this too, we get mad with our sisters over men! Is that you, young lady or ladies, did you have a misunderstanding with your sister over a man, a story told, a dress that she took and nobody believed you, your car, your friend, your job, your inheritance, your dignity, your hope, your identify, or maybe even your whole life or something else? Ask yourself, what is it you feel that your sister stole from you to hinder your place, your stance? Are you a half-sister that feels that you didn't get your "justice"? Do you feel like you missed out on a lot, because you didn't bear the same room, but you all came from the same seed? These are thoughts that was told to me, by sisters and things I researched. Some are willing to admit, while others are not. I am here to set you free, whether you disclose it openly or secretly, it doesn't matter, just so long as it comes out. You can hear people on their cell phones, in the grocery stories, in the park, talking on some outlandish drama filled scene or story regarding something their sister has done to them or has happened. I have seen so many crime shows of sisters talking about how much their sister's meant to them after the loss of their sister, I hear Tamron Hall (news reporter) speak of her concern and regret with a lot pertaining to the loss of her sister. They almost, always say, "I wished, she would have told me, or I wish would not have done or known this or that." I know that none of us, want to be in those shoes, I know that you want to learn how to be a better sister, in order to leave no stones unturned. Let's live, love and grow. Let's DO so NOW! Let's be like my two granddaughters Melianna and Chrissy that reap love from each other. My two granddaughters pictured in this book (below) exhibit the love that I wish that many of us wish we had, when I watch them only three years old and 9 months old interact, Chrissy is always looking at her sister for some touch, some pull some attention, she stops at her sister's movement and Meliana the oldes that refers to "Chrissy" as "baby" is always trying to help her, hold her and give her things, even if she doesn't know what it is, she has a undying love for her sister that she calls "baby", shows the love that is so obvious and so clear. They are bonded and connected. Lets all take a lesson from my grandbabies Melianna and Chrissy.

"My grandbabies/sisters (this is how love of sisters
should be, they started as infants)"!

Growing and Glowing as a sister should be your focus in this new year 2021, especially as we experience a devastating world lynching disease called or referred to as the Coronavirus, COVID 19 or referred to as the pandemic. Learn to grow with your sister. Learn to glow, by being open, honest, frank, sincere, no matter if it hurts. Don't allow so much time to pass or "pass over" you, and you forfeit the glorious opportunity to bond and mate in the deepest place that God intended with your sister. I have learned something about time, that if you don't take on opportunities that presents itself at the time you need to, then it "never really comes back the same time as before." Bondages are built, hindrances are stayed and nothing never really feels the same, if you wait too long to fix or mend it. Don't miss deep inner connection, over strife, jealousy, misery, distance or any other barrier that may cause estrangement.

I know for some of you, this book is helping you realize the importance of having your sister, being with her and sitting by her through this journey of life. I hope that you have become aware through this memoir. It is time, My Dear Queen Sisters … It's Time (Sisters I hope you enjoyed this book and if the response is good, I may do an extension of My Sister, My Enemy and by that time- let's just hope this time, your sister is no longer your enemy)Thanks Readers I hope to hear your feedback soon!

Love Peace and Blessings!

Dr. Pamela Renee Applewhite
I finally finished on-May 26, 2020!!!
After almost six to seven years or up to a decade- and now all of my edits on July 30, 2020, October, and now November 29, 2020! Now, after one more round of edits on December 29, 2020!
Hallelujah!!

Printed in the United States
by Baker & Taylor Publisher Services